SOME PIONEER DELAWARE FAMILIES

Donald Odell Virdin

HERITAGE BOOKS
2007

HERITAGE BOOKS
AN IMPRINT OF HERITAGE BOOKS, INC.

Books, CDs, and more—Worldwide

For our listing of thousands of titles see our website
at
www.HeritageBooks.com

Published 2007 by
HERITAGE BOOKS, INC.
Publishing Division
65 East Main Street
Westminster, Maryland 21157-5026

Copyright © 1992 Donald Odell Virdin

All rights reserved. No part of this book may be reproduced or transmitted in any form or by any means, electronic or mechanical, including photocopying, recording or by any information storage and retrieval system without written permission from the author, except for the inclusion of brief quotations in a review.

International Standard Book Number: 978-1-55613-608-5

CONTENTS

PAGE

Chapter 1.	Background	1
Chapter 2.	The Virdin Family	3
Chapter 3.	The Broadway Family	123
Chapter 4.	The Carter Family	131
Chapter 5.	The Gilder Family	145
Chapter 6.	The Lowber Family	151
Chapter 7.	The Marvel Family	163
Chapter 8.	The Register Family	167
Chapter 9.	The Reynolds Family	171
Chapter 10.	The Rodney Family	187
Bibliography		195
Subject Index		197
Name Index		201

Chapter 1.   Background

BACKGROUND

After <u>The Virdins of Delaware and Related Families</u> was published in 1976, new information was developed. With this data, and with unpublished family history which had not been used in the original book, it seemed that an effort should be made to publish that which has been collected. The years of work involved will benefit no one unless it is printed. Accordingly, the writer has again attempted to publish a genealogy, or rather a compilation of genealogical facts, knowing that it is incomplete and that it primarily covers the early periods of our history.

There are many missing links in this book. Further, in an undertaking of this kind, with so many individuals and dates to be verified, there is always a possibility for error. The writer believes that such errors are few; certainly, none are intentional.

For much of the material on the Virdin family credit must be given to James R. Virden, Russia, Ohio, and his sister, Mrs. Ruth (Virden) Shoup, Chula Vista, California. Most of the census data, and much of the data on the Virdin family in the Midwest and the West, has been contributed by James R. Virden as the result of almost twenty years of research. Without his gift of time and information this book would not have been as complete.

Some of the family histories concerning the other Delaware families was prepared by Mr. Herman Carter before 1900 with the assistance of Mr. John C. Gooden of Wyoming, Delaware. They were given to Samuel A. Virden with a note which said:

> "The source of information in these sheets is found in county records, public documents, church records, family bibles, and tombstones...Mr. John C. Gooden, genealogist and historian, made this subject the study of his life. To him are due the credit for much of the data here arranged. He does not strain lines to make family connections, but is truthful and records only such data for which he has positive evidence."

It will be noted that some of these family records are incomplete and do not give dates and citations. However, by making a spot check of several of the families from public records, it appears that the work of Mr. Carter and Mr. Gooden is accurate, and they are included with the hope that they will enable someone to find a family tree.

There is additional data concerning the Virdin family of Mississippi (who are descendants of John and Ellinor (Sipple) Virdin of Kent County) available in a manuscript prepared by Mrs. Edythe W. Thoesen of Boulder, Colorado, in 1963. This document, the writer understands, is available in the Delaware Hall of Records, Dover, Delaware.

The two illustrations in this book were prepared by Thomas Wayne Major (a direct descendant of John and Ellinor (Sipple) Virdin) of Wilmington, Delaware. "By-Fields", located near Dover, Delaware, was the birthplace of Ceasar Rodney, signer of the Declaration of Independence. The Lowber House, Magnolia, Delaware, was built in 1774 and is presently owned by the State Archives Commission of Delaware. It is on the National Register of Historical Places.

Chapter 2.   The Virdin Family

THE VIRDIN FAMILY

Insofar as the writer has been able to determine, the Virdins mentioned in this book (with two or three exceptions specifically discussed) are descendants of HUGH VIRDEN and his wife Elizabeth (White) Virdin who were in Sussex County, Delaware, in 1719, or JOHN VIRDIN and his wife Ellinor (Sipple) Virdin who were in Kent County, Delaware, in 1732. Although extensive research has been conducted, both in America and in England, no records have been found to determine when Hugh Virden and John Virdin arrived in America.

However, the conclusion must be reached (based upon the known facts) that Hugh Virden and John Virdin arrived in America sometime prior to 1720. It is quite likely that they were brothers. Although there have been many stories written and printed as to how the first Virdins arrived in America, none that have come to the attention of the writer have been more than theories, unsupported by facts. The two most logical stories are these: According to Mrs. Samuel Warren Hall, who was a descendant of John Virdin of Kent County and a professional genealogist, three Virdin brothers who served in the English Navy went from England to Holland. From there they took a ship to America, landing at Jamestown, Virginia. The other story was told by William Virdin (son of Matthew Lowber Virdin) who was born in 1807, and died in 1888. According to William Virdin there were three Virdin brothers who left Liverpool, England, after 1700 and came to America, finally arriving at Lewes, Delaware.

Notwithstanding the genealogical axiom that any "three brother" story is untrue, it seems to the writer that in this instance there may be some element of truth. However, it is probable that there were two brothers rather than three. Indeed, ENGENIOR VIRDEN, who was in Virginia in 1760, is probably the son of Hugh Virden of Sussex County, Delaware, or John Virdin of Kent County, Delaware. Engenior Virden had to be at least 21 years of age when he witnessed the will of John Wright in Augusta County, Virginia, on September 27, 1760. Thus, he was probably born between 1730 and 1740--a decade when he could have been a son of either Hugh Virden or John Virdin. He may have left home upon reaching maturity, or prior to that time, and moved from Delaware, his place of birth, to nearby Virginia.

ENGENIOR (ENGENIAR, AGENIAH) VIRDEN was probably born between 1730 and 1740 since he had to be 21 years of age on September 27, 1760, when he witnessed the will of John Wright in Augusta County, Virginia. He was one of the two persons who proved the will on November 18, 1762. Further records of Engenior Virden in Augusta County, Virginia, show that: (1) On December 10, 1764, he witnessed a document transferring a large tract of land at Snodons Spring from Daniel Young to Samuel Beard; (2) On May 23, 1765, he witnessed a document concerning a tax exemption for Robert McGee because of great age and infirmity. Engenior Virden was shown on the land records of Wilkes County, Georgia (the parent county of Warren County) as early as 1783, so one can assume that after the Revolutionary War he moved from Virginia to Georgia. He was in that war; his grave in Warren County, Georgia, is marked by the DAR. In 1793 both Engenior Virden and William Virden appeared on the tax rolls of Wilkes County, afterwards known as Warren County, Georgia. Engenior Virden and William Virden were also listed on the 1794 tax records of Warren County. In 1805 Engenior Virden, William Virden, and John Virden, were listed in the Land Lottery. Engenior (Ageniah) Virden owned at one time some 300 acres of land on Rocky Comfort Creek, Georgia. On land records in 1784 Engenior Virden's wife is listed as Jane Virden, but in his will dated in 1808 his wife is listed as Winney. Thus, it must be assumed that he was married twice and that his second wife was much younger than he was, since records of Houston County, Georgia, as late as 1830 indicate that Winney Virden was still living.

The will of Engenior (Engeniar) Virden, dated August 14, 1808, lists his wife Winney Virden, and sons James Virden, John Virden, and William Virden. In the will he refers to his very old age and low state of health, so it is quite likely that he is the same Engenior Virden who is shown in the early Virginia and Georgia records rather than being father and son by the same name. William Virden, born in 1791 in South Carolina, who spent most of his life in Georgia, is reportedly the son of Engenior Virden. John Virden, who was born in South Carolina, and later listed in Georgia records, and James Virden, who was born in South Carolina, could have been sons of Engenior by his first wife. Both John Virden and James Virden were listed in the 1790 census of South Carolina.

Will of Engeniar Verdan of Warren County, Georgia

"IN THE NAME OF GOD AMEN:

I Egeniar Verdan of the State of Georgia and County of Warren being verry old and in a low State of health but in my proper Senses which I thank God for the same I will to my wife Winney Verdan her first choice bed and furniture also one Bay Mare and Saddle and Bridle also one dud Side cow and her own calf also five head of hogs and one Sow and four one year old also Seventy five Bushels of corn and Eight hundred Weight of fodder also one hundred Weight of See Cotton also one pair of Trunks also one dutch oven and the small pot also her choice Pewter Dish and Boson and Three Earthen plates also one Earthen pitcher I give the said mentioned thing to her and her heirs forever also one spinning Wheel and a pair of Cards and her first two choice chairs and also Seventy Dollars in cash and then

"all the Rest of my Estate Both Real and
Personal Shall be Equally Divided amongst
my two Sons James and John Verdan also I give
to my Son William Verdan three hundred
dollars, one hundred Dollars, on a note upon
Thomas Davis due the first January 1809 and
Two hundred Dollars on the Note due the first
of January 1810 - After my Son John Verdan
paying all my Just debts I give the Ballance
of the Note to him Namely one note due Last
January to the Amount of one hundred and
Twenty Dollars and one hundred due on a
Note the first of January 1809 and Twenty
Dollar Note due the Same time and Twenty
Dollars due on a note 1810 Also I devise
my wife and my son John Verdan to Executor
to my Will and being my last Will Testament
In Witness Whereof I have set my hand and
Seal this 14th of August 1803."

                                          his

                              Egeniar X Verdan (Seal)

                                        mark

Test

Reuben Reese
Edw. Mathews   his
Aaron Aldred   X
                    mark

PROBATE

GEORGIA
WARREN COUNTY

Personally appeared in open Court Reuben Reese
Edward Mathews and Aaron Aldred and being duly
Sworn Saith that they Saw the within named
Egenia Verdan Sign Seal and heard him publish
and declare the Within Instrument of Writing
to be his Last Will and Testament and that at
the time of his So doing he was of Sound mind
and memory and that at his Request and in his
presence and in the presence of Each other they
Subscribed their Names as Witnesses to the Same

Sworn to in Open Court 5th of September 1808

Septimus Weatherby
C.C.O.W.

Reuben Reese
Edward Mathews
Aaron X Aldred
    his mark

WILLIAM VIRDEN (son of Egenior and Jane Virden) was born February 27, 1791, in South Carolina, and died November 13, 1841, in Georgia. He is buried in the Virden-Moore Cemetery near Topeka Junction, Upson County, Georgia. On June 3, 1809, he married Elizabeth--who was born June 9, 1793, in North Carolina. The William Virden homestead was located in the northeast corner of Upson County, Georgia, near the Pike County line. His daughter, Julia Ann (Virden) Adams inherited the property and lived there until her death in 1905. The cemetery in which he is buried is located on property that was a part of the Virden homestead. In addition to the graves of William Virden and his wife, Elizabeth Virden, graves of several of the children are there: Julia Ann (Virden) Adams and her husband, Jeremiah Adams; Priscilla (Virden) Elliott and her husband, Thomas Elliott; Thomas G. Virden and his wife Zilphia (Brown) Virden; and Elizabeth (Virden) Corley. William Virden was listed in the 1820 Census of Warren County, Georgia. He also drew in the Land Lottery of 1827, and in the Cherokee Lottery. William Virden appeared on the 1830 Census of Pike County, Georgia, but records show him to be a resident of Upson County prior to 1835. He appeared on the 1820 Census of Warren County, Georgia, with a wife and five children--one son and four daughters. During the War of 1812 he served as a soldier and after that war returned to Warren County. The 1818 tax records of Warren County show that he owned 71 acres of land on Big Briar Creek.

The 1860 Census of Upson County, Georgia, shows that his widow, Elizabeth Virden, was 67 years of age and was born in South Carolina. The 1850 Census of Upson County, Georgia, shows that there were four persons in the household: (1) Elizabeth Virden, age 56, born in North Carolina; (2) Thomas Virden, age 18, born in Georgia; (3) Priscilla Virden, age 16, born in Georgia; and (4) Benjamin Virden, age 14, born in Georgia. The last two children were not in the bible records supplied by Mr. Jason Eugene Virden (wife: Flora Virden), such records being verified and enlarged upon in History of Upson County, Georgia, 1930.

The will of William Virden, dated January 21, 1839, mentions children Eliza Virden, Samuel Virden, William Virden, Mary Virden, and Martha Virden. (Upson County Wills, page 253.) His wife, Elizabeth Virden, was given certain land to use during her lifetime, and then to her children. Will was probated January 21, 1842.

The children of William and Elizabeth Virden, all born in Georgia, were:

(1) Samuel Virden, born February 17, 1811;
(2) Mary C. Virden, born April 5, 1813;
(3) Martha Virden, born July 11, 1815;
(4) Elizabeth Virden, born February 9, 1821;
(5) James Virden, born October 31, 1822;
(6) William Virden, Jr., born September 18, 1824;
(7) Sarah Virden, born May 28, 1825;
(8) John Virden, born May 27, 1826;
(9) Julia Ann Virden, born October 12, 1828;
(10) Thomas G. Virden, born October 4, 1831;
(11) Priscilla Virden, born April 5, 1834; and
(12) Benjamin Virden, born December 15, 1835.

SAMUEL VIRDEN (son of William and Elizabeth Virden) was married twice. He married his first wife, Laura Ann Wood, the daughter of Rev. David Wood, a Baptist Minister, on December 20, 1843, in Pike County, Georgia. The name of his second wife is not known, nor is there proof that the following are all the children he had:

(1) Alexander G. Virden, born June 24, 1846. He was born in Barnsville, Georgia. He married Martha Ann Swann. He died in Victoria, Texas, September 19, 1926;
(2) Nancy E. Virden, born about 1848;
(3) Samuel Virden;
(4) Thomas Virden;
(5) John Virden; and
(6) William David Virden, born near Atlanta, Georgia, January 26, 1854. He married Willie Lenora Youngblood in Bell County, Texas, and they lived in Winters, Texas.

Alexander Virden, William David Virden, and Thomas Virden went to Texas together. Thomas Virden was buried in the same cemetery in Texas with his uncle, Benjamin Franklin Virden, and his headstone reads "Uncle Tom Virden", having been put up by his brother's children. The 1850 Census of Pike County, Georgia, lists: (1) Samuel Verdin, age 38, born in Georgia; (2) Laura A. Verdin, age 24, born in Georgia; (3) Alexander Verdin, age 3, born in Georgia; and (4) Nancy E. Verdin, age 1, born in Georgia.

Mary C. Virden (daughter of William and Elizabeth Virden) married _____ Woodall.

Martha Virden (daughter of William and Elizabeth Virden) married Richard Brown in Upson County, Georgia, on December 25, 1838.

Elizabeth Virden (daughter of William and Elizabeth Virden) married John Corley on December 21, 1843. She died June 14, 1847, and is buried in the Virden-Moore Cemetery. She was referred to as Eliza in her father's will.

JAMES VIRDEN (son of William and Elizabeth Virden) married Maria (or Monah) Stephens. He is listed in the Warren County, Georgia, Census of 1870 with this family: (1) James N. Virden, age 46, born in Georgia; (2) Monah Virden, age 34, born in Georgia; (3) Willie L. Virden, age 13, born in Georgia; (4) Fannie Virden, age 12, born in Georgia; (5) Milton Virden, age 11, born in Georgia; (6) Jenny Virden, age 7, born in Georgia; (7) John Virden, age 5, born in Georgia; and (8) James Virden, age 1, born in Georgia.

WILLIAM VIRDEN, JR. (son of William and Elizabeth Virden) married Patience McDaniel on December 9, 1846, in Upson County, Georgia. William and Patience (McDaniel) Virden had two children:

(1) John James Virden, born June 15, 1853, in Georgia. He married Julia Octavia Densen. John Virden died January 29, 1919, in Cedartown, Georgia. Julia Virden died April 28, 1928. John and Julia Virden had nine children: (1) William P. Virden; (2) James A. Virden; (3) Oscar C. Virden; (4) a son who died as a baby; and five girls, one of whom was Mrs. Minnie Suratt of Baylor, Mississippi. (The information concerning John James Virden was furnished by James R. Virden, who obtained it from Oscar C. Virden, Alhambra, California.)
(2) William Virden was killed in the Civil War.

JOHN VIRDEN (son of William and Elizabeth Virden) married Mary _____ on March 7, 1850, in Pike County, Georgia. The 1870 Census of Warren County, Georgia, shows these family members: (1) John Virden, age 44, born in Georgia; (2) Mary M. Virden, age 40, born in Georgia; (3) Martha A. Virden, age 17, born in Georgia; (4) Christopher C. Virden, age 15, born in Georgia; (5) John W. Virden, age 13, born in Georgia; (6) Mary C. Virden, age 11, born in Georgia; (7) Nancy A. Virden, age 7, born in Georgia; (8) William Virden, age 5, born in Georgia; (9) Emma Virden, age 3, born in Georgia; and (10) James P. Virden, age 1, born in Georgia.

Julia Ann Virden (daughter of William and Elizabeth Virden) married Jeremiah Adams on December 21, 1843, in Upson County, Georgia. She died in 1905 and is buried in the Virden-Moore Cemetery.

THOMAS G. VIRDEN (son of William and Elizabeth Virden) married Zilphia (or Zelphey) Brown in Pike County, Georgia, on January 7, 1853. She was born October 8, 1835 and died October 12, 1913. Thomas G. Virden died June 13, 1903. He was a veteran of the Civil War. Both are buried in the Virden-Moore Cemetery.

Priscilla Virden (daughter of William and Elizabeth Virden) married Thomas D. Elliot on March 10, 1853. They had one son, Eugenia F. Elliot, born November 28, 1866, and died November 28, 1889. Both Priscilla and Thomas Elliot died in Georgia and are buried in the Virden-Moore Cemetery.

BENJAMIN FRANKLIN VIRDEN was born December 15, 1835, probably in Barnsville, Georgia, in the Pike-Upson County area. He was the youngest child of William Virden (who was born in 1791) and Elizabeth Virden (whose maiden name is unknown). William and Elizabeth were married either January 3 or June 3, 1809. William Virden is listed in the 1820 Census of Warren County, Georgia. Elizabeth Virden was called "Queen Elizabeth" by her family. Benjamin Franklin Virden died February 14, 1903.

Benjamin Franklin Virden married Nancy Thomas Mathews July 10, 1854, probably in Calhoun (formerly Benton) County, Alabama. Nancy Thomas Mathews was born January 29, 1835, and died January 9, 1881. She was the daughter of John T. Mathews and was shown with her parents in the 1850 Upson County, Georgia, Census. Her father was listed in the 1860 Polk County, Texas, Census. Benjamin F. Virden was also listed in the 1860 Polk County, Texas, Census with three children, William, Queen Elizabeth, and Mary, all born in Alabama.

Benjamin Franklin and Nancy Thomas (Mathews) Virden had nine children:

(1) William Hamilton Virden, born May 20, 1855, in Alabama;
(2) Queen Elizabeth Virden, born May 11, 1857, in Alabama. She died April 29, 1955. On August 15, 1873, she married Leonard Covington, and reared the family in Mills County, Texas. She was known by her nieces and nephews as "Aunt Queenie." She had a daughter, Nettie Covington, who married William Jackson Hall. (He was a grandson of Jackson J. Hall who was born in 1815 in Jackson County, Illinois, and moved to Texas about 1829 with his father, James Hall, Jr.;
(3) Mary Daniel Virden, born July 4, 1859, in Alabama. On November 7, 1867, she married Edward Parker, and had a son, Benjamin Parker, who married Ida Henson. She died April 20, 1931;
(4) John Josiah Virden, born November 18, 1861, in Polk County, Texas. On December 24, 1885, he married Alice Carey Thompson in Mills County, Texas, and had a son, Edward Franklin Virden, who married Ava Susannah Henson, a sister of Ida Henson;
(5) Benjamin Thomas Virden was born April 30, 1864, in Texas;
(6) Henry Hill Virden was born May 8, 1866;
(7) Julius Allen Virden was born March 9, 1869;
(8) Martha Caroline Virden was born September 21, 1871. She married John N. Keese on December 2, 1898; and
(9) James Mathews Virden was born May 4, 1874.

Benjamin Franklin Virden, after the death of his first wife, married Mary E. Giles in Mills County, Texas, in 1884. They had five children: (1) Ennis E. Virden, born in 1885; (2) Edna Priscilla Virden, born November 16, 1886, who married _____ Fry and lived in Abiline, Texas; (3) Joseph Marion Virden, born September 12, 1888; (4) Tommy Terrell Virden, born September 12, 1890; and (5) Virginia Bell Virden, born March 28, 1893, who married Charles Boyd.

JOHN JOSIAH VIRDEN and Alice Carey (Thompson) Virden had nine children:

(1) William Francis Virden, born November 16, 1894, in Mills County, Texas;
(2) Nellie Pearl Virden, born March 15, 1897;
(3) Mary Elizabeth Virden, born March 15, 1897;
(4) Martha Bell Virden, born September 6, 1899;
(5) Georgia Mae Virden, born June 12, 1904;
(6) Eliza Thomas Virden, born November 17, 1891;
(7) Alice Laura Virden, born March 27, 1902;
(8) Nora Edward Virden, born June 23, 1909; and
(9) Edward Franklin Virden, born June 23, 1909. He married Ava Susannah Henson and had two sons, John Wesley Virden and Edward Franklin Virden, Jr. John Wesley Virden had two sons: Robert Wesley Virden (who also had two sons, Robert Virden and Ryan Virden, and a daughter, Rita Virden) and Glenn Virden. (The information concerning Benjamin F. Virden and descendants was furnished by James R. Virden, Russia, Ohio, based upon data supplied by Mrs. T.H. Corley of Houston, Texas, whose mother was T. Cora Henson, a sister of Ava Susannah Henson.)

JAMES VIRDEN (VERDEN, OR VERDIN) SR., was born in South Carolina on August 25, 1756. In August 1784 he married Sarah Cater (or Caten) also of South Carolina. They had eleven children, all born in South Carolina. James Virden and a brother, John Virden, are listed in the 1790 Census of Newberry County, South Carolina. James Virden died in Illinois on June 18, 1843, and Sarah Virden died on September 3, 1845. James Virden served for 15 months (from June 1777 until September 1778) in the Revolutionary War. He filed a pension application for that War from South Carolina in 1790, No. W-22485. He also filed a claim for a pension from Missouri in 1827, stating that he had never filed a claim before. However, the Missouri claim indicates that it is an Original Claim. In the claim filed from Missouri he stated that 6 children were living, all outside the state of Missouri. In fact, there were 7 children living when he filed the application, probably all living in Illinois. After James Virden died, his widow, Sarah Virden, filed a claim for a widow's pension in the State of Illinois.

On March 17, 1846, Levi Verden and Isaac Verden, son of Levi, filed a claim for benefits for the surviving children of Sarah Verden, a pensioner. The surviving children listed were: (1) Elizabeth Davis and (2) Radford Verden of Montgomery County; (3) William Verden and (4) Jane Gordon of Christian County; (5) James Verden and (6) Charity Cisco of Shelby County; and (7) Levi Verden of Fayette County, all of Illinois.

James and Sarah (Cater) Virden had eleven children, according to family Bible records:

(1) Elizabeth Verdin, born July 4, 1785. She married George Davis;

(2) James Verdin, born November 8, 1787. He married Nancy _____ who was born in 1790 in South Carolina. Her name is listed as Nancy on her tombstone, but as Elizabeth in the 1850 Census;

(3) Jane Verdin, born November 3, 1789. She married John Gordon (Gorden);

(4) Sarah Verdin, born December 28, 1791. She died prior to 1827;

(5) William Verdin, born March 23, 1794. He married Nancy _____;

(6) Levi Verdin, born April 4, 1796. He married as his first wife, Rachel _____, who died in Illinois in 1826. As his second wife he married Catherine Reese, who was born in 1812 in South Carolina;

(7) Margaret Verdin, born June 13, 1798. She died prior to 1827;

(8) Mary Merick Verdin, born October 14, 1800. She died prior to 1827;

(9) Charity Cater Verdin, born May 5, 1803. She married Daniel Francisco on January 10, 1822;

(10) Ann Cater Verdin, born September 25, 1805. She died young; and

(11) Hugh Radford Verdin, born in 1807. He married Margarett Wilson on April 10, 1828. She was born in 1807 in South Carolina.

(Note: Sarah (Cater) Virden in her application for a pension after the death of her husband, James Virden, attached to her file a page torn from her bible in which were listed the names and dates of birth of all the above children except James Virden (November 8, 1787) and Hugh Radford Virden (1807).)

Original Claim of James Verden for Revolutionary War Pension

"Declaration to be placed on the pension list under the act of the 18th of March 1818. State of Missouri, County of Scott, S.S.: On the fifteenth day of October in the year of our Lord Eighteen hundred and twenty-seven personally appeared in open Court in the County Court for the said County of Scott, being a Court of Record, and State aforesaid, James Verden, a resident of said County aged seventy three years who being first duly sworn according to law, doth on his oath make the following declaration in order to obtain the provisions made by the acts of Congress on the 18th of March 1818 and the 1st of May 1820. That the said James Verden enlisted as a private for the term of fifteen months on or about the first day of June A.D. 1777 in the State of South Carolina and Charlestown in the company commanded by Frank Boykin the second regiment of Riflemen commanded by Colonel William Thompson in the line of the State of South Carolina in the continental establishment, that he continued to serve in the said corps until on or about the first day of September A.D. 1778 during the full term of fifteen months from the said time of his enlistment when he was honorably discharged from the service in Charlestown in the State of South Carolina. That he hereby relinquished every claim whatever to a pension except the present, that his name is not on the roll of any State except that made by this application, and that the following are the reasons for not making earlier application for a pension. I lived... where I could obtain but little information and did not know what to do to obtain a pension, thinking it more trouble and expense to take the necessary steps to obtain the pension than it would be worth. But the increased feebleness of my body and debility owing to my more advanced age making me less able to support myself by manual labour compels me to endeavour to obtain the pension.

And in pursuance of the Act of the 1st day of May 1820, I do solemnly swear that I was a resident citizen of the United States on the 18th day of March 1818 and that I have not since that time by gift, sale, or in any manner disposed of my property or any part thereof

with the intent thereby so to diminish it as
to bring myself within the provisions of an act
of Congress entitled 'An Act to provide for
certain persons engaged in the land or naval
services of the United States in the Revolutionary
War', passed on the 18th day of March 1818 and
that I have not nor has any person in trust for
me any property, securities, contracts, or
debts due to me, nor have I any income other
than what is contained in the schedule hereto
annexed and by me subscribed consisting of one
horse of the value of thirty dollars and two
heifers each of the value of five dollars lately
bought and not by me or yet paid for. That
since the 18th of March 1818 the following
changes have taken place. I then owned one
horse of the value of forty dollars and three
cows each of the value of ten dollars, and
I swapped the horse for the horse I now have
when a colt and fifteen dollars, and from
necessity have lived on the money as far as it
went. One of the cows died, another I killed
for meat for the use of myself and family, the
other from necessity I sold to one James Matley
for ten dollars in meat for the use of myself
and family. That I am by occupation a farmer
and that from my advanced age am unable to
persue it, that I have a wife and six children
all of whom are married and do not reside in
this State and are not in a situation to assist
me...."

Sworn and subscribed to in open Court on the
fifteenth day of October in the year of our Lord
Eighteen hundred and twenty seven

                                                       His
                  Signed   James Verdin X
                                                       Mark

(Note: The file shows that his pension of $8.00
per month began November 25, 1828, and he was
sent $26.63 on March 4, 1829. The file also shows
that his widow, Sarah Verden, received a pension
of $50.00 per year after his death. He died
June 19, 1843.)

JAMES VIRDEN (son of James and Sarah (Cater) Virden) was born November 8, 1787, in South Carolina. He married Nancy (Elizabeth) _____ about 1807 in South Carolina. Nancy was born in 1790 in South Carolina. The older children of James and Nancy Virden were also born in South Carolina. James and Nancy Virden moved from South Carolina to Kentucky, and may have spent some time in Missouri, but finally moved to Illinois between 1821 and 1823, where James younger brothers, Levi Virden and William Virden had already settled. James Virden died January 10, 1859; his wife, Nancy Virden, died August 13, 1860. Both are buried in Tolly Cemetery in Shelby County, Illinois. The children of James and Nancy Virden, were:

(1) Margaret Virden, born in 1808 in South Carolina. She married Jonathan B. Howard, who was born in Maryland in 1803. They had several children, all born in Illinois: (1) Dekalb Howard, born in 1834; (2) Palaskie Howard, born in 1836; (3) Nancy Howard, born in 1838; (4) Baltimore Howard, born in 1840; (5) Madison Howard, born in 1842; (6) Rachel Howard, born in 1844; (7) Randolph Howard, born in 1846; and (8) Thomas Howard, born in 1848;

(2) Cynthia Virden, born in September 1809. She married Andrew South (or Smith) February 4, 1830;

(3) Norman (or Naoman) Virden, born in Kentucky in 1815 or 1820. He married Ann _____, also born in Kentucky, and they had five children: (1) Narcissa Virden, born in 1837; (2) Luiza Virden, born in 1840, in Illinois; (3) Elisha Virden, born in 1842, in Illinois; (4) James Virden, born in 1844, in Illinois; and (5) Jane Virden, born in 1848, in Illinois;

(4) Nancy Virden who married William Templeton on January 6, 1840;

(5) Sarah Virden, born January 13, 1821, in Kentucky. She died November 12, 1897, in Illinois. She married Levi Casey, Jr. (who was born July 23, 1817, and died March 6, 1893) and they had four children: (1) Elizabeth Casey, born in 1842; (2) Samuel Casey, born in 1844; (3) Ann Casey, born in 1847; and (4) James Virden Casey, born in 1849;

(6) Hugh Virden, born in 1822 in either Missouri or Illinois;

(7) Lucinda Virden, born April 17, 1823, at Shoal Creek, Illinois. She married William Smith. (He was born January 30, 1820, in Nicholas County, Kentucky, and was a son of Nathan Smith of Maryland.) on March 2, 1843. They had five children: (1) Sarah Smith who died at age 3;

(2) Josephus (or Josephson) Smith, born in 1849; (3) Nancy A. Smith who married R.H. Bullington; (4) Mary Smith who died in February 1867 at age 13; and (5) Elizabeth Smith;

(8) Jacob Virden, born in 1824. He evidently never married since he was living in the home of Elizabeth Gordon in 1850 and with a cousin, John Virden, in 1880;

(9) Willis Virden, born April 17, 1825, and died September 18, 1901. His name was listed as Willis Virden on his marriage certificate, as William Virden on Census records, and as Willie Virden on his tombstone. He married Sarah Jacobs, born in 1823 in Kentucky. William and Sarah (Jacobs) Virden had seven children: (1) Lavina Virden, born October 4, 1848, died September 6, 1867; (2) Margaret Virden, born in 1849; (3) Nancy Virden, born in 1857, died September 19, 1858; (4) George A. Virden, born in 1867, who married Jane _____ in 1881; (5) William Jacobs Virden, born in 1852, and died about 1872; (6) Willis Virden, who married Sarah _____ in 1880; (7) Abner Virden, who married Mary E. _____ as his first wife. She died January 6, 1879, and he married Sydia Hinkle as his second wife in 1889. Abner and Mary Virden had a son, Willie Virden, who died October 6, 1878. Abner Virden died in 1931;

(10) Elizabeth Virden, born in 1829, in Illinois. She married Benjamin Gordon, a cousin, who was born in 1820 in Kentucky; and

(11) Emiline Virden, born in 1830 or 1831. She married Beverly Armstrong who was born in Illinois about 1828.

WILLIS VIRDEN (son of Willis and Sarah (Jacobs) Virden) married Sarah _____ in 1880 and had three children: (1) Charles Virden, born in 1881, died in 1932. He married Cora Neighswander in 1903. (2) Ida May Virden, born in 1882. She married Onily Little in 1903; (3) Eugene Virden, born in 1888; and (4) Christopher Virden, born in 1895. He lived in Upland, Nebraska.

Jane Virden (third child of James and Sarah (Cater) Virden) was born November 3, 1789, in South Carolina. She married John Gordon, probably in South Carolina or Kentucky, lived in Kentucky for a while, and then moved to Illinois between 1820 and 1825. It is likely that they moved at the same time James Virden, her brother, moved to Illinois. The 1830 Census shows James Gordon with a wife and 5 sons and 2 daughters. The 1840 Census shows Jane Gordon with 5 sons and 2 daughters. The known children of John and Jane (Virden) Gordon are:

(1) Levi Gordon, born in 1819 in Kentucky. He
married Mary _____ and they had three children:
(1) Nathaniel Gordon, born in 1845 in Illinois;
(2) Sariah Gordon, born in 1847 in Illinois;
and (3) Jane Gordon, born in 1849 in Illinois;
(2) Benjamin Gordon, born in 1820. He married a
cousin, Elizabeth Virden, who was a daughter of
James Virden;
(3) William Gordon, born in 1825 in Illinois. He
married Mary _____ and had two children: (1)
Melissa Gordon, born in 1848; and (2) Malvina
(or Malida) Gordon, born in 1849;
(4) Mary Gordon, born in 1827;
(5) Pheby Gordon, born in 1828; and
(6) Thomas Gordon, born in 1822.

WILLIAM VIRDEN (son of James and Sarah (Cater) Virden) was born in South Carolina, March 23, 1794. He was in Illinois as early as 1815 and was listed in the 1820 Census of Bond County, Illinois, as was his brother, Levi Virden. William Virden was also shown on the 1830 Census of Bond County, and on the 1840 Census of Christian County, Illinois. His will was dated March 7, 1848, naming his wife Nancy _____ Virden, four sons, and seven daughters. All of his children apparently were born in Illinois. The children of William and Nancy Virden were:

(1) Elizabeth Virden;
(2) Sarah Virden. (She may be the Sally Virden who
married James W. Gordon.);
(3) Susan Virden, born in 1821, married John D.
Ishmael on September 23, 1841. They had these
children: (1) Nancy S. Ishmael, born in 1842;
(2) Julia A. Ishmael, born in 1844; (3) Polly
Ishmael, born in 1846; (4) Amanda J. Ishmael,
born in 1848; and (5) Patia M. Ishmael, born in
1850;
(4) Charity Virden, born in 1823, married as her
first husband, John D. Davis, on July 4, 1844.
As her second husband she married John McKinza
(or McKinzie) on December 20, 1849;
(5) Minerva Virden, born in 1826, married James
Card on May 23, 1844. They had these children:
(1) Sarah Card, born in 1847; and (2) America
Card, born in 1849. Minerva (Virden) Card
died before 1855 and her husband, James Card,
married as his second wife, Elizabeth _____
and they had two children: (1) Hester Card,
born in 1855; and (2) Levi Card, born in 1857;
(6) William Virden, born in 1827. He married
Elizabeth _____ and they had one son, James
Samuel Virden, born in 1849. It is likely
that both William Virden and his wife, Elizabeth
Virden, died in the 1850's;

- (7) James Virden, born in 1829; and
- (8) Samuel Virden, born in 1831. He married Patience Meads on November 24, 1851. Samuel and Patience (Meads) Virden had a son, John Edward Virden, born November 16, 1853, and two other children, a boy and a girl. Samuel Virden died, probably a victim of cholera, and Patience (Meads) Virden married Andrew J. Oller as her second husband on October 30, 1859. Patience died, together with two of the children, leaving John Edward Virden an orphan before he was 10 years of age. He was raised by Gabe Durbin, a relative of his mother's;
- (9) Jane Virden, born in 1835;
- (10) John Virden, born in 1837; and
- (11) Nancy Virden. She married George McKinzie on May 30, 1853.

JOHN EDWARD VIRDEN (son of Samuel and Patience (Meads) Virden) was born November 16, 1853, in Christian County, Illinois, and died in 1945 in Kenosha, Wisconsin. On July 1881 he married Mary Ellen Painter in Talorville, Illinois. She was born in Illinois June 28, 1863, the daughter of Christopher "Kit" Painter and Margaret Matilda (Durbin) Painter. Her father was a Civil War Veteran. She died in 1928. John Edward and Mary Ellen (Painter) Virden had these children, all born in Illinois:

- (1) Edward Virden, born March 1885, died October 1886;
- (2) Nonie Agnes Virden, born April 18, 1887, died February 17, 1954;
- (3) Effie Margaret Virden, born in 1888, died in 1974;
- (4) Christopher Elmer Virden, born May 19, 1890, died July 21, 1964;
- (5) Alice Virden. She died March 2, 1969;
- (6) Mary Freda Virden. She died in 1959;
- (7) and (8) Two sons, who were stillborn, one named Charles Leo Virden.

Nonie Agnes Virden (daughter of John Edward and Mary Ellen (Painter) Virden) married Jesse Berry on February 23, 1909. He was born about 1884 and died October 3, 1972. Jesse and Nonie Agnes (Virden) Berry had these children:

- (1) Everett Berry, born February 27, 1911. In June 1936, he married Rose Kreagle and they had these children, all being born in Kenosha, Wisconsin: (1) Frederick Berry, born January 4, 1937; (2) Barbara Berry, born June 29, 1938; (3) Robert Berry, born December 12, 1939; and (4) Thomas Berry, born January 29, 1943;

(2) Ruth Berry, born June 6, 1913. On January 17, 1931, she married Oliver Shields, and they had a daughter, Audrey Shields, who married James Aceto on February 1, 1952;

(3) Edward Berry, born April 22, 1917. He married Angelina Nacolazzi and they had these children: (1) Catherine Berry (an adopted daughter) born June 1, 1936; (2) Helen Berry, born August 22, 1946; (3) Patricia Berry, born October 20, 1948; (4) James Berry, born March 28, 1950; and Susan Berry, born January 11, 1952;

(4) Gertrude Berry, born May 26, 1918. She married Harold John Horne and they had these children: (1) Judith Horne, born August 2, 1936; (2) Sharon Horne, born February 16, 1945; (3) John Horne, born November 5, 1946; (4) James Horne, born March 27, 1949; and (5) Sandra Horne, born June 11, 1951.

Effie Margaret Virden (daughter of John Edward and Mary Ellen (Painter) Virden) married Roy Deweese in 1908. Roy and Effie Margaret (Virden) Deweese had these children: (1) Eva Deweese, who married Harry Myers on December 24, 1938, in St. Charles, Missouri. They had no children; (2) Marjorie Deweese, who married Paul Oller, on March 9, 1940, at St. Charles, Missouri. They had no children; and (3) Ormand Deweese, who married _____ Oller--a daughter of George Oller. They had a daughter, Betty Deweese, who married Oscar Green.

Alice Virden (daughter of John Edward and Mary Ellen (Painter) Virden) married Francis H. Corr. They had no children.

Mary Freda Virden (daughter of John Edward and Mary Ellen (Painter) Virden) married Jerry Agazzi. They had no children.

CHRISTOPHER ELMER VIRDEN (son of John Edward and Mary Ellen (Painter) Virden) was married twice. As his first wife he married Alice Anderson on July 16, 1915. She was born in Salisbury, Missouri, about 1895. They had one child, Amy Virden, who only lived three months and 13 days. Alice (Anderson) Virden died from childbirth on July 18, 1916.

Christopher Elmer Virden was born in Clarksdale, Christian County, Illinois, May 12, 1890. During his early years he travelled a great deal. He worked on the railroad, lived in hobo "Jungles", helped lay railroad tracks, was a railroad detective, a justice of the peace, a telegrapher and agent on a number of railroads in the Midwest. He served in World War I. In his later years he was a carpenter. He moved many times during his life, living in Illinois, Indiana, Mississippi, Arkansas, Missouri, and California. His last residence was in Oakdale, California, where he moved in 1951, and where he died in 1964 while fishing--one of his favorite pastimes. He used the name "John Christopher" most of his life.

As his second wife he married Cora Ellen Wells (daughter of John and Lillie Frances (Mitchell) Wells) who was born September 6, 1900, in Kingman, Indiana. Cora Wells Virden died in Yucca Valley, San Bernadino, California, July 15, 1975. Both she and Christopher are buried in Golden Gate National Cemetery, San Bruno, California. Christopher Elmer and Cora Ellen (Wells) Virden had nine children.

(1) Ellen Frances Virden, born November 7, 1918, in Glenarm, Illinois, and died December 11, 1921, at Pawnee, Illinois;

(2) Christopher Edward Virden, born January 17, 1920, at Glenarm, Illinois. He was in World War II. He lives in Yucca Valley, California;

(3) Mildred Eva Virden, born July 6, 1921, in Glenarm, Illinois. She lives in Minneapolis, Minnesota;

(4) Charles Laurence Virden, born May 19, 1924, at Kenney, Illinois. He died in December 1944 in Germany while serving in the U.S. Army during World War II;

(5) James Robert Virden, born July 17, 1925, in Fort Wayne, Indiana. He served during World War II. He lives in Russia, Ohio;

(6) Joseph William Virden, born February 26, 1928, in Fort Wayne, Indiana. He served in Germany during the occupation of that country after World War II. He lives in Hollywood, California;

(7) John Edward Virden, born February 19, 1931, in Houston, Mississippi. He served for some 22 years in the Marine Corps during both the Korean War and the Vietnam War. He lives in Joshua Tree, California;

(8) JoAnn LaVerne Virden, born September 13, 1937, in Garrett, Indiana. She lives in San Clemente, California; and

(9) Ruth Ann Virden, born February 16, 1941, in Garrett, Indiana. She now lives in Chula Vista, California.

CHRISTOPHER EDWARD VIRDEN (son of Christopher Elmer and Cora Ellen (Wells) Virden) married Zella Lavonne Pulver on February 6, 1939. She was born January 20, 1922, in Indiana. Christopher Elmer and Zella Lavonne (Pulver) Virden had seven children:

(1) Gwenlyn Yuvonne Virden, born July 27, 1939. She married Charles David Chenelle on August 9, 1959, and they had these children: (1) David Chenelle, born May 14, 1960; (2) Colin Chenelle, born December 2, 1961; (3) Francis Chenelle, a son, born January 31, 1962; and (4) Delsey Chenelle, a daughter, born August 31, 1964. The Chenelles live in Peru, South America;

(2) Rochelle Marie Virden, born August 29, 1941. She married John Garcia on December 17, 1956, and they had these children: (1) John Garcia, born July 4, 1957; (2) Christopher Garcia, born August 19, 1958; (3) Lori Garcia, born August 14, 1960; (4) Robert Garcia, born August 1, 1963; and (5) Shelly Garcia, born December 25, 1967;
(3) John Edward Virden, born July 11, 1943;
(4) Michael Allen Virden, born July 13, 1947;
(5) Noel Francis Virden, born December 27, 1948;
(6) Mathew Virden, born December 21, 1961, a twin; and
(7) Christine Virden, born December 21, 1961, a twin.

Mildred Eva Virden married James Durr on October 27, 1945. James and Mildred Eva (Virden) Durr had these children: (1) Charles William Durr, born January 29, 1947. He married Terry Stuart; (2) Mary Jean Durr, born September 12, 1948. She married Bill Bodine; and (3) Timothy Durr, born January 17, 1951.

JAMES ROBERT VIRDEN (son of Christopher Elmer and Cora Ellen (Wells) Virden) married Lucille Peltier on June 26, 1946. James Robert and Lucille (Peltier) Virden had three children: (1) Angela Virden, born November 28, 1947; (2) Christina Virden, born March 30, 1949; and (3) Dennis Virden, born February 25, 1954.

JOSEPH WILLIAM VIRDEN (son of Christopher Elmer and Cora Ellen (Wells) Virden) married Frances Arlene Hefty on May 17, 1945. Joseph William and Frances Arlene (Hefty) Virden had five children:

(1) Judith Frances Virden, born August 28, 1946, and died September 22, 1946;
(2) Gloria Ann Virden, born October 27, 1948, in Geissen, Germany. She married Willie Crider June 18, 1966. They had one son, William Crider, born October 13, 1973, in Deland, Florida. They were divorced in 1975;
(3) Joseph Robert Virden, born December 9, 1949, in Winter Park, Florida. He married Pamela Jean Mounts on August 25, 1967, in Franklin, Kentucky. They had these children: (1) Joseph L. Virden, born August 18, 1967, in Kentucky; (2) Jeanne Frances Virden, born November 23, 1970, in Florida; (3) Jeffrey Virden, born July 29, 1972, in Florida; and (4) Jennefer Judith Virden, born January 20, 1974, in Florida;
(4) Marilyn Frances Virden, born November 15, 1951, died December 9, 1951; and
(5) Beverly Jean Virden, born October 24, 1952, in Los Angeles, California. She married Allen Rhoades May 1, 1970. They had no children. They were divorced in 1974.

JOHN EDWARD VIRDEN (son of Christopher Elmer and Cora Ellen (Wells) Virden) married Virginia Marques in December 1956. She was born October 30, 1935. She is the great-great-granddaughter of Pio Pico, the first Governor of California. John Edward and Virginia (Marques) Virden had three children: (1) Jonathan Virden, born July 13, 1957; (2) Ellen Virden, born October 20, 1958; and Roxane Virden, born August 21, 1963.

JoAnn LaVerne Virden married John Dwane Pirkle at Oakdale, California, on November 5, 1955. He was born October 20, 1939, in Oakdale, California. John Dwane and JoAnn LaVerne (Virden) Pirkle had four children: (1) Kathleen Ellen Pirkle, born May 12, 1956; (2) Gerald Dwane Pirkle, born March 17, 1958; (3) Robert Jeffrey Pirkle, born October 31, 1959; and (4) Brian Scott Pirkle, born December 7, 1964.

Ruth Ann Virden (daughter of Christopher Elmer and Cora Ellen (Wells) Virden) married Cecil Leroy Shoup on July 13, 1959. Cecil Leroy and Ruth Ann (Virden) Shoup had five children: (1) Edward Lawrence Shoup, born January 4, 1960; (2) Jennifer Aleen Shoup, born May 6, 1961; (3) Jeffrey Paul Shoup, born November 15, 1962; (4) Thomas Michael Shoup, born December 21, 1963; and (5) Kenneth Patrick Shoup, born February 22, 1965.

LEVI VERDEN (the son, and sixth child, of James and Sarah (Cater) Verden of South Carolina) was born April 4, 1796, in South Carolina. When he was 17 years of age he moved to Kentucky. Reportedly, he met his first wife, Rachel _____, in Kentucky. From there he moved to Illinois where he lived by 1818, probably the same year he married Rachel. Levi Verden is listed in the 1820 Census of Bond County, Illinois (as was his brother William Verden). Levi Verden was then listed in the Census of Shelby County, and afterwards in Fayette County, Illinois, until his death. He died after the age of 80. His first wife, Rachel, died in Shelby County, Illinois, in 1826. Levi and Rachel Verden had four children, all born in Illinois:

(1) Sarah Verden, born in 1819. She married Thomas Ishmael on July 24, 1845. He was born in Kentucky in 1819. Sarah (Verden) Ishmael died young. Thomas and Sarah (Verden) Ishmael had four children: (1) Benjamin Ishmael, born in 1842. (Note: This son was probably a son of Thomas Ishmael by a prior marriage since he and Sarah did not marry until 1845.); (2) Rachel Ishmael, born in 1846; (3) Elizabeth Ishmael, born in 1847; and (4) Andrew Ishmael, born in 1849.

(2) John Verden, born in 1822. He married Elizabeth _____ sometime before 1848. John and Elizabeth Verden had two children: (1) Melvina Verden, born in 1848; and (2) Levi Verden, born in 1849, died in 1941. John Verden died young and his widow, Elizabeth Verden, may have been the woman who married

Wooten Harris on November 22, 1854. Levi Verden married Frances Sears (she was born in 1852 and died in 1920) and they had three children: (1) Amelda Verden, born in 1873, died in 1894; (2) William Eugene Verden, born in 1875, died in 1954; (3) Fonaire Verden who was born and died in 1877; and (4) Frederick Verden, born in 1879;

(3) Isaac Verden, born in 1824. He died about 1864. He married Serilda (or Surrelda) Jane Ishmael on February 4, 1844. She was born in Illinois in 1846;

(4) Catherine Verden, born in 1825, died in 1854. She married John Massey on April 28, 1845, and they had a son, William Radford Massey, born after 1850. John and Catherine Massey died in 1854 leaving their son an orphan.

ISAAC VERDEN (son of Levi and Rachel Verden) and Serilda Jane (Ishmael) Verden had these children:

(1) Samuel Verden, born in 1844. He married Sarah _____, who was born in 1846, and they had two children, a daughter, born in 1875 and a son, William Verden, born in 1877;

(2) James F. Verden, born November 28, 1846, and died March 2, 1916. He had these children (wife's name unavailable): (1) Katie K. Verden, born in 1874, died June 9, 1949; (2) Orville Verden, born in 1879, died 1957; (3) Martin I. Verden, born January 21, 1881; (4) Ira Verden, born about 1888; and (5) Bessie Verden, also born about 1888;

(3) Levi Verden, born in 1848;
(4) Martha Verden, born in 1850;
(5) John Verden, born in 1854; and
(6) Radford Verden, born in 1856.

LEVI VERDEN, after the death of his first wife, Rachel Verden, married as his second wife, Catherine Reese, on October 30, 1828. She was born in 1812 in South Carolina. Levi and Catherine (Reese) Verden had these children:

(1) Margaret Verden, born in 1830. She married James Ishmael about 1848 and they had two children, Catherine Ishmael, born in 1849, and Elizabeth Ishmael, born in 1850;

(2) William Verden, born about 1831, died after he was 21, probably in 1854 when other members of the family died;

(3) Mahala Verden, born in 1836, died in 1854. Since Catherine and John Massey died of cholera

in 1854, it is reasonable to assume that Mahala Verden, and other brothers and sisters who died about 1854, all died from the same disease;

(4) Levi David Verden, born April 7, 1839, died February 5, 1917; and

(5) Eli Verden, born in 1841. He married Susan T. Price February 10, 1867. She was born April 20, 1839, and died November 23, 1888. Eli and Susan T. (Price) Verden had these children: (1) William H. Verden, born in 1868; (2) Joseph P. Verden, born in 1870; (3) Mandy G. Verden, born in 1875; and (4) Melvina Verden, born in 1789 or 1780.

LEVI DAVID VERDEN (son of Levi and Catherine (Reese) Verden) married Martha Thorpe, who was born May 13, 1844, and died March 20, 1884. Levi David and Martha (Thorpe) Verden had these children:

(1) A child who died while an infant on February 18, 1873;
(2) Emma Verden, born in 1875. She married Franklin Davis;
(3) William Edward Verden, born January 24, 1877, died May 19, 1964. He married twice. His first wife was Bertha Lavina Hamblen who died in 1916. There were at least six children, four daughters and two sons, Donald Verden, and Luther Verden. Apparently the children were by his first wife. His second wife was Hazel _____;
(4) Mary Verden, born in 1879;
(5) Lulu Almira Verden;
(6) Homer Levi Verden, born in 1883, died in 1947. He married Martha _____, who was born in 1888 and died in 1926; and
(7) Mina Verden.

Charity Virden (the daughter, and ninth child, of James and Sarah (Cater) Verden) was born in South Carolina May 5, 1803. She probably went to Kentucky with her older brothers and sisters and then to Illinois, where she married Daniel Francisco on January 10, 1822. Her brother, William Verden, gave his consent. Daniel Francisco was born in Alabama and went to Illinois in 1813 as a young boy. He died November 18, 1859. Charity died November 30, 1853. Daniel and Charity (Virden) Francisco had fourteen children:

(1) Zimeria Francisco, a daughter, who died in 1835;
(2) Sarah Francisco, who died young;
(3) Rachel Francisco, who died young;
(4) Alfred Francisco, born in 1825. Served in Civil War. Died May 12, 1864. He married Mary _____ and they had three children: (1) Elsen Francisco, born in 1845; (2) Elizabeth Francisco, born in 1848; and (3) Elander Francisco, a daughter, born in 1849;

(5) Allen Francisco, born in 1825, and probably a twin to Alfred. He married Mary Terry January 8, 1846. She was born in Kentucky in 1825, and died July 6, 1851. Allen and Mary (Terry) Francisco had three children, William Francisco, born in 1848, Elizabeth Francisco, born in 1849, and another child whose information is lacking. After the death of his first wife he married Ellen Waller on November 19, 1851;

(6) Eli Francisco, born in 1826. He married Rosseline ____ who was born in 1830, and they had a daughter, Charity Francisco, born in 1849;

(7) Izri (or Izah, or Jazah - Joseph) Francisco, born in 1829;

(8) Daniel Francisco;

(9) Levi Francisco, born in 1832;

(10) Howard Francisco, born in 1835, died in 1927;

(11) John Francisco, born in 1837, died in 1916;

(12) Jacob Francisco, born in 1839, died in 1893. He married Susan J. ____, who was born in 1832 and died October 11, 1886;

(13) James Francisco, born in 1841, died in 1904; and

(14) Peter Francisco, born in 1842, died February 18, 1917. He married twice, his first wife being C.A. ____, who was born in January 1843 and died October 23, 1865. They had a son, Dennis Francisco who died August 6, 1861, when only 7 days of age. As his second wife Peter Francisco married Nancy E. ____, who was born in 1843 and died November 9, 1897. They had a daughter, Elizabeth Francisco, who died July 10, 1868, when only 1 day of age.

(See also: *Moultrie County Heritage*, Vol. 1, No. 2, February 1974.)

HUGH RADFORD VIRDEN (a son and the last child of James and Sarah (Cater) Verden) was born in South Carolina in 1807. He married Margarett Wilson on April 10, 1828. She was born in South Carolina in 1807. Hugh Radford Virden was in Illinois early in his life and settled in Montgomery County, Illinois. All of his children were born in Illinois. Hugh Radford and Margarett (Wilson) Virden had eight children:

(1) James Virden, born in 1830. He married Edith Wilson, born in 1838 in Kentucky. They had two children: (1) Hiram Virden, born January 9, 1859, died March 13, 1930. (He married twice. His first wife's name is unknown. As his second wife he married Mrs. Barbara ____ Massey, the widow of William Massey who died in 1902.); (2) Nettie Virden, who married ____ Ishmael;

(2) John Virden, born in 1833, who married Ester _____.
They had three children: (1) Addie Virden, born
in 1872; (2) Mary Jane Virden, born in 1873;
and (3) John R. Virden, born in 1876;
(3) Hiram Virden, born in 1836;
(4) Elisha Virden, born in 1837;
(5) Joseph Virden, born in 1839;
(6) Rutha Virden, born in 1841;
(7) Martha Virden, born in 1843. (This Martha
Virden married William Hinson on July 3, 1872;
if it was not her that married, then it must
have been the daughter of Isaac Virden who
married him.);
(8) Bub Virden, born in 1849 or 1850. (This is
probably a nickname.)

Cecil Leroy Shoup, Jr., born December 22, 1937, in Washington Township, Pennsylvania, married Ruth Ann Virden on July 13, 1959, at St. Mary's Catholic Church, Oakdale, California. (He was the son of Cecil Leroy Shoup and Nora B. (Serafine) Shoup.) She was born February 16, 1941, in Garrett, Indiana, the daughter of Christopher E. and Cora E. (Wells) Virden. Cecil Leroy and Ruth Ann (Virden) Shoup have five children: (1) Edward Lawrence Shoup, born January 4, 1960, in San Diego, California; (2) Jennifer Aleen Shoup, a daughter, born May 6, 1961, in La Mesa, California; (3) Jeffrey Paul Shoup, born November 15, 1962, in La Mesa, California; (4) Thomas Michael Shoup, born December 21, 1963, in La Mesa, California; and (5) Kenneth Patrick Shoup, born February 22, 1965, in La Mesa, California.

JOSEPH WILLIAM VIRDEN, born February 26, 1928, in Ft. Wayne, Indiana, married Frances Arlene Hefty, May 17, 1945, in Garrett, Indiana. (He was the son of Christopher Elmer Virden and Cora Ellen (Wells) Virden.) She was born January 1, 1929, in Auburn, Indiana, the daughter of Otto Earl and Ethel Lenore (Stone) Hefty. Joseph William and Frances Arlene (Hefty) Virden have five children:

(1) Judith Frances Virden, born August 28, 1946, in
Auburn, Indiana, and died September 22, 1946;
(2) Gloria Ann Virden, born October 27, 1948, in
Geissen, Germany. On June 18, 1966, she married
William Crider and they had one child, William
Mathew Crider, born October 13, 1973. They
were divorced in 1975;
(3) Joseph Robert Virden, born December 9, 1949, in
Winter Park, Florida. On August 25, 1967, he
married Pamela Jean Mounts in Franklin, Kentucky.
Joseph Robert and Pamela Jean (Mounts) Virden
live in St. Petersburg, Florida, and have four
children: (1) Joseph Lee Virden, born August 18,
1967, in Franklin, Kentucky; (2) Jeanne Frances
Virden, born November 23, 1970, in Orlando,
Florida; (3) Jeffry David Virden, born July 29,
1972, in Orlando, Florida; and (4) Jennifer
Judith Virden, born January 20, 1974, in Ft.
Myers, Florida;

(4) Marilyn Frances Virden, born November 15, 1951, in Los Angeles, California, and died December 9, 1951; and

(5) Beverly Jean Virden, born October 24, 1952, in Los Angeles, California. On May 1, 1970, she married Allen Dale Rhodes. They were divorced May 1, 1974. There were no children.

ISAAC VIRDEN was born January 10, 1779, in either Maryland or Virginia (one son gave his birthplace as Maryland, another gave it as Virginia). He went to Ohio in the early part of the settlement of that state and was one of the early pioneers of Ross County, Ohio. On April 9, 1809, he married Amelia Saddler, who was born in Ohio on June 10, 1791. Sometime between 1832 and 1839 Isaac and his family moved to Illinois, and he settled on Buckhart Creek, in Christian County, Illinois. He lived on the property until his death in 1846. He was listed in the 1840 Census of Christian County, as was his son William Virden. Isaac and Amelia (Saddler) Virden had eleven children:

(1) William Virden, born about 1810 or 1811, in Ohio;
(2) John W. Virden, born about 1812, in Ohio;
(3) Samuel Virden, born about 1812, in Ohio;
(4) A son, name unknown;
(5) A son, name unknown;
(6) A son, name unknown;
(7) Archibald L. Virden, born October 27, 1823, in Ohio;
(8) Isaac Virden, born October 23, 1824, in Ohio;
(9) Wilson Virden, born in 1827, in Ohio;
(10) A daughter, born between 1825 and 1830, in Ohio; and
(11) J.W. or F.W. Virden, born about 1828, in Ohio.

(Note: The writer believes that Isaac Virden was probably the grandson of John Virdin and Ellinor (Sipple) Virdin of Kent County, Delaware, since they had a son Isaac Virdin, who would quite likely have named his son Isaac Virdin. Further, it is known that John and Ellinor Virden had a granddaughter, Mary Virdin, who married and moved to Ohio.)

William Virden (son of Isaac and Amelia (Saddler) Virden) was listed in the 1840 Census and the 1850 Census of Christian County, Illinois. The 1850 Census gave his age as 39 and that of his wife, Elizabeth Virden, as age 39. William Virden was listed as a tavernkeeper. According to the 1850 Census they had these children, although it is possible that there were other children who died young: (1) Amelia Virden, age 13, at time of 1850 Census; (2) Nelson Virden, age 12, at time of 1850 Census; (3) Francis Virden, age 9, at time of 1850 Census; and (4) William A. Virden, age 6 months, at time of 1850 Census.

JOHN W. VIRDEN (son of Isaac and Amelia (Saddler) Virden) was listed in the 1850 Census of Macoupin County, Illinois. His wife, Emily Virden, was shown as age 37 in that census. His occupation in 1850 was listed as farmer. The town of Virden, Illinois, is named after him because he was the owner of a stage stand south of the site selected for the town. He reportedly opened the stand about 1838 at the intersection of the Springfield and St. Louis stage line and the Springfield and Vandalia Stage line. The location was widely known as the Virden Stand. The first building erected in Virden was a hotel built by John Virden. The 1850 Census lists John and Emily Virden as having four daughters: (1) Eleanor Virden, age 12; (2) Cornelia Virden, age 6; (3) Harriet Virden, age 8; and (4) Emeline Virden, age 4.

SAMUEL VIRDEN (son of Isaac and Amelia (Saddler) Virden) was born in Ross County, Ohio, about 1812. He was shown on the records of Dane County, Illinois, in 1839. But the 1850 Census of Grant County, Wisconsin, shows him with his wife, Margaret (Kendall) Virden. Afterwards, he may have moved to St. Louis, Missouri.

> (Note: Although he is listed here as the son of Isaac Virden, and available evidence seems to indicate this, there is no absolute proof that he is Isaac's son.)

ARCHIBALD VIRDEN (son of Isaac and Amelia (Saddler) Virden) married Henrietta Dyson on August 18, 1844, and settled in Christian County, Illinois. In 1852 he moved to Virden, Illinois, and first worked as a plasterer and later as a druggist. He was listed with his wife and two children in the 1850 Census of Montgomery County, Illinois. He was listed in the 1870 Census of Macoupin County, Illinois, with a wife and three children. His occupation was listed as druggist. He was an important business man in Virden, Illinois, and was elected to the State Legislature in 1872. Based upon Census records Archibald and Henrietta (Dyson) Virden had several children: (1) Samira Virden, age 3, during 1850 Census. She died young; (2) Ann Virden, age 1, during 1850 Census. She was listed as 21 during the 1870 Census; (3) William Virden, age 18, during 1870 Census; and (4) Edgar Virden, age 12, during 1870 Census.

Ann Virden (daughter of Archibald and Henrietta (Dyson) Virden) married Otho Williams.

EDGAR VIRDEN (son of Archibald and Henrietta (Dyson) Virden) married Jennie Piper.

WILLIAM VIRDEN (son of Archibald and Henrietta (Dyson) Virden) married Sarah Wilcox. William and Sarah (Wilcox) Virden had three children: (1) Homer Virden, born in 1876, who married Laura _____ and had a daughter, Betty Virden; (2) Henrietta Virden, born in 1877, who married Dieter Rathgeber, and had a daughter, Katheryn Rathgeber; and (3) Archibald Virden, born after 1880, who married Orah _____, and had two sons, Archie Virden and Homer Virden.

ISAAC VIRDEN (son of Isaac and Amelia (Saddler) Virden) married Rachel Nester in 1845. She was born in Bath County, Kentucky. Isaac and Rachel (Nester) Virden lived in Christian County, Illinois, and had six children: (1) Anne Virden, born in 1848; (2) Harriett Virden, born in 1850; (3) Julie Virden, born in 1853; (4) May Virden, born in 1855; (5) William Virden, born in 1858; and (6) Molly Virden, born in 1861.

WILSON VIRDEN (son of Isaac and Amelia (Saddler) Virden) married Mary _____, who was born in 1833. The 1850 Census of Sangamon County, Illinois, showed Samuel Dixon, age 20, living with them. He could have been Mary's brother.

J.W. (or F.W.) VIRDEN was married twice. He was listed in the 1860 Census of Macoupin County, Illinois, with his wife, Margaret Virden, and four children. Living with them at that time was Rebecca Cox, age 20. His occupation was shown as plasterer. The children of J.W. and Margaret Virden in 1860 were: (1) Henry Virden, age 16; (2) Fannie Virden, age 4; (3) Isaac Virden, age 9; and (4) Charles Virden, age 1.

The 1880 Census of Illinois shows his wife to be Harriet Virden, and the following children are shown: (1) Fanny Virden, age 24 (daughter of Margaret); (2) Charles Virden, age 21 (son of Margaret); (3) Fred Virden, age 15; (4) Nellie Virden, age 13; (5) Earl Virden, age 6; (6) Stella Virden, age 3; and (7) Archie Virden, age 7 months. (Note: He is listed as J.W. Virden in the 1860 Census and as F.W. Virden in the 1880 Census.)

ISAAC VIRDEN (born January 10, 1779; died in 1846) was a native of Maryland and emigrated to Ohio at an early date where he married Amelia Sadler. She was born June 10, 1791 in Ohio. They had eleven children born in Ohio--ten boys and one girl. He was a farmer who in 1832 moved to Illinois and settled on Buckhart Creek, four miles west of Grove City. When he settled on Buckhart Creek it was a howling wilderness and pigs and sheep were kept in pens near the house so that the wolves would not destroy them. The family had to go sixteen miles to a mill to do their own grinding of grain, which was accomplished by having a yoke of oxen to the wheel for the grinding. (From an old news clipping, unidentified.)

I.Q. Virden (eighth son of Isaac and Amelia (Saddler) Virden) was born in Ross County, Ohio, October 24, 1824. He lived at home until he was twenty-one years of age. He then married Rachel Nester, of Bath County, Kentucky. He was a farmer. They had six children, five daughters and one son. The daughters all married. The son was William E. Virden. (From an old news clipping, unidentified.)

ARCHIBALD L. VIRDEN (seventh son of Isaac and Amelia (Saddler) Virden) was born in Ross County, Ohio, October 27, 1823. On August 18, 1844, he married Henrietta Dyson, who was the daughter of William Dyson and a native of Maryland. He lived most of his life in Virden, Illinois, a town named after an older brother of his, John Virden. He and his wife had seven children of whom only three were living in the 1880's:

(1) Anna Maria Virden who married Otho Williams; (2) William H. Virden; and (3) Edgar L. Virden. Henrietta (Dyson) Virden was born January 8, 1827, in Montgomery County, the daughter of William Dyson and Annie (Darnall) Dyson (who was the daughter of Thomas and Henrietta (Fish) Darnall of Delaware).

Otho and Anna Marie (Virden) Williams had three children: (1) Mariel Williams; (2) Archie Williams; and (3) Lamira Williams.

WILLIAM H. VIRDEN, born June 28, 1852, married Sarah Wilcox and had three children: (1) Homer W. Virden; (2) Henrietta E. Virden; and (3) Archie L. Virden. William H. Virden died in December 1882.

EDGAR L. VIRDEN married Jennie Piper and moved to Cincinnati, Ohio. (See Portrait and Biographical Record of Macoupin County, Illinois, 1882.)

LACY S. VIRDEN married Delileh Coffman on May 13, 1817, near Zanesville, Ohio, Muskingum County. He was five feet ten inches tall with dark brown hair and brown eyes. He had never been married before and his wife did not marry after his death. They lived in Zanesville for nine years and near Zanesville for eleven years. After his death Delileh Virden filed a claim for one hundred sixty acres of land and on May 10, 1878, she filed a claim for a pension based on the service of Lacey S. Virdin in the War of 1812. At that time she listed her age as seventy eight. Her Post Office address was Bridgeville, Ohio. Lacy S. Virden died September 4, 1834. He volunteered for service in the Army on June 18, 1812, in Captain William Reynold's Company. He was a prisoner of war at the time of the surrender of Brigadier General Hull and remained a prisoner for about six months, until he was honorably discharged at Detroit.

SAMUEL VIRDEN, who was born in 1812 in Ohio, and lived in Grant County, Wisconsin in 1850, married Margaret Kendall (Kindle). She was born March 9, 1823, in Pennsylvania, the daughter of James and Margaret (Noble) Kendall. James Kendall was born February 6, 1778, in Pennsylvania and died May 10, 1868, in Lafayette County, Wisconsin. Margaret (Noble) Kendall was born October 11, 1804, in Crawford County, Pennsylvania.

> "This Kendall family came across Ohio to Sangamon County, Illinois, prior to going to Wisconsin. They lived in Kendall Township, named after the Kendall's. In 1839 Dane County, Illinois, was formed from part of Sangamon, Montgomery, and Shelby Counties. The name was changed to Christian County in 1840. The first election for county officers was held in Dane County in 1839. Samuel Virden served as a clerk on the election board. Samuel Virden does not show up on the 1840 Census.

1850 Census of Grant County, Wisconsin shows:

Samuel Virden, age 38, merchant, born in Ohio
Margaret Virden, age 27, born in Pennsylvania
Harrison West, age 34, born in New York
Hannah Irene West, age 17, born in Kentucky

"Samuel Virden left Wisconsin and supposedly went to the St. Louis, Missouri, area. I have never found any further trace of him. By the fact that the Kendall family lived in the area when Dane County was formed, I have always believed that she married the Samuel Virden mentioned in 1839, and that he had to be a son of Isaac Virden, since Isaac settled on Buckhart Creek when the first County election was held in 1839...."
(Letter dated March 19, 1977, from James R. Virden, of Russia, Ohio.)

OSCAR VIRDEN was born June 19, 1819, in Tompkinville, Monroe County, Kentucky, June 19, 1819. He died March 2, 1905, in Waterloo, Iowa. He married Love Charity Powell, who was born December 25, 1822, in Massachusetts, and died November 28, 1910, at Waterloo, Iowa. Oscar and Love Charity (Powell) Virden had these children:

(1) George Virden, born in 1837, in Wayne County, Indiana, died in the State of Washington;
(2) Charles Virden, born in 1839, in Illinois, died in Waterloo, Iowa;
(3) Norman Virden, born in 1852 in Iowa, died in 1865, age 14, at Waterloo, Iowa;
(4) Elizabeth Virden, born July 1, 1954, died October 25, 1943, at Osakis, Minnesota. She married David Orville Bly, October 30, 1875;
(5) Emma Martha Virden, born February 5, 1857, at Waterloo, Iowa, died September 17, 1957, at Osakis, Minnesota. She married Jacob Artemus Coons; and
(6) William Virden, born in 1860, died in 1865.

Isaac Virden, son of William Virden, died in Mobile, Alabama, September 10, 1865, age 35 years, 4 months, 15 days. He was buried in Waterloo, Iowa. Eliza Virden was probably his wife since she is buried in the same cemetery having died January 1, 1883, age 50 years, 26 days.

James Virden, son of William Virden, was born in 1823. He married Charlotte Platt as his first wife and they had two children: (1) George Virden, born in 1852, and (2) Willard Virden, born January 8, 1854. After the death of his first wife, James Virden married Harriet Rathbone (?).

According to Mrs. Ruth Shoup, Ralph Virden, of La Jolla, California (who died in 1974) told her that there were half brothers and half sisters in the family of James Virden. He also mentioned the Rathbones. He said that he did not know of the other children after the marriage of James Virden to Harriet Rathbone. George Virden, the first son, was lost track of, but Mrs. Philip L. White, of Denver, Colorado (who was a sister of the late Ralph Virden, of La Jolla, California) believes that he had a son who lived in Santa Rosa, California. She furnished the following information about Willard Virden to Mrs. Ruth Shoup.

WILLARD VIRDEN, was born January 8, 1854, in Waterloo, Iowa. He died March 25, 1933, in San Diego, California. He married Mary Brockway, who was born June 21, 1860, in Frederickton, New Brunswick, Canada, and who died April 25, 1952, in Denver, Colorado. William and Mary (Brockway) Virden had these children:

(1) Lottie Virden, born August 12, 1880, in Loveland, Colorado, and died November 4, 1956, at San Diego, California. She married Jesse Jay Brown, who was born March 14, 1882, in Illinois, and died October 13, 1953, in San Diego, California;

(2) Ray Willard Virden, born March 23, 1885, in Loveland, Colorado, and died December 19, 1970, in Denver, Colorado. He married Margaret Beynon, who was born February 3, 1888. They had no children;

(3) Lulu Virden, born November 26, 1888, at Douglas, Wyoming, died April 13, 1972, at Carmichael, California. She married Finn J. Angell, who was born May 3, 1891, in Oslo, Norway, and died February 2, 1952, in Los Angeles, California;

(4) Jessie Mary Virden, born June 9, 1890, at Douglas, Wyoming. She married Lawrence Robert Kershner on March 20, 1909. He was born March 21, 1888, at Indianapolis, Indiana, and died October 20, 1935, at San Diego, California;

(5) Ralph J. Virden, born April 24, 1895, in Douglas, Wyoming, died January 7, 1974, in La Jolla, California. He married as his first wife Beatrice Russell, who was born October 6, 1895, in San Diego, California, and died about July 26, 1922, in San Diego. As his second wife he married Agnes Ridgeway Steinmann, who died April 17, 1966, in La Jolla, California;

(6) Alice B. Virden, born November 24, 1897, in Douglas, Wyoming. She married Philip L. White on February 7, 1920, in Denver, Colorado. He was born May 10, 1898, in Denver, Colorado. They had no children; and

(7) Harold Virden, born November 24, 1897, in Douglas, Wyoming, and died in August 1898 in Douglas. He was a twin to Alice.

Jesse and Lottie (Virden) Brown had one child, Clifford Willard Brown, who was born August 14, 1919, in Denver, and died November 5, 1974, in San Diego, California. He married Rita Patricia Brychel, who was born December 18, 1949, in San Diego. They had no children.

Finn J. and Lulu (Virden) Angell had a child, Winifred Lois Angell, born June 3, 1913, in San Francisco, California. She married Charles H. Trudrung (who was born December 17, 1912) on October 15, 1938, and they had a son, Richard Charles Trudrung, born December 13, 1945, in Vacaville, California.

Lawrence Robert and Jessie Mary (Virden) Kershner had a daughter, Mildred Kershner, born December 14, 1909, in Los Angeles, California.

RALPH J. VIRDEN and Beatrice (Russell) Virden had a son, Willard Russell Virden, born June 14, 1922, in San Diego, California. Ralph J. Virden had no children by his second wife.

HIRAM P. VIRDEN was the son of James and Edith (Wilson) Virden, James Virden being born in Illinois and Edith Virden being born in Kentucky. He was married twice. The children of his first marriage were: (1) Ellie Litts Virden; (2) Edith Virden; (3) George Virden; (4) Roscoe Virden; (5) Onee Virden (the mother of Ruth Finnegan Meire); and (6) Gertrude Switzer Virden. Hiram died in March 1930. As his second wife he married Mrs. Barbara Ellen Massey, the widow of William Massey, who died in 1902. She and Hiram were married in 1920. She was born in Bond County, Illinois, August 27, 1866, and died September 10, 1945, age 79 years. She had been a resident of Decatur, Illinois, for 48 years. (From Decatur Review, Decatur, Illinois, obituary notice) When Hiram P. Virden died March 13, 1930, the Decatur Herald, Decatur, Illinois, in his obituary notice, stated that he died in the home of his daughter, Mrs. Leota Coriell, and that he was born January 9, 1859, in Montgomery County, Illinois. He left his wife, Barbara Virden, and 6 children, all living in the Decatur area: Mrs. Leota Coriell, Mrs. Edith Mercker, George Roscoe Virden, Mrs. Ellen Litts, and Mrs. Gertrude Shartzer. He also left 4 step-children: Elmer Massey, George Massey, Mrs. Kate Morgan, and Mrs. Martha Atwood, all of Decatur. He had 16 grandchildren, and one great granddaughter, and one sister, Mrs. Nettie Ishmael.

LEVI D. VIRDEN was born April 7, 1841, in Fayette County, Illinois. (He was the son of Levi and Catherine (Reese) Virden; Levi was a native of South Carolina and Catherine was a native of North Carolina. They met and were married in Kentucky.) Levi D. Virden married Martha A. Thorp, a native of Ramsey Township, Illinois, and the daughter of Cal and Ann Thorp. She died in 1887. Levi D. and Martha A. (Thorp) Virden had several children: Emma Virden, who married Franklin Davis, a farmer in Hurricane Township; (2) William Edward Virden, a farmer in Hurricane Township; (3) Lulu Almira Virden, a milliner; and (4) Homer Levi Virden.

Levi D. Virden was a farmer, owning about 220 acres which was used mostly in growing corn, breeding cattle, and raising Poland China hogs. He was an active member of the School Board for many years. (History of Fayette County, Vol. II)

LEVI VIRDEN, the father of Levi D. Virden, mentioned above, went to Illinois with his wife when it was still a Territory, and voted on its admission to the Union. For some time he was Supervisor of Hurricane Township. He died when he was over eighty years of age, having survived his wife by five years. Levi and Catherine (Reese) Virden had several children:

(1) Isaac Virden, who died on a farm in Shelby County when he was about forty;
(2) John Virden, who died young on a farm in Shelby County;
(3) Kate Virden, who married J. Massey, and died while a young woman;
(4) Sarah Virden, who married Thomas Ishmael, and also died while a young woman;
(5) Margaret Virden, who married James Ishmael, and also died young;
(6) Mahala Virden, who died at age eighteen;
(7) William Virden who died when about twenty-one;
(8) Levi D. Virden, previously referred to; and
(9) Eli Virden.

(History of Fayette County, Vol. II)

THEODORE W. VIRDEN was born September 24, 1817, in Delaware. He moved to Montgomery Township, Marion County, Ohio, sometime before 1838 where he married Sarah Davis of Ohio on October 23, 1838. He had at least four sons and one daughter: (1) William A. Virden, born July 6, 1839; (2) Mary Virden, born August 9, 1841 (my great-grandmother); (3) T.D. Virden, born September 1, 1847 (the fourth son). Theodore Virden died in Marion County, Ohio, December 5, 1899. I have been unable to find his father. (From a letter dated March 4, 1977, from Mrs. E.A. Cole, Akron, Ohio.)

Elizabeth Virden married as her first husband William Harrington, who died in 1862. They had two children: (1) John Virdin Harrington who was killed during the Civil War at Cold Harbor; and (2) Samuel Harrington, born October 26, 1833, at Viola, Delaware. He married Catherine Lofland, daughter of John and Marial Hamilton, on April 8, 1876. They had three children, Bertha Harrington, Lillie Harrington, and Samuel M. Harrington. (Biographical and General History of Delaware, page 857)

JOHN VIRDIN married Sarah Purdin December 21, 1790. He died December 3, 1796. John and Sarah (Purdin) Virdin had two children: (1) Andrew Virdin, born February 15, 1792; and (2) Elizabeth Virdin, born September 8, 1795. She married William Harrington.

After the death of her husband Sarah (Purdin) Virdin married Thomas Green on March 13, 1798. Thomas and Sarah Green had five children: (1) Amelia Green, born August 23, 1799, died April 19, 1805; (2) Kelly Green, born September 14, 1801; (3) William Green, born February 11, 1804; (4) Sarah Green, born June 14, 1806; and (5) John Green, born July 4, 1808. (From Bible record, gift of Mrs. James McNeil, of Newark, Delaware, in Genealogical Surname File, Delaware Historical Society)

WILLIAM VIRDIN, born in Delaware January 26, 1767, married Martha Williamson in Lexington, Kentucky, on April 20, 1815. (From letter from Mrs. James Duffy, Glenwood Springs, Colorado, in Delaware Historical Society, Genealogical Surname File. This file also indicates that he may have been the son of William and Prudence (Jerrard) Virdin, she being the daughter of Matthew Jerrard whose will was made in 1788.)

WILLIAM VIRDIN, born in 1768, died in 1817, of Canterberry, Delaware, married Mary Berry, born in 1769, died in 1818, also of Canterberry, Delaware. They had a daughter, Mary Berry Virden, born 1812, died 1890, who married Thomas Sipple, of Kent County, Delaware. Thomas Sipple was born in 1811, died in 1853. Thomas and Mary Berry (Virden) Sipple had a son, William Virdin Sipple, who married Ruth Anna Holland, born in 1853, in Milford, Delaware. William Virdin and Ruth Anna (Holland) Sipple had a daughter, Mary Sipple, born February 27, 1875, who married Howard Hendrickson Bromley of Milford, Delaware. (Note: William Virdin, born in 1768, served in the War of 1812. See Delaware Historical Society, Genealogical Surname File.)

Will of William Virdin, Sr., of Kent County (Born March 16, 1807 and died December 12, 1888)
___

"I, William Virdin of Kent County and State of Delaware, hereby make this my last will and testament--

First: I direct that my just debts be paid by my executors hereinafter named, as soon after my death as may by them found to be convenient.
Second: I release Samuel C. Wallace from all indebtedness to me and my estate.
Third: I devise and bequeath to my daughter Ellen Wallace wife of Samuel C. Wallace the sum of fifty dollars annually during her natural life to be paid to her by my son Alexander Virdin--said annuity to commence immediately after the death of her husband Samuel C. Wallace and the first payment to be made one year from the date of his decease.
Fourth: I hereby release my son James Virdin from all indebtedness to me and my estate.

"Fifth: I hereby release my son William Virdin from all indebtedness to me and my estate.

Sixth: I give and bequeath to Emily Virdin wife of my son William Virdin the horse-cart which the said William Virdin has now in his possession.

Seventh: I bequeath to my son Alexander Virdin that part of the "Stout" farm where my son William Virdin now resides and that was surveyed and laid off by Thomas B. Johns on the 24th day of December A.D. 1885, and represented on the plot of the same made by him by the letter "K" and containing fifty-seven acres and one hundred and thirty-five square perches of land--excepting and reserving the graveyard or burying ground on said land, said graveyard to be thirty feet square--also all that tract of woodland which has been used in connection with the whole of the aforesaid "Stout" farm--said woodland lying and being on the west side of the public road leading from "Bethesda" M.P. Church to Davis Cross Roads and containing about twenty-five acres of land, both tracts in trust for my son William Virdin and his wife Emily Virdin during the natural life of my son William Virdin, then for Emily Virdin so long as she shall remain the widow of William Virdin, and upon the death of both William Virdin and Emily Virdin his wife or the remarriage of the said Emily Virdin, I direct and empower my trustee Alexander Virdin aforesaid or his survivors to sell at public sale all the aforesaid tracts or parcels or land last devised on what terms he shall deem most for the interest of all concerned and apply the proceeds of said sale in the following manner, to wit: First, to pay to Eunity Elderdice my daughter or her heirs the sum of six hundred dollars ($600) and remaining proceeds to the heirs or lawful issue of my son William Virdin and should my son William Virdin die and leave no lawful issue, I direct that the portion or part that I directed to be paid to his heirs to be equally divided and paid over to the heirs of John W. Virdin and Lizzie B. Schafer to their use forever.

Eighth: I hereby release my son John W. Virdin from all indebtedness to me and my estate and I give and bequeath unto him the said John W. Virdin that part of the "Hour Glass" farm surveyed and laid off by Thomas B. Johns on the 12th day of December A.A. 1885 and represented on a draught of the "same made by him by the letter "B" and contains eighty acres and eighty-one square perches of land to have and to hold the same to his use forever.

Ninth: I give and bequeath to my daughter Lizzie B. Schafer that part of the "Hour Glass" farm lying on both sides of the public road leading from "Bethesda" M.P. Church to Hazlettville as surveyed and laid off by Thomas B. Johns December 12, A.D. 1885 and represented on a draught of the same made by him by the letter "H" and contains eighty-seven acres and ninety-nine perches of land to have and to hold the same during her natural life and should she leave issue to her and her heirs forever, but if the said Lizzie B. Schafer should die and leave no living issue, then upon the death of her I direct the said tract of land or the proceeds from sale of said trace of land be divided into two equal parts and one of said parts I direct to be given to heirs of John W. Virdin and the other part to the heirs of Ellen Wallace to them and their use forever. All of the last (ninth) bequest to be effected after a certain Bond given by William Schafer, Lizzie B. Schafer, William Virdin and Philip D. Marvel to the Farmer's Bank of the State of Delaware for the sum of six hundred dollars is paid or my entire estate released therefrom, otherwise I direct that this last (ninth) bequest be applied to the payment of said Bond and interest thereon and the residue to my daughter Lizzie B. Schafer.

Tenth: To my son Alexander Virdin I give and bequeath two Judgments on the Prothonotary's docket in Dover in my favor, and all my other personal property and effects of whatsoever kind not otherwise disposed of to him and his use forever. I also give and bequeath to him Alexander Virdin upon the payment of my entire indebtedness or provision for the same not otherwise provided for that part of the "Hour Glass" farm whereon the aforesaid Lizzie B. Schafer and William H.S. Schafer her husband now reside and in their tenure and which was surveyed and laid off by Thomas B. Johns on the 12th day of December A.D. 1885 and represented on a draught of the same made by him by the letter "A" and contains one hundred and three acres and one hundred and seven

"square perches of land. I also give and
bequeath to my son Alexander Virdin that part
of the "Stout" farm lying between that part
bequeathed to Alexander Virdin in trust for
William Virdin and Emily Virdin his wife and
the public road leading from Bethesda M.P.
Church to Davis Cross Roads and was surveyed
by Thomas B. Johns December 24, A.D. 1885,
and represented on the plot made by him of
the same by the letter "M" and contains
sixty-five acres and one hundred and fifteen
square perches of land excepting and reserving a road or right of way twelve feet in
width through said tract of land on a line
between the dwelling house now in tenure of
my son William Virdin and some direct point
on the public road leading from Bethesda M.P.
Church to Davis Cross Roads, said point to be
determined by my executors hereinafter named,
said right of way or road reserved and excepted
to and for the use of the farm and premises
bequeathed to Alexander Virdin in trust for
William Virdin and Emily Virdin his wife,
both of said tracts to the use of Alexander
Virdin aforesaid forever after the payment
of my debts or provisions made for the same.
Eleventh: I hereby direct that if any of my
heirs or devisees to whom I have made a bequest
shall in any way or manner either directly or
indirectly attempt to contest or set aside,
alter, change or break this my last will the
heir or heirs so doing shall forfeit all right
to any inheritance in my estate and the
bequest or bequests that I have heretofore made
for them shall be null and void and no effect,
and I direct that my executors do pay over
or give said bequests to my other heirs at law
in an equitable manner to their children.
Twelfth: I hereby appoint Alexander Virdin
my son and Philip D. Marvel executor to per-
form the trusts and execute this will.

In testimony whereof I have hereunto set my
hand and seal this twenty-ninth day of
August eighteen hundred and eighty-eight."

       William Virdin (Seal)

On this twenty-ninth day of August A.D.
eighteen hundred and eighty-eight the said
William Virdin signed the foregoing instrument
in our presence, declaring it to be his last
will and as witnesses thereof we have in his

presence and in the presence of each other hereunto
subscribed our names as witnesses.

      Thomas B. Johns
      Kate Johns

"I William Virdin of Kent County and State of
Delaware hereby make this codicil to my last will
and testament made and published by me and dated
this twenty-ninth day of August A.D. eighteen
hundred and eighty-eight which will I ratify and
confirm in all respects except as the same shall
be changed hereby--

Whereas by my will, I gave a certain tract of
land to my son Alexander Virdin in trust for my
son William Virdin and Emily Virdin his wife,
reserving a certain graveyard or burying ground,
now I hereby reserve the right of entrance and
exit to said burying ground, said reservation
to and for the use of persons using said graveyard forever.

In testimony whereof I have set my hand this
twenty-ninth day of August eighteen hundred and
eighty-eight."

      William Virdin

Signed and published by William Virdin as a
codicil to his last will and testament in our
presence and we in his presence and in the presence
of each other have at his request, hereunto subscribed our names as witnesses on this twenty-
ninth day of August, 1888.

      Thomas B. Johns
      Kate Johns

  JAMES VIRDIN (son of William and Mary (Hargadine) Virdin) was
born April 12, 1840, and died in 1916. He married Mary Wallace November
8, 1865, in Kent County. James and Mary (Wallace) Virdin had these
children:

  (1) Minnie Virdin, who married George Cook and had
    four children: (1) Beatrice Cook; (2) James
    Cook; (3) Eliza Cook; and (4) Bessie Cook;
  (2) Harry Virdin;
  (3) Dr. Frank Virdin;
  (4) Bessie Virdin;
  (5) Ralph Virdin; and

(6) Marion Wallace Virdin who married Irene Hawkins. As his second wife he married Orra Hawkins on December 3, 1885, in Kent County. They had a son, William Virdin, who married Madeline Sackett. (From information in Delaware Hall of Records, family letters, and information from Mrs. Gertrude S. Hall and Mrs. Edythe W. Thoesen.)

Unity Virdin (daughter of William and Mary (Hargadine) Virdin) was born November 21, 1841. She married Rev. James Elderdice. Apparently, her father, William Virdin, did not want her to marry Rev. Elderdice, because he sent her to visit some of the Virdin relatives in Mississippi for more than a year, hoping that she would lose her interest. That was not to be the case. She and Rev. Elderdice arranged by correspondence to meet in Alexandria, Virginia, upon her return from Mississippi and were married. (From a letter written by her granddaughter.) Rev. James and Unity (Virdin) Elderdice had these children:

(1) Dr. John Elderdice who married Edna Adkins and had these children: (1) Robert Elderdice; (2) John Elderdice; and (3) Frances Elderdice;
(2) Mabel Elderdice who married Dr. Lawrence C. Freenay and had three children: (1) Lawrence Freenay; (2) John Freenay; and (3) Alice Freenay;
(3) Augustus Webster Elderdice, who died in 1948.

HARRY VIRDIN (son of James and Mary (Wallace) Virdin) married Anna Belle Thompson on December 26, 1900. Harry and Anne Belle (Thompson) Virdin had these children:

(1) Grace Eunity Virdin, born October 23, 1910, died September 7, 1916;
(2) Lucy Mae Virdin, born May 1, 1903;
(3) James Virdin, born May 26, 1904;
(4) Robert Clifton Virdin, born August 7, 1905;
(5) Anna Hazel Virdin, born October 21, 1906, died in February 1931;
(6) Mary Eliza Virdin, born January 24, 1908;
(7) Harry Franklin Virdin, born March 18, 1909;
(8) Helen Love Virdin, born August 1, 1910, who married David Wright;
(9) Howard Thompson Virdin, born September 29, 1913;
(10) Virginia Belle Virdin, born May 15, 1915;
(11) Bessie Elma Virdin, born July 29, 1916.

(From data furnished by James R. Virden, of Russia, Ohio, information in Delaware Hall of Records, and family records.)

FRANK VIRDIN (son of James and Mary (Wallace) Virdin) married Margaret May Authors on October 16, 1900, in Kent County. Frank and Margaret May (Authors) Virdin had two children: (1) Allen Virdin; and (2) Marjorie Virdin.

RALPH VIRDIN (son of James and Mary (Wallace) Virdin) married Louisa Marvel in Philadelphia, Pennsylvania, on February 3, 1921. They lived in Wyoming, Delaware. They had one child, Charlotte Ann Virdin.

WILLIAM VIRDIN (son of James and Mary (Wallace) Virdin) married Madeline Sackett, and they had a son, Roy Virdin.

Lucy Mae Virdin (daughter of Harry and Anne (Thompson) Virdin) married Harry E. Short and they had three children: (1) Harry Raymond Short; (2) Geraldine Dianne Short; and (3) Barbara Mae Short.

JAMES VIRDIN (son of Harry and Anne (Thompson) Virdin) married Mary Shane. James and Mary (Shane) Virdin lived near Kenton, Delaware. They had these children: (1) James Glen Virdin; (2) Robert Dale Virdin; (3) Ronald Lee Virdin; and (4) Kenneth Allen Virdin.

ROBERT CLIFTON VIRDIN (son of Harry and Anne (Thompson) Virdin), born August 7, 1905, married Ethel Bailey. The lived at Smyrna, Delaware.

Mary Eliza Virdin (daughter of Harry and Anne (Thompson) Virdin), born January 24, 1908, married August V. Lane. August V. and Mary Eliza (Virdin) Lane had two children: (1) Penelope Ann Lane, and (2) Philip Allen Lane.

HARRY FRANKLIN VIRDIN (son of Harry and Anne (Thompson) Virdin), born March 18, 1909, married Elizabeth Bennet, and lived at Smyrna, Delaware. Harry Franklin and Elizabeth (Bennet) Virdin had these children: (1) Frances Jane Virdin; (2) Doris Marie Virdin; and (3) Harry Arthur Virdin.

HOWARD THOMPSON VIRDIN (son of Harry and Anne (Thompson) Virdin), born September 29, 1913, married Ruth Blendt and lived at Clayton, Delaware. Howard Thompson and Ruth (Blendt) Virdin had these children: (1) Marjorie Carol Virdin; (2) William Howard Virdin; and (3) Vivian Ruth Virdin.

Virginia Belle Virdin (daughter of Harry and Anne (Thompson) Virdin, born May 15, 1915, married Clyde Miller. Clyde and Virginia Belle (Virdin) Miller had these children: (1) Patsy Ruth Miller; (2) John Clyde Miller, Jr.; (3) Virginia Lee Miller; (4) Beverly Rebecca Miller; (5) Donald Virdin Miller; (6) Helen Joanne Miller; and (7) Paula Janet Miller.

Bessie Elma Virdin (daughter of Harry and Anne (Thompson) Virdin), born July 22, 1916, married as her first husband Jefferson Scout, and they had a son, Jefferson Scout, Jr. As her second husband she married John

Kates. John and Bessie Elma (Virdin) Kates had these children:
(1) David Virdin Kates; (2) John Rowen Kates, Jr.; (3) Susanna Kates;
(4) Joseph Kates; and (5) Sally Ann Kates.

Copy of Undated Newspaper Clipping Concerning Dr. Frank Virdin of Wilmington, Delaware

"Councilmen Vote for Dead Man.

Wilmington, Del., Jan. 7 - A dead man was almost nominated by City Council last night. As it was, he received three votes for city vaccine physician, while his 'live' competitor received five votes. The man placed in nomination was Dr. Frank Virdin. None of the Councilmen knew he was dead, although they argued for and against his abilities. Dr. P.A.M. Rovitti received five votes, which were not enough to elect. After the voting a newspaperman informed Council Dr. Virdin had been dead several months."

Herman Wallace (son of Samuel Craig and Ellen (Virden) Wallace) married Florence Boggs and they had these children: (1) Henry Wallace; (2) Samuel Wallace; (3) Ellen Wallace; (4) Mary Wallace; (5) Hannah Wallace; (6) Evelyn Wallace; (7) Nellie Wallace. (From information compiled by Mrs. Edythe W. Thoesen and other family records.)

Herman Cook married Mabel Wallace (daughter of Samuel Craig and Ellen (Virden) Wallace) and they had these children: (1) Wallace Cook; (2) George Cook; and (3) Elizabeth Cook. (From same sources as above.)

WILLIAM E. VIRDEN (son of James and Sarah (Lynch) Virden) was born October 29, 1877 at Five Points, near Dover, Delaware. His father reportedly was born in Mississippi and his mother in Delaware. His father, James Virden, was a ship's carpenter by trade who moved to Wilmington, Delaware, in the late 1870's, and died at the age of seventy-three years. His mother, Sarah Virdin, died at the age of seventy-nine. James and Sarah had one daughter and four sons, of whom William E. Virden is one.

William E. Virden began work with a firm engaged in the manufacture of glass, then learned the trade of millwright. In 1900 he was appointed bridge tender of the Third Street Bridge in Wilmington where he worked for several years. Later, he had positions at the New Castle County Courthouse, the Market Street Bridge, Wilmington, and as supervisor of the city incinerator plant. In 1920 he was elected to the Delaware State Legislature from the Fourth District and served in that body for six consecutive terms. In 1941 he was appointed Collector of Taxes for the southern district of Wilmington; in June 1943 he was elected to that office and reelected in 1945.

On July 19, 1899, he married Anna M. Reed of Wilmington and they had three children: (1) Grace Virden, who married Thomas J. Gainor, who was a police sergeant in Wilmington; (2) Mary Virden who died when nine years of age; and (3) William Virden who died in infancy.

WILLIAM VIRDIN lived in Philadelphia, Pennsylvania, where he was a successful produce merchant. His family lived in prosperity and affluence until his death about 1861. After that time his family was said to have lived in poverty. He married Kathryn Brady. William and Kathryn (Brady) Virdin had six children: (1) William Virdin, who served in the Civil War; (2) George Virdin; (3) Frank Virdin; (4) John Virdin, born in 1852, died May 2, 1918; (5) Kathryn Virdin; and (6) Victoria Virdin. (Information supplied by John Virdin, a descendant.)

JOHN VIRDIN (son of William and Kathryn (Brady) Virdin) married Estelle Smulling. John and Estelle (Smulling) Virdin had three children: (1) a daughter, Mrs. Stella (Virdin) Wilgus; (2) Alfred C. Harmer Virdin; and (3) Clifford Virdin. (Letter from John Virdin dated, October 3, 1976.)

ALFRED C. HARMER VIRDIN (son of John and Estelle (Smulling) Virdin) married _____ and had one son, John Virdin II.

JOHN VIRDIN II (son of Alfred C. Harmer and _____ Virdin) was born December 27, 1914. He married Margaret G. _____ and they had these children: (1) John Virdin, Jr. who married and has a son, John Walker Virdin; (2) Paul Richard Virdin; and (3) a daughter.

Copy of Undated Newspaper Clipping Concerning John Virdin while He was Recorder of Deeds of Philadelphia

"John Virdin, the Recorder of Deeds, of Philadelphia, and founder and mainstay of the Harmer Club was born on Marlborough street above Beach, in the old District of Kensington, early in the fifties.

Up to John's 9th year, the Virdin family lived in prosperity and affluence. His father was in the produce business and highly successful. But when John was nine, his father died, and as Mr. Montaline would say, things went to the 'Demd Bow-wows.'

The family becoming quite poor, John was sent on a farm, when for four years he "did the roughest and the hardest work. But though he suffered hardships, his frame and his strength developed, and his present magnificent physique he owes to those early days on the farm.

At the age of 15--a boy in years, but a man in stature--he returned to Philadelphia, and sought employment at Cramp's ship yard at laboring work, being ambitious to earn a man's wages. At that time John King, a well-known Kensingtonian was foreman of the riggers at Cramps. To him the boy applied for work. 'I don't want boys,' was King's reply as he glanced into the youth's face.

The applicant turned away disheartened. Just then he caught sight of a number of the riggers trying one at a time to lift a large, heavy hydraulic jack. They all gave it up in despair. After the men had left, John Verdin tried his hand. He lifted it with some _____

This act of strength was witnessed by an aged rigger, named Jack Cook, who made a mental memorandum of the same.

Shortly afterward Charles W. Cramp, the president of the Cramp Shipbuilding Company, happened along and to him the boy applied for work. Mr. Cramp hesitated a moment and then calling the foreman of the riggers directed him to give John employment.

The foreman demurred, but as the president insisted, the foreman had to submit. Then arose another obstacle. The riggers work in pairs. All of them objected to the boy for a mate until old Jack Cook sang out:

'I'll take the boy! He has more strength than any man among ye. He is good enough for my mate.'

And from that moment John Verdin and Jack Cook were sworn friends, a friendship that lasted until the old man's death.

John was receiving $1.75 a day at Cramp's, but he threw this up for $2.50 per week to go as an apprentice boy to Bartle's Mast Yard and learn spar making.

"When about 21 years of age he got into the Navy Yard, as stated above. This was the old Navy Yard, at Front and Federal streets. When work at League Island was started he went there first as carpenter, and was afterward appointed to be master spar maker, passing a civil examination for the position by a board, of which Admiral Hitchborn was one of the members. To this day the Admiral remains one of the ex-spar maker's firmest friends.

When Mayor Fitler was in office Mr. Virdin made application for the position of Inspector of Highways, five of whom were to be appointed. The lucky applicants at the time were Messrs. Berkelback, Hensy, Stull, Bullock, and John Virdin.

In this position Mr. Virdin remained until elected Recorder of Deeds in the fall of 1898.

For nearly thirty years, Mr. Virdin has been an untiring political worker. Twenty-six years ago he was elected to the Republican committee of the Eighteenth ward, representing his division, the second, in which he has always lived. He has been chairman of the ward committee for many years and has represented his ward in the City Committee.

As Recorder of Deeds he has proved himself an excellent executive officer, and is well liked by all his subordinates."

Copy of Newspaper Clipping from a Philadelphia paper, dated May 3, 1918, concerning the Death of John Virdin
---

"JOHN VIRDIN DIES AT PATRIOTIC RALLY

Widely Known Politician Suddenly Stricken
While Delivering Address at Harmer Club

VARE LEADER IN 18TH WARD

John Virdin, chief of the Bureau of Weights and Measures and for years an active figure in local politics, died from heart disease while delivering a patriotic address in the

"A.C. Harmer Club, 1130 Shackamaxon st., last night.

He was the Vare leader of the Eighteenth Ward and he helped to organize the Harmer Club. He was sixty-six years old.

The Rev. Henry Hess, of the Kensington (Old Brick) Methodist Church, delivered an address in which he invited the club members to attend a patriotic rally in the church May 12.

Chief Virdin was later called upon to speak. He became so enthusiastic over the Allies cause in the war and Liberty Loan that he overtaxed his strength. He had spoken about five minutes when he stopped and staggered to a chair.

'Boys,' he said, 'I feel myself going. I'm getting weak. I must sit down.'

Dr. Alfred G. Smith and Dr. Henry L. Sidebotham, who were present, applied first aid treatment in an effort to revive him. Dr. Smith said death resulted from acute dilation of the heart.

The body was taken to Mr. Virdin's home, 324 Richmond st. The funeral will be held Tuesday afternoon at 2 o'clock with services in his home.

Chief Virdin had always been active in Republican politics in the Eighteenth Ward, where he was born. Both his parents died before he was eleven years old, and he was compelled to make his own way. For four years after their death he worked for a farmer in New Jersey, attending school in the winter. Then he returned to this city and obtained employment as a laborer at Cramps' Shipyard.

He early became interested in politics. When he was twenty-one he met Alfred C. Harmer, Congressman from his district. The Congressman obtained a position for young Virdin at the Philadelphia Navy Yard as sparmaker. Years later when Virdin helped to organize the Republican Club in the Eighteenth Ward he had named the Harmer Club in gratitude to the man who obtained him his first Government position.

"During the term of Mayor Fitler, Virdin was appointed an inspector in the bureaus of highways. In 1898 he became the Republican candidate for recorder of deeds, serving until January, 1902, when he was succeeded by William S. Vare, now Congressman. Virdin broke away from the organization temporarily and supported the Union Party.

Later he became a clerk in the city solicitor's office, and in 1907 he was made assistant chief of the highway bureau. He served in this office for five years, when the Blankenburg administration forced his resignation.

In 1913, by legislative act, the bureau of weights and measures was established in Philadelphia, and the county commissioners appointed Virdin its first chief.

He was a member of Mozart Lodge, Masons; the Shriners and the Knights Templar; Ionic Lodge, Royal Arcanum, and former president of the Pilots' Association. He is survived by a widow, one daughter, Mrs. Stella Wilgus, and two sons, Alfred C. Harmer Virdin and Clifford Virdin."

Philadelphia, Pennsylvania, Notes

John Verdin - of Greene County, Wayne Township, was listed in the 1810 Census of Pennsylvania.

Thomas Verden - of Spring Garden, Philadelphia, was listed in the 1830 Census of Pennsylvania.

1868 City Directory of Philadelphia lists these Virdins

Daniel Verden - brickmaker, 1914 Ringold Place.
Frank Verden - roller, rear 912 Marlborough.
Henry Verden - Lewes, Delaware.
Henry F. Verden - pilot, Pine Street at 33rd.
Isaac Verden - police, 922 Catherine.
James Verden - brickmaker, 1914 Ringold Place.
James Verden, Jr. - brickmaker, 1914 Ringold Place.
Richard Verden - tanner, rear 967 North Front.
Sarah Verden - widow of John Verden, seamstress, 64 North 37th.
Thomas B. Verden - plasterer, 105 State, West Philadelphia.
William Verden - 726 Richmond.

1871 Philadelphia Directory lists these Virdins

Francis Virden   -   sparmaker, 6 Belgrade Place.
George W. Virdin   -   sparmaker, 436 Dreer.
Henry Virden (Pedrick and Virden)   -   Lewes, Delaware.
Henry F. Virden   -   pilot, 426 South Delaware Avenue. (Business address)
                      307 Pine. (Home address)
Isaac Virden   -   brickmaker, 922 Catherine.
Peter L.S. Virden   -   grocer, 2520 Gray's Ferry Road.
Thomas Verdan   -   plasterer, North 3501 Market, West Philadelphia.
William Virden   -   726 Richmond.
William H. Virden   -   brickmaker, 2055 Evergreen.

HENRY VIRDEN (March 14, 1815 - October 4, 1884) of Lewes, Delaware, married on November 1, 1837, Elizabeth Carpenter (January 24, 1818 - January 19, 1893) of Lewes, and they had seven children:

(1) Thomas J. Virden, born August 4, 1838, died July 24, 1856;
(2) Margaret C. Virden, born February 27, 1841;
(3) Henry F. Virden, born January 2, 1843;
(4) Mary Helen Virden, born March 6, 1845;
(5) Annie Virden, born February 24, 1847, died October 5, 1871;
(6) John Penrose Virden, born April 8, 1849; and
(7) Walter L. Virden, born December 19, 1861.

(This information duplicates, but also supplements the data given on page 20 of The Virdins of Delaware and Related Families.)

It was found by John Virdin, of Philadelphia, in a Bible given to him by a lady who owned a rooming house in which the owner of the Bible lived at the time of his death. The Bible is embossed on the cover in gold "E.W. Verden," but there is no notation regarding E.W. Verden. However, it is probable that this Bible originally belonged to Elizabeth W. (Carpenter) Virden, and that the man who died was one of her descendants.

Copy of Undated Newspaper Clipping (probably about 1955) from the Philadelphia Inquirer concerning the Death of Captain Thomas J. Virden, of Lewes, Delaware

CAPT. VIRDEN, PILOT, DIES AT 80

Special to The Inquirer

LEWES, Del., Nov. 18.--Capt. Thomas J. Virden, former president of the Pilots' Association for the Bay and River Delaware, died last night in Beebe Hospital. He was 80.

"Capt. Virden, who lived at 344 Pilot Town rd., served his apprenticeship on one of the sail pilotboats which predated the steam pilotboat, Philadelphia, which was built by his father, Capt. John Penrose Virden. He launched a Diesel-powered craft, the Delaware, in 1926, and was active as a pilot for nearly 50 years, retiring in 1946.

During the First World War, Capt. Virden served in the Navy as executive officer on the hospital ship Relief and the submarine chaser repair ship Prairie. He was assigned to convoy duty in the Atlantic in the final months of the war.

He was a past president of the Delaware State Pilot Commissioners, a Mason, a former member of the Lewes Board of Town Commissioners, former president of the Lewes Chamber of Congress, a charter member of the Rehoboth Beach Country Club and a member of the Lewes Yacht Club.

Surviving are his wife, Eva Kneale Virden; a daughter, Marjorie P., and a sister, Mrs. Arthur West Marshall, Sr. Services will be held at 2 P.M. Tuesday in St. Peter's Episcopal Church. Burial will be in the churchyard.

RUSSELL VIRDIN, SR. (son of Olin and Nettie (Artis) Virdin), was born in Kent County, Delaware, August 11, 1911, one of eleven children. He married Marie Rosengren of Hartly, Delaware, who was born April 15, 1914, the seventh child in her family. Russell and Marie (Rosengren) Virdin had these children:

(1) Russell Virdin, Jr., born October 12, 1935. He is married and has two children;
(2) A child who died at birth and was not named; and
(3) A foster son, born May 30, 1945, who was raised to maturity, and is married with two children.

Russell Virdin was the third child of eleven children (not seven as previously indicated). His oldest brother, Artis Virdin, died in 1960. (From letters dated October 12, 1976, and March 1, 1977, from Mrs. Russell Virdin, Sr.).

PAUL CRAIG VIRDIN (son of Samuel A. and Lela C. (Ludwig) Virdin) was born January 31, 1926. He married Virginia (Durham) Lidke on April 10, 1962. They have two children: (1) William Jeffery Virdin, born January 26, 1965; and (2) Susan Crystal Virdin, born April 5, 1966.

There are also other members of the family, children of Virginia (Durham) Lidke by her first marriage: (1) Cynthia Dell Lidke, born in November 1959, and (2) Maclyn Kay Lidke, born in October 1954.

William Virden, date of birth unknown, died about May 6, 1803. He married Anne _____. He was a soldier from Delaware in the Revolutionary War. (DAR Patriot Index)

Steven Virden, born June 6, 1754, died in 1821. He was married. He was a drummer from Virginia in the Revolutionary War. (DAR Patriot Index)

John C. Virden, Decatur, Macon County, Illinois, was an agent with the Southwestern Detective Agency, of Paris, Texas, in 1914. (From copy of certificate issued at Montgomery, Alabama, on August 3rd, 1914, by Chief of Agents, M.N. Greene.)

Chris E. Virden, was a Justice of the Peace, in the Town of Ball, County of Sangamon, Illinois, in April 1921. (From certificate issued by Len Small, The Governor of Illinois, on April 29, 1921.)

Moses Verdain, was a witness to the will of Jacob Wilkinson on November 14, 1760, in Accomack County, Virginia. (1663-1800 Wills and Administrations of Accomack County, by Stratton Nottingham.)

ELMINA VIRDEN (SEARS), Mrs. Louis C. (Elmina Virden) Sears, 95, of Pana, formerly of Ramsey, died December 30, 1976, at Pana. She was born in Fayette County, Illinois, the daughter of Levi and Martha Virden. Her husband, Louis C. Sears, died in 1954. (From obituary notice in Decatur, Illinois, newspaper, of December 31, 1976.)

Sally Virden, married Micajah H. Foster in 1827, in Laurence County, Indiana. They had a son, Jacob Virden Foster, who lived in Baxter County, Arkansas, and in Ozark County, Missouri. Although the 1820 Census of Washington County, Indiana, listed Hugh Virden, there was no record in Laurence County, where Sally Virden lived. The Foster family had moved from Louisa County, Virginia, and Bullitt and Nelson Counties, Kentucky, to Indiana. (Letter from James Holmes, a descendant, dated December 3, 1976.)

RICHARD VIRDIN, age 24, came to the Virginia Colony from London on August 21, 1635, on the ship George Jo. According to records about this voyage he had conformed to the Church of England discipline and had taken the oath of allegiance. The writer has been unable to find any further record of him or his descendents, if any. The assumption must be made, therefore, that he died sometime after arriving in America.

STEPHEN VERDEN, born June 6, 1754, in France came to Virginia and served during the American Revolution. He received of Lt. Samuel Gill, of the 4th Virginia Regiment, pay for March 1788. He was also listed as Stephen Vardine, of the 8th Virginia Regiment. (Virginia Magazine of

History and Biography, Vol. I, page 206) He died in 1821. He was married but his wife's name is unknown. He served as a drummer, at least during part of his service. (DAR Patriot Index)

    Note: There is no evidence available to the writer that either Richard Verdin or Stephen Verden are related in any way to the Virdins discussed in this book. However, it seemed appropriate to include this information about the Virdin family as a matter of history, if not relationship. Indeed, it seems conclusive that Richard Verdin of Virginia died without heirs, and since no information has been developed about any heirs of Stephen Verden, he too may have died without offspring.

The following information was furnished by James R. Virden,
of Russia, Ohio, by letter dated February 10, 1977

EGENIOR VIRDEN	- of Augusta County, Georgia. His name was found in many spellings: Egniar, Egenior, Ezemah, Ajemiah, etc.
Sept. 27, 1760	- Egenior Virden was a witness to the will of John Wright, and was one of the executors of the will which was probated Nov. 18, 1762.
Dec. 10, 1764	- Egeniah Virden was a witness to a document transferring land (260 acres at Snodons Spring) to Samuel Beard.
May 13, 1765	- Egenior Virden was a witness to a document exempting Robert McGhee from levy (evidently a tax levy) because of his great age and infirmity.

"I find mention of Egenior Virden in South Carolina will briefs. No county is mentioned. Egenior had to be twenty-one years of age to witness a will in 1760; so he was born prior to 1740 in South Carolina."

Dec. 11, 1770	- Engenior Virden was a witness to the will of Frederick Imer of the fish dam ford, Broad River, near Little St. Simons Island, which will was probated this date.
1793 - 1794	- Engenior Virden appeared on the tax roll of Wilkes County, Georgia, in 1784. In 1793 he and a William Virden appeared on the tax rolls of Wilkes County.

Egenior Virden was in the American Revolution as his grave is marked in Warren County by the DAR of Georgia. He was married twice. Land records in 1784 show his wife's name to be Jane. But his will named his wife as Winny. She was apparently a young woman since she appeared in records in Houston County, Georgia, after 1830. She disappeared from Warren County after the death of Egenior.

1805	- Engenior Virden was in Warren County, Georgia, in 1805. John Virden was also living in that county. (This may be the John Virden of Newberry County, South Carolina, as shown in the Census of 1785 and 1790.)
Jan. 24, 1795	- Ezemah Virden and wife Jane Virden, of Warren County, Georgia, deeded land to James Osborne.

1803. - The will of Engenior Virden mentions three sons, William Virden, James Virden, and John Virden.

1830 - A James Virden is shown on the 1830 Bibb County, Georgia, Census, age 40-50.

1805 - A William Virden appeared on a land lottery in 1805 and received 2 draws given to man and wife, or child. A requirement was a one year residence in Georgia and U.S. citizenship. (This could not be Engenior's son since he was born in 1791 and married in 1809.)

Engenior Virden could possibly be the father of James Virden and grandfather of John Virden of Newberry, South Carolina, but it seems unlikely that he named two sets of sons the same name. I am more inclined to think James Virden and John Virden of Newberry were sons of the William Virden in Wilkes County, Georgia, in 1793, or sons of another brother. I have found no further mention of Engenior Virden and son John Virden, and James Virden listed in Bibb County is probably the son James Virden, although the date is off a little.

It appears that the older William Virden was the father of three sons: (1) Samuel Virden, born in 1789; (2) Hugh A. Virden, born in 1798; and (3) William Virden, born in 1805, that migrated to Cape Girardeau, Missouri. Hugh A. Virden migrated to Arkansas prior to 1850.

The older William Virden appeared on the 1793 and 1794 tax rolls. William Virden appeared on the 1805 land lottery with Engenior Virden and son John Virden. The older William Virden does not appear any more.

WILLIAM VIRDEN, son of Engenior Virden, was born February 27, 1791, in South Carolina. He died November 13, 1841, age 50 years. He is interred in the Virden-Moor Cemetery near Topeka Junction, Upson County, Georgia. On June 3, 1809, he married Elizabeth _____, who was born June 9, 1793. Bible records show that they had twelve children:

(1) Samuel Virden, born February 17, 1811. He married Louisa Ann Wood in Pike County, Georgia, December 20, 1843. He was married a second time. He had fifteen children but all data is not available. His known sons were: (1) Alexander G. Virden, born June 24, 1846, in Barnsville, Georgia, was the oldest son. He died September 19, 1926, in Victoria, Texas; (2) Samuel Thomas Virden; (3) John Virden; (4) William David Virden, born January 26, 1854, near Atlanta, Georgia. He married Willie Leona Youngblood in Bell County, Texas, and later moved to Winters, Texas. Alexander Virden and William David Virden went to Texas together.

(2) Mary Virden, born April 5, 1813. She married a Mr. Woodall.

(3) Martha Virden, born July 11, 1815. She married Richard Brown in Upson County, Georgia, December 25, 1838;

(4) Elizabeth Virden, born February 9, 1821. She married John Corley (Colley) on December 21, 1843. She died June 14, 1847, and is buried in the Virden-Moore Cemetery at Topeka Junction, Upson County, Georgia;

(5) James Virden, born October 31, 1822. The 1870 Census of Warren County, Georgia, shows him with the following family, all having been born in Georgia: (1) James Virden, age 46; (2) Monah Virden, age 34; (3) Willie Virden, age 13; (4) Fannie Virden, age 12; (5) Milton Virden, age 11; (6) Jenny Virden, age 7; (7) John Virden, age 5; and (8) James Virden, age 1;

(6) William Virden, Jr., born September 18, 1824. On December 9, 1845, he married Patience McDaniel of Upson County, Georgia. (See letter from Mrs. Minnie Surratt, great granddaughter of William Virden.) He was killed in the Civil War on the Confederate side. James John Virden, a son, had nine children, born in Georgia, Alabama, and Mississippi;

(7) Sarah Virden, born May 28, 1825;

(8) John Virden, born May 26, 1826. The 1870 Census of Warren County, Georgia, shows him with the following family, all born in Georgia: (1) John Virden, age 44; (2) Mary M. Virden, age 40; (3) Martha A. Virden, age 17; (4) Christopher C. Virden, age 15; (5) John N. Virden, age 13; (6) Mary C. Virden, age 11; (7) William Virden, age 5; (8) Emma Virden, age 3; and (9) James P. Virden, age 1;

(9) Julia Ann Virden, born October 12, 1828. She married Jerimiah Adams of Upson County, Georgia on December 21, 1843. Part of this family went to Texas;

(10) Thomas G. Virden, born October 4, 1831. He was in the Civil War. He married Zilphey N. _____, who was born October 8, 1855, and died October 12, 1913. Thomas G. Virden died June 13, 1903, and is buried in the Virden-Moore Cemetery in Upson County, Georgia;

(11) Pricilla Virden, born April 5, 1834. She married a Mr. Elliot (probably Thomas D. Elliot) and she and her husband are buried in the Virden-Moore Cemetery, which is also known as the Salem Cemetery. They are believed to have had a daughter, Eugenia B. Elliot, born November 28, 1866, who died November 28, 1889; and

(12) Benjamin Virden, born in 1835. (see separate information relating to Benjamin Virden.) The Hamilton County, Texas, Census for 1880 shows him with the following family, all born in Texas except where specified here: (1) Benjamin Virden, age 45, born in Georgia, while his father and mother were born in South Carolina; (2) Nancy T. Virden, age 45, born in Georgia; (3) William Virden, age 25, born in Alabama; (4) John J. Virden, age 18; (5) Benjamin T. Virden, age 16; (6) Henry M. Virden, age 14; (7) Julius F. Virden, age 11; and (8) James M. Virden, age 6.

The 1850 Upson County, Georgia, Census shows this

Elizabeth Virden - age 56, born in North Carolina.
Thomas Virden - age 18, born in Georgia.
Pricilla Virden - age 16, born in Georgia.
Benjamin Virden - age 14, born in Georgia.

These last two children were not shown in the original Bible records. I have contacted several descendants of this line, but all are too busy to do anything, or just don't want to fill in the blank spaces.

The 1850 Census of Pike County, Georgia, shows the following relating to Samuel Virden, the oldest child listed

Samuel Virden - age 38, born in Georgia.
Laura A. Virden - age 24, born in Georgia.
Alexander Virden - age 3, born in Georgia.
Nancy E. Virden - age 1, born in Georgia.

The 1850 Census of Cape Girardeau, Missouri, shows the following

Samuel Virden - age 61, born in Georgia.
Fanny Verden - age 49, born in North Carolina.
William Verden - age 23, born in Missouri.
John Verden - age 22, born in Missouri.
Enoch Verden - age 20, born in Missouri.

Ajeniah Verden - age 18, born in Missouri.
Lyrilda Verden - age 18, born in Missouri.
Sarah Verden - age 17, born in Missouri.
George Verden - age 15, born in Missouri.
Annie Verden - age 12, born in Missouri.

Angeline Verden - age 10, born in Missouri.
John Verden - age 10, born in Missouri.
James Verden - age 5, born in Missouri.

The 1850 Census of Cape Girardeau, Missouri, shows the following

William Verden - age 45, born in Georgia.
Elizabeth Verden - age 24, born in Missouri, as were the rest of
    the family.
Nelson Verden - age 20.
Lerena Verden - age 19.
William Verden - age 12.
James Verden - age 2.
Nancy Verden - age 2.
Elizabeth Verden - age 8.

The 1850 Census of Cape Girardeau, Missouri, shows the following

John Verden - age 23, born in Missouri.
Sarah Verden - age 22, born in Missouri.
Mary E. Verden - age 2, born in Missouri.
James W. Verden - age 1, born in Missouri.

This John Verden appears to be the son of William Verden.

The following two families do not seem to fit into the Georgia Virden family. They do seem to fit James Virden, Jr. Of course, James Virden (my third great uncle) could have gone to Missouri from Kentucky, where his father lived, prior to moving to Illinois. The printed Census records show Missouri as the location of the following Virdens. All were born in Missouri unless otherwise specified. (From 1850 Census)

Hugh A. Virden - age 28, born in Missouri.
Mary Virden - age 28, born in Illinois.
Sophia Virden - age 8 (she married a Mr. Borders, listed as Virgin
    in marriage record)
Frena C. Virden - age 7.
James H. Virden - age 5.
Amanda J. Virden - age 4.
David Virden - age 2.
Lina Virden - age 1.

The 1850 Census cited above also shows the following family

John Verden - age 25, born in Missouri.
Ann Verden - age 30, born in North Carolina.

The 1850 Census of Pope County, Arkansas, shows

Hugh A. Verden   -   age 52, born in Georgia.
Elizabeth Verden   -   age 43, born in Tennessee.
Louisa Verden   -   age 17, born in Missouri.
Hugh A. Verden   -   age 15, born in Missouri.
Thomas B. Verden   -   age 10, born in Arkansas.
Felix G. Verden   -   age 7, born in Arkansas.
James B. Verden   -   age 1, born in Arkansas.

      The above Census of Pope County also shows a Calvin Verden, age 22 (enumerated with Reuben Mothern), born in Missouri.

The 1870 Census of Pope County, Arkansas, shows

James B. Virden   -   age 21, born in Arkansas.
Elizabeth Jane Virden   -   age 22, born in Arkansas.
Dora A. Virden   -   age 6 months, born in Arkansas.
Melinda Bynum   -   age 40, born in Arkansas.
Felix J. Bynum   -   age 9, born in Arkansas.
George W. Bynum   -   age 9, born in Arkansas.

The same Census shows

John C. Virden   -   age 41, born in Missouri.
Catherine Virden   -   age 37, born in Alabama.
Margaret A. Virden   -   age 17.
Hugh A. Virden   -   age 16.
John M. Virden   -   age 14.
Mary L. Virden   -   age 8.
Calvin J. Virden   -   age 5.
Mary M. Virden   -   age 6 months.

Another Family Shown on the 1870 Census of Pope County is

Felix G. Virden   -   age 29, born in Arkansas.
Ellen Virden   -   age 25, born in Arkansas.
Matilda A. Virden   -   age 2, born in Arkansas.
Elizabeth A. Virden   -   age 1, born in Arkansas.

The 1870 Pope County Census also Shows the Following Two Families

James Verdon   -   age 51, born in Missouri.
George W. Verdon   -   age 19, born in Arkansas.
Francis Verdon   -   age 17, born in Arkansas.
Franklin P. Verdon   -   age 16, born in Arkansas.
Willis Verdon   -   age 14.

```
Catherine Verdon   - age 13.
Robert J. Verdon   - age 12.
Margaret Verdon    - age 8.
Polly Verdon       - age 6.
Cardie Verdon      - age 2.
Elizabeth Verdon   - age 1, born in Arkansas, as were the other children.
```

The second family is that of Henderson Virden

```
Henderson Virden      - age 40, born in Missouri.
Picey (Scott) Virden  - age 38, born in Tennessee.
John W. Virden        - age 15.
Louisa Jane Virden    - age 13.
Lydia Ann Virden      - age 11.
Catherine Virden      - age 9.
Willie H. Virden      - age 5.
Ellen Virden          - age 3.
Eveline Virden        - age 1.
```

This James Verdon (first family above) does not seem to fit the Georgia branch of the family either. Have been trying to place him as a brother of Hugh A. Virden and John Virden of Cape Girardeau, Missouri, of 1850 Census, as a son of James Virden, born in 1787 in South Carolina, but have had no luck.

A James Virden showed up in Pope County, Arkansas, in 1845 when he married Sally Gray, age 28. He gave his age as 26. They were married November 30, 1845.

A James Verden in Pope County in 1856. He married Lucinda Butler September 15, 1856. He gave his age as 40 while she was 23.

A Sarah Virden married Reuben Campbell November 23, 1856. She gave her age as 35 while Reuben gave his as 35.

<u>The 1860 Census of Pope County, Arkansas, lists this family!</u>

```
James Virden    - age 39, born in Missouri.
Lucinda Virden  - age 23, born in Tennessee.
Matilda Virden  - age 3, born in Arkansas.
Felix Virden    - age 1, born in Arkansas.
```

This James Virden is apparently the same man, but I have four different birth dates--1819, 1816, and two in 1821. There is too much age difference for him to be the son of Hugh A. Virden, born in 1798 in Georgia. Samuel Virden, age 61, born in Georgia, has a son, James Virden, and he does not fit the William Virden either. This James Virden also had a son, Thomas Benton Virden, born in 1865, but I can't locate him.

From pension records and marriage records of Pope County I have put together the following: Hugh A. Virden, born 1798, in Georgia, married Elizabeth _____, born 1807, in Tennessee, and they had these children:

(1) Calvin Virden, born 1828, in Missouri. He married Sarah Bewley on July 9, 1850;
(2) John C. Virden, born 1829. Did not find his marriage, but 1860 Census shows: John C. Virden, age 30, born in Missouri; Margaret E. Virden, age 8, born in Arkansas; Henly A. Virden, age 7, born in Arkansas; John M. Virden, age 5, born in Arkansas; and William J. Virden, age 3, born in Arkansas;
(3) Henderson Virden, born 1830. He married Dicey Scott on October 31, 1851;
(4) Louisa Virden, born 1833. She married Wiley G. Hillis December 9, 1850;
(5) Mary Virden, born 1834. She married Asa Wade June 3, 1848;
(6) Hugh A. Virden, born 1835, in Missouri;
(7) Thomas Virden, born 1840, in Arkansas. He married Margaret L. Williamson, July 6, 1858;
(8) Felix G. Virden, born 1843, in Arkansas. He married Ellen _____ about 1867; and
(9) James B. Virden, born 1849, in Arkansas. He married Elizabeth J. Bynum about 1868.

THOMAS BENTON VIRDEN (son of James Virden and Lucinda Butler) was born June 1, 1865, in Dover, Pope County, Arkansas. On September 1, 1889, he married Sarah Elizabeth Watson, who was born February 2, 1873, in Atkins, Arkansas. Thomas Benton Virden died January 21, 1953, in Quinton, Oklahoma. Sarah Elizabeth Virden died January 3, 1963, in McAllister, Oklahoma. (Her father, Arthur Lee Watson, married Louisa Jane Virden, born January 27, 1857, the daughter of Henderson Virden and Dicey (Scott) Virden.) The children of Thomas Benton Virden and Sarah Elizabeth (Watson) Virden were:

(1) Lucinda Virden, born July 23, 1890, in Russellville, Pope County, Arkansas. On July 25, 1908, she married Wylie Frank Scott. After the death of Wylie she married Elmer Frazier. She died November 11, 1967;
(2) William Oscar Virden, born August 19, 1892, in Enterprise, Hasknell County, Oklahoma. On February 20, 1913, he married Flossie Ann Jones, who was born March 12, 1897, at Kinta, Oklahoma. He died September 13, 1956, in McAllister, Oklahoma. The children of William Oscar and Flossie Ann (Jones) Virden were: (1) Nowassa Juanita Virden, born November 10, 1913, in Quinton, Oklahoma. On July 25, 1933, she married Woodrow Wilson Folsom; (2) Emerson Virden, born February 28, 1915, in Blocker, Oklahoma. He married Fern Marie Jones; (3) Nolan Virden, born March 26, 1917, in Quinton, Oklahoma, and died November 1, 1917; (4) Virginia Virden, born August 26, 1920. She

married Roy William Martin on March 8, 1939;
(5) Hazel Lee Virden, born August 7, 1922, in
Quinton, Oklahoma. She married Howard Norwood
Duff on January 8, 1941; (6) a son, stillborn,
in 1924; and (7) Willie Wanda Virden, born
May 11, 1926. She married James Virgil Carney
on February 6, 1943. As her second husband
she married Paul Grant, and as her third husband
she married James Watkins;

(3) James Jefferson Virden, born September 11, 1898, in Russellville, Arkansas. He married Lulu Risen Hoover;
(4) Elvin Guy Virden, born August 1, 1901, in Enterprise, Oklahoma. He married Pearl Jenkins;
(5) Dovie May Virden, born September 28, 1903, in Enterprise, Oklahoma. Her first husband was Ernest Cherry; her second husband was Ode Shelton; and
(6) Evlyn Alice Lee Virden, born April 9, 1906, in Enterprise, Oklahoma. She married as her first husband Joseph Snow; as her second husband she married Clifford Webber.

Arthur Lee Watson (son of Decater Watson) was born June 12, 1853, in Independence County, Arkansas. He died in March 1931, in Quinton, Oklahoma. In 1872 he married Louisa Jane Virden (daughter of Henderson and Dicey (Scott) Virden), who was born January 27, 1857, in Pope County, Arkansas, and died February 27, 1943, in Sand Springs, Oklahoma. Their children were:

(1) Sarah Elizabeth Watson, born February 3, 1873, in Atkins, Arkansas. She married Thomas Benton Virden September 1, 1899;
(2) William Elton Watson, born 1875, in Atkins, Arkansas. He married Arvie James;
(3) James Elmer Watson, born July 12, 1881. In 1904 he married Dicey Hill. He died March 24, 1938;
(4) Oliver Rudolph Watson, born 1879;
(5) Emma May Watson, born May 8, 1887, in Atkina, Arkansas. She married a Mr. Upton. She died March 13, 1904;
(6) Benjamin Harrison Watson, born 1883, Pope County, Arkansas.
(7) Wiley Arthur Watson, born September 25, 1891, in Enterprise, Oklahoma. He married Hattie King. He died in 1963; and
(8) Thomas Edgar Watson, born December 18, 1893, in Enterprise, Oklahoma. He married Mae Lentz. He died September 8, 1968.

Some Notes

Lacey Virden's widow is on the 1883 pension list of Mt. Pleasant, Henry County, Iowa.

The 1860 mortality list of Henry County, Iowa, shows Harriet Virden, age 13, born in Ohio, died in August. Also, Jesse Virden, age 3 months, died in January.

1850 Census of Muskingum County, Ohio, shows

Lewis Virden - age 65, born in Delaware.
Ruth Virden   - age 64, born in Pennsylvania.

* * *

Jerome Virden - age 36, born in Ohio. (This family moved to Iowa.)
Sarah (Fleming) Virden - age 35, born in Ireland.
John L. Virden - age 15, born in Ohio, as were the succeeding children.
Edward R. Virden - age 14.
Jane Virden - age 10.
Levi Virden - age 8.
Mary Virden - age 7.
Lewis Virden - age 5.
Henrietta Virden - age 3.
Jerome Virden - age 8 months.

* * *

Lewis Virden   - age 28, born in Ohio.
Mary J. Virden - age 21, born in Ohio.
James H. Virden - age 2, born in Ohio.

* * *

Delilah Virden - age 49, born in Pennsylvania. (Wife of Lacey Virden who died prior to 1850.)
Caroline Virden - age 26, born in Ohio.
Rufus Virden - age 19, born in Ohio.
Sarah J. Virden - age 12, born in Ohio.

* * *

LEVI VIRDEN (son of Jerome and Sarah (Flemming) Virden) was born in Zenesville, Ohio, October 21, 1841. He died May 9, 1883, in Mt. Pleasant, Henry County, Iowa. He married Virginia Ann Rowe on March 15, 1866, in Blakesburg, Iowa. She was born January 15, 1849, at Navoo, Illinois, and died March 4, 1926, at Albia, Monroe County, Iowa. (She was the daughter of John T. and Rebecca Jane (Heller) Rowe.) Levi and Virginia Ann (Rowe) Virden had eight children but all except three died young:

(1) Lewis Rowe Virden, born December 27, 1871, at Mt. Pleasant, Iowa. On December 4, 1884, he married Mary Elizabeth Judd. He died November 6, 1954. She died in Simla, Colorado, September 15, 1943. Their known children are: (1) Lodina Virden, (2) Herbert Virden, and (3) Cora Virden;

(2) Franklin Jerome Virden, born July 19, 1873, in Blakesburg, Iowa. He died January 21, 1925, in Long Beach, California. On December 12, 1894, he married Fanny Louise Weidman. Both husband and wife are buried in the family crypt at Sunnyside Cemetery, Long Beach, California. Their known children are: (1) Jerome Virden and (2) Francis Virden;

(3) Freddie Virden, born Blakesburg, Iowa, April 30, 1876, and died May 27, 1876;

(4) L. Virden (male child), born June 7, 1877, died June 9, 1879;

(5) A. Virden (female child), born June 7, 1877, died June 9, 1879;

(6) William Elmer Virden, born Blakesburg, Iowa, August 28, 1878. He died December 4, 1935, in Long Beach, California. On August 17, 1899, he married Nancy Angeline Thompson at Colorado Springs, Colorado. Nancy died in 1953. Both are buried in the family crypt in Long Beach, California;

(7) Lidonia May Virden, born August 7, 1880, in Mt. Pleasant, Iowa, and died February 15, 1885; and

(8) Johnnie Virden, born October 21, 1882, Mt. Pleasant, Iowa, died June 15, 1885.

WILLIAM ELMER VIRDEN and Nancy Angeline (Thompson) Virden had these children:

(1) E. Virgil Virden, born January 19, 1900, at Fountain, Colorado. In July 1921, he married Florence Edith Doile at Long Beach, California. Florence was born in 1903 at Emporia, Kansas. They had three children. ("I met him and since he did not know who his grandparents were, I gave him his line back to Lewis Virden, born in 1785 in Delaware.")

(2) Cordelia May Virden, born January 19, 1902, in Fountain, Colorado. On June 16, 1930 (?) she married Frank G. Hink (?) in Long Beach, California;

(3) Levi Cecil Virden, born in Fountain, Colorado, March 7, 1904. On June 6, 1925, he married Pearl Ried, at Long Beach, California. As his second wife he married Clasetta Houig. Levi died February 16, 1959, and was buried in Greenwar Memorial Cemetery, San Diego, California;

(4) Lorena Viola Virden, born February 15, 1906, in Fountain, Colorado. On September 15, 1932 (?)

she married Hassell L. Mervin at Long Beach,
California; and
(5) Glenn Wilson Virden, born September 18, 1908,
in Loveland, California.

1860 Census of Mt. Pleasant Township, Henry County, Iowa, shows

L.H. Virden   - age 38, born in Ohio.
Matilda Virden   - age 38, place of birth unknown.
James Virden   - age 12, born in Ohio.
Lucy Virden   - age 10, born in Ohio.
Mary Virden   - age 8, born in Ohio.
Isaac Virden   - age 5, born in Ohio.
Lucretia Virden - age 3, born in Ohio.

* * *

Jerome Virden   - age 45, born in Ohio.
Sarah Virden   - age 48, born in Ireland.
Jane Virden   - age 18, born in Ohio.
Ellen Virden   - age 16, born in Ohio.
Louis Virden   - age 14, born in Ohio.
Levi Virden   - age 11, born in Ohio.

* * *

H.S. Virden   - age 39, born in Ohio, as were all this family except
                   Benjamin Virden who was born in Missouri.
Elizabeth Virden - age 37.
Ruth Virden   - age 14.
Louis Virden   - age 12.
Robert Virden   - age 11.
Arthur Virden   - age 10.
Lacey Virden   - age 9.
Jane Virden   - age 8.
Isabelle Virden - age 7.
John Virden   - age 4.
Benjamin Virden - age 2.

* * *

1850 Census of Waterloo, Blackhawk County, Iowa, shows

Charles Mullin   - age 35, born in Pennsylvania.
America (Virden) Mullin - age 28, born in Kentucky.
James Virden   - age 26, born in Kentucky.
Daniel Virden   - age 25, born in Kentucky.
Isaac Virden   - age 22, born in Illinois.
Elizabeth Mullin   - age 6, born in Illinois.

Charles Mullin   -   age 4, born in Illinois.
William H. Mullin -   age 2, born in Iowa.

* * *

William Virden   -   age 29, born in Kentucky.
Rebecca Virden   -   age 26, born in Illinois.
Martha Virden   -   age 7, born in Illinois.
Louisa Virden   -   age 3, born in Iowa.

* * *

1860 Census of Blackhawk County, Iowa, shows

James Virden   -   age 37, born in Kentucky.
Harriet Virden -   age 27, born in Kentucky.
George Virden   -   age 8, born in Iowa.
Willard Virden -   age 6, born in Iowa.

Note: Martha (Williamson) Virden was living with Charles and America
       (Virden) Mullin in the 1860 Census.

* * *

Oscar Virden   -   age 40, born in Kentucky.
Love Charity (Powell) Virden   -   age 27, born in Massachusetts.
George Virden   -   age 13, born in Illinois.
Charles Virden -   age 11, born in Illinois.
Norman Virden   -   age 8, born in Iowa.
Elizabeth Virden - age 5, born in Iowa.
Emma Virden   -   age 3, born in Iowa.
William Virden -   age 8 months, born in Iowa.
Eliza Virden   -   age 27, born in Indiana.
Estella Virden -   age 2, born in Iowa.

Note: This is the wife of Isaac Virden, born 1828, in Kentucky.
       Isaac died September 10, 1865, age 36 years, 4 months, and
       15 days, in Mobile, Alabama. Eliza Virden died January 1,
       1883, age 50 years, 26 days, at Clarksville, Iowa.

    Elizabeth Virden, born July 1, 1854 (daughter of Oscar Virden)
married David Orville Bly October 30, 1875. She died October 20, 1943.

    Emma Virden, born February 5, 1857 (daughter of Oscar Virden)
married Jacob A. Coons, born in 1854. She died September 17, 1957. The
families of both Elizabeth Virden and Emma Virden migrated to Minnesota
about 1895.

1850 Census of Wayne County, Illinois, shows

William Verden - age 65, born in Delaware.
M. Verden - age 57, born in New Jersey.
Th. Verden - age 19.
Eliz. Verden - age 17.
F.M. Verden - age 14. (probably Frank Verden)
Mary Verden - age 12.

* * *

Osker Verden - age 30, born in Kentucky.
L.C. Verden - age 37, born in Massachusetts. (Error in birth date; should probably be 17 years of age.)
George Verden - age 4, born in Illinois.
Charles Verden - age 2, born in Illinois.

Note: The Census taker really made a mess out of this. He could not spell and in most cases he just used initials.)

* * *

1880 Soundex Film of Iowa shows

Charles Virden - age 31, born in Illinois. (Lived Waterloo Township)
Nelits Virden - age 28, born in Illinois.
Bertrand Virden - age 3, born in Iowa.
Maud _____ - age 10 months. No relation.

* * *

Frank Virden - age 44, born in Illinois. (Lived in Butler Township)
Hattie Virden - age 24, born in Iowa.
Howard Virden - age 3, born in Iowa.
Martha Virden - age 87, born in New Jersey. (Mother)

* * *

John Virden - age 30, born in New York. (Lived in Lafayette Township)
Madeline Virden - age 29, born in Iowa.
Peter Virden - age 9, born in Iowa.
Maggie Virden - age 5, born in Iowa.
John Virden - age 3, born in Iowa.
Salena Virden - age 1, born in Iowa.

* * *

Josiah Varden - age 25, born in Pennsylvania. (Lived in Sioux City)
Mary Varden - age 22, born in Minnesota.
Bertha Varden - age 3, born in Iowa.
Bird Varden - son, age 1, born in Iowa.

Levi Virden   - age 41, born in Ohio.
Virginia Virden - age 30, born in Illinois.
Lewis Virden   - age 8, born in Iowa.
Franklin Virden - age 5, born in Iowa.
Elmer Virden   - age 1, born in Iowa.

* * *

Berryman Virden - age 53, born in Illinois. (Lived in
                    Whitebreast Township)
Susan Virden   - age 48, born in Illinois.
Lewis B. Virden - age 20, born in Illinois.
Charles W. Virden - age 18, born in Illinois.
Ellen Phillips - age 31, born in Illinois. (A niece)
George Virden   - age 2, born in Missouri. (Adopted son)

Note: There was a Joe Virden, age 33, born in Mississippi, living in
      Jones County, Iowa, in 1880. He was a negro with a family.)

* * *

1880 Soundex Film of West Virginia shows

Absolom Virden - age 39, born in Virginia. (Lived in Pleasants County)
Rachel Virden   - age 36, born in Pennsylvania.
Anna R. Virden - age 15, born in West Virginia.
James S. Virden - age 13, born in West Virginia.
Irene P. Virden - age 7, born in Ohio.
Angie N. Virden - age 4, born in Ohio.
Lizzie Harlan   - age 14, born in Ohio.

* * *

Thomas Virden   - age 36, born in Virginia. (Lived in Pleasants County)
Ellen Virden   - age 24, born in Virginia.
Flossie L. Virden - age 6, born in West Virginia.
Robert Lawson Virden - age 1, born in West Virginia.
Catherine Keeder - age 65, born in Pennsylvania. (Mother-in-law)

* * *

Hamilton Virden - age 35, born in Virginia. (Lived in Pleasants County)
Lucretia Virden - age 33, born in Virginia.
C. Jane Virden - age 15, born in Virginia.
Prissila A. Virden - age 11, born in Virginia.
Fanny L. Virden - age 3, born in Virginia.
Park C. Virden - age 1, born in Virginia.

* * *

Martin Virden - age 27, born in Virginia. (Lived in Pleasants County)
Letha Ellen Virden - age 23, born in Virginia.
Sarah F. Virden - age 4, born in Virginia.
Margaret Virden - age 2, born in West Virginia.
John F. Virden - age 4 months, born in West Virginia.

* * *

Thomas Virden - age 48, born in West Virginia. (Lived in Tyler County)
Rebecca Virden - age 45, born in West Virginia.
Clarra Virden - age 26, born in West Virginia.
Clark Virden - age 24, born in West Virginia.
Mary B. Virden - age 21, born in West Virginia.

* * *

Martha Virden - age 17, born in West Virginia.[1]
Susan Virden - age 14, born in West Virginia.[2]
Fred Virden - age 3, born in West Virginia.

[1] Martha married Joseph W. Johnson, September 17, 1882.
[2] Susan married Edgar M. Bell July 2, 1889.

* * *

Thornton Virden - age 45, born in West Virginia. (Lived in Tyler County)
Ammie Virden - age 43, born in Pennsylvania.
George W. Virden - age 19, born in West Virginia.[1]
Andrew J. Virden - age 13, born in West Virginia.[2]
Friend Virden - age 8, born in West Virginia.
Annie L. Virden - age 1, born in West Virginia.

[1] George married Marilla H. Wells, March 9, 1889.
[2] Andrew married Martha Williamson, September 5, 1890.

* * *

David Williamson Virden - age 38, born in West Virginia.
(Lived in Tyler County)
Mary (Bogard) Virden - age 33, born in West Virginia.
Russell Virden - age 12, born in West Virginia.
Lillian A.E. Virden - age 10, born in West Virginia.
Ella N. Virden - age 7, born in West Virginia.
Edward Warren Virden - age 3, born in West Virginia.[1]
Willie W. Virden - age 9 months, born in West Virginia.
J.M. Bogard - age 74, born in Pennsylvania. (Father-in-law)

[1] This Edward Virden had a son, Captain Robert Warren Virden, living in California.

Notes: There was an Absolom Virden who married Alice J. Fuller, June 8, 1866, in Tyler County, West Virginia.

There was a John Virden who married Margaret Boyd, January 1, 1850, in Monongalia, West Virginia.

1880 Soundex Film of Ohio shows

John Virden - age 29, born in West Virginia.[1] (Lived in Columbiana County, Ohio)
Mary E. Virden - age 26, born in Pennsylvania.
Jennie Virden - age 2, born in Pennsylvania.
Lucy Virden - age 2 months, born in Pennsylvania.

[1] Probably a brother of Thomas, Thornton, and David Virden of Tyler County, West Virginia.

1883 Pension Records show

Thomas W. Virden - Pleasants County, West Virginia, received a pension of $50.00 for entire helplessness November 1881. (No. 74885)

John R. Virden - Received a pension of $4.00 per month in August 1882. He lived at Connersville, Fayette County, Indiana. (No. 216387)

Edward Virden - Tippencanoe County, Indiana, received a pension of $8.00 per month in November 1882. (No. 204071)

John Virden - Humbolt County, California, received a pension of $8.00 per month in December 1867. (He must have gone gold mining.) (No. 28714)

Microfilm Records of Revolutionary War Soldiers show

David Varden - North Carolina, private.
John Varden - 3rd Artillery, Continental Troops, Major Ross.
Thomas Varden - 1st Pennsylvania Regiment, private.
Samuel Varden - 2nd Massachusetts Regiment.
Stephen Varden - 3rd and 4th Virginia Regiment, Drum and Fife Corps.

Thomas Verdin - Regular Continental Troops.
Thomas Varden - 5th Battalion, Pennsylvania Regiment.
Thomas Varden - 6th Battalion, Pennsylvania Regiment.
John Vardon - Hall's Delaware Regiment.
John Verdin - Captain William Perry's Independent Company, Delaware.

Hugh Virden   - Haslet's Delaware Regiment, private.
Marriet Virden   - Haslet's Delaware Regiment, corporal.
Marnix Virden   - Haslet's Delaware Regiment, corporal.
Levi Virden   - Haslet's Delaware Regiment, private.

This completes the letter dated February 10, 1977, from James R. Virden.

The Virdens from Christian County, Illinois, by Mrs. Ruth A. Shoup, Chula Vista, California.

"My name is Ruth (Virden) Shoup, youngest child of Christopher E. Virden, of Christian County, Illinois. I've just read your book <u>Virdins of Delaware and Related Families</u>. My brother, Joseph Virden, of Hollywood, California, purchased your book and loaned it to me to read as he knew that my brother James and I had been working on genealogical records for years.

I was very pleased and interested in all of the records of the Delaware Virdens listed in your book. But I have to admit that when I went to look for Virdens in Illinois and other states that I was disappointed. But I do realize that the book is primarily about the Delaware Virdins and therefore wouldn't have the other lines in it. It is my belief that the other Virdens did originate from the original families in Delaware as that seems to be the earliest record of any Virdens (outside of the Virginia Virden).

My brother James who now lives in Russia, Ohio, and I have been working for a number of years. He has the Georgia Virdens, also Virdens in Arkansas, Missouri, Texas, Ohio, and Illinois. We are descendants of James Virden of South Carolina, listed on page 69 of your book....We have the pension application that he filed in Missouri, obtained from the National Archives, claiming that he had never filed before and entitled 'Original Claim.'...

James and a brother, John, are listed in South Carolina, Newberry County, in 1790. James served 15 months in the South Carolina line during the Revolutionary War from June 1, 1777, to September 1, 1778. In his application filed in Missouri he claimed to have six children still living and all out of state. He in fact had seven living and all probably lived in Illinois at that time.

We believe James Virden to be a brother of Egenior Virden of Georgia. Egenior (Ajeniah) (Egeniah) was a Revolutionary War Soldier from Warren County, Georgia. His grave is marked by the D.A.R. He is listed on land "records in Virginia at an early date (in 1760's). His will is dated 1808 in Warren County, Georgia, and lists sons James, John, and William. (William was born in 1791...) Egenior was married twice it seems. On Virginia land records his wife was Jane, and in Georgia records later on his wife was Winney (Winnifred) and a good deal younger than him. Egenior was probably born as early as 1740....

James Virden, Verden, Verdin, Virdin, Verdan, etc., used Verdin and Verden on his records most commonly, although I have all the different spellings on his family. (My grandfather, John Edward, was orphaned as a small boy. He spelled the name Virden but always claimed as he grew older that the original spelling was Verdin. It seems that many of the early Virdens didn't know how to write and signed their mark. James was born August 25, 1756, in Newberry or Pendleton District, South Carolina. He married Sarah ____ (Cater?) also of South Carolina in 1784. They had a family of eleven children, all born in South Carolina. They moved to Missouri, where in 1827 James applied for a pension. Then they moved to Illinois where Sarah applied for a pension after James died. James died in Fayette or Shelby County, Illinois, June 18, 1843. Sarah died September 3, 1845, also in Illinois. In a claim filed March 17, 1846, son Levi and his son Isaac filed a claim for benefits for the surviving children, all in Illinois. Children:

(1) Elizabeth Verdin. Born July 4, 1785. Married ___ Davis and went to Kentucky then to Illinois.
(2) James Verdin. Born November 8, 1787. Married Elizabeth (could be Nancy) ___. Born in 1790 in South Carolina. James moved to Kentucky and then to Illinois. He had his children in Kentucky. Some of the children remained in Kentucky. A few went to Illinois with him.
(3) Jane Verdin. Born December 28, 1789. Married ___ Gordon. Went to Illinois.
(4) William Verdin. Born March 23, 1794. Married Nancy ___ who was born in South Carolina. William moved to Illinois about 1815. We know that he was there when it became a state in 1818. (He is listed in your book on page 25 as a son of Isaac Virden...). More on Isaac later, but William listed as No. (1),

Radford No. (3), Levi No. (5), were brothers but not sons of Isaac and Amelia Saddler Virden. William and his brother Levi are listed on the 1820 Bond County, Illinois, Census. William died about 1849. His will is dated 1848. It lists all of his children: Sarah, Elizabeth, Susan (or Suka), Charity, Minerva, Jane, Nancy, William, Samuel, James, and John Verdin. Samuel Verdin, born in 1831, married Patience Meads in 1851. He died around 1857 leaving his wife and three children, John Edward Verdin, and a boy and a girl. Samuel's wife remarried and she and the other two children died of colds contracted from measles. John Edward Verdin was raised by Gabe Durbin, an uncle of his mother's, as Andrew Oller, his step-father, was not good to him. John Edward Verdin married Mary Ellen Painter and had seven children: Christopher Elmer Verdin (my father) was the only son who lived. Christopher Elmer was known as John Chris most of his life. He married Cora E. Wells in 1917 and had nine children of whom I am the ninth.

(5) Levi Verdin. Born April 4, 1796. Married twice. His first wife was Rachel ___ who died in Illinois in 1826. His second wife was Catherine Reese. Their children were: Isaac, Jacob, John, Catherine Mahala, Levi, and Eli. Isaac Verdin married Surelda Jane Ishmael; they were the parents of James F. Verdin, father of Martin I. Verdin. All of Levi's children were born in Illinois.

(6) Margaret Verdin. Born June 13, 1798. Died prior to 1827.

(7) Mary Meniale Verdin. Born October 14, 1800. Died prior to 1827.

(8) Charity Cater Verdin. Born May 5, 1803. Married Daniel Francisco (Cisco). Lived in Illinois.

(9) Ann Cater Verdin. Born September 25, 1805. Died young.

(10) Hugh Radford Virden. Born 1807 in South Carolina. Married Margaret Wilson. (He is listed in your book on page 25 as a son of Isaac. On page 28 the Hiram Virden listed as Radford's son was not

his son although he did have a son named Hiram, born in 1836. Hiram Virden listed on page 28 was born in Ohio. He was a brother to Jerome Virden and was the son of Lewis Virden, a brother to Lacy Virden, son of Levi Virden of Delaware. Hugh Radford Virden lived in Illinois. These brothers and sisters did not have a brother named John although James, the eldest son, had a son named John who may have gone to Illinois from Kentucky with his father. My brother and I have the dates and most of the children of all of these if you are interested.

Isaac Virden. Born January 10, 1779, either in Pennsylvania, Virginia, or Maryland. (One son's biography states Virginia; the other states Pennsylvania; and I have Maryland on other records.) He married Amelia Saddler in Ohio. She was born June 10, 1791. Isaac was an early pioneer to Ross County, Ohio. They had a family of ten sons and one daughter. They moved to Illinois (Christian, Sangamon, Macoupin Counties) in 1834. I have three different dates but 1834 appears to be correct. Archibald, a son, claims 1834 in one biography and 1839 in another. When Christian County was formed in 1839 Isaac Virden and son William Virden were residents. In the 1840 Census Isaac and his son William S. are listed, and also our William from South Carolina. We have not been able to name all the sons of Isaac yet. Samuel may have been a son. He is listed on records in 1836. Or it could be that he is a son of James - son of James of South Carolina. Anyway, these sons we are certain were all born in Ohio. Isaac died in 1846.

(1) William S. Virden. Born in 1811;
(2) John W. Virden. Born in 1812. Virden, Illinois, was named after him;
(3) Archibald Virden. Born October 27, 1823;
(4) Isaac Q. Virden. Born October 25, 1824;
(5) Wilson Virden. Born in 1827;
(6) J.W. (or F.W.) Virden. Born in 1828. J.W. shows on the 1850 Census and F.W. shows on the 1880 Census.

....We can provide more information on the Illinois and Georgia Virdens if you are interested. And I want to tell you how much I have enjoyed your book. I know that you have put a lot of work into it.

"As for me, I am married and have five children. The oldest is sixteen, the youngest is eleven. I was born in Garrett, Indiana, DeKalb County, February 16, 1941. My parents came to California in 1951. Both of my parents are now dead."

The Virdens from Musgingum County, Ohio, and Adair County, Missouri, by Mrs. Jean C. Breese, Berlin, Maryland

"My husband, Thomas Wilson Virden, is a descendant of Lewis Virden, born in Delaware about 1790, who migrated to Muskingum county, Ohio, with his brother Lacy, later moving to Adair county, Missouri, where my husband was born July 7, 1913. His parents were William Thomas Virden and Edna Clea Evans. William and Edna were divorced when Thomas was about two years old and Edna married Albert Roy Breese, which explains why our name is now Breese.

I first found Lewis and Lacy Virden in the 1820 US Census in Muskingum Co. Ohio. Although I have no proof I feel that Lewis Virden was the father of Hiram. I also believe that Lewis and Lacy were brothers, at least there was a relationship. You will see from the following census records why I have come to these conclusions.

Lacy Virden was in the war of 1812. He is listed in the Ohio Roster. He married Delilah Coffman 13 May 1817 in Muskingum Co. Ohio (recorded in Muskingum County marriage records. I found no marriage record for Lewis. Both Delilah and Ruth (wife of Lewis) were born in Pa. so perhaps Lewis was married there before migrating to Ohio. Perhaps Lacy and Lewis were in Pa. for some time before Ohio. All this I have yet to prove.

<u>1820 Census</u> Muskingum Co. Zanesville Twp. Ohio

Lacy Virden   1 Male 45 & over   1 Female 10-15
                                   1   "   16-25

Lewis Virden   3 Males under 10   1 Female 10-15
               1   "   26-44   1   "   16-25
                                   1   2   45 & over

<u>1830 Census</u> Muskingum Co. Perry Twp. Ohio

Lacy Virden   1 Male 40-50   1 Female under 5
                                   2   "   5-10
                                   1   "   10-15
                                   1   "   20-30

"Note - Lacy had all girls so Hiram must have been the son of Lewis. There were no other Virdens in Muskingum County in those early days.

Lewis Virden	1 Male	5-10	1 Female	5-10
	2 "	10-15	1 "	10-15
	1 "	40-50	1 "	40-50

<u>1840 Census</u>   Muskingum Co.   Union Twp. Ohio

Lewis Virden	1 Male	50-60	1 Female	15-20
			1 "	20-30
			1 "	50-60

Jerome Virden	1 Male	under 5	2 "	under 5
	1 "	5-10	1 "	20-30
	1 "	20-30		

<u>1840 Census</u>   Perry Twp.

Mrs. Delilah Virden	No males	1 Female	under 5
		1 "	5-10
		1 "	20-30
		1 "	30-40
		1 "	40-50

Note - Lacy died in Sept 1834.

<u>1850 Census</u>   Muskingum Co. Ohio   Union Twp.

Lewis Virden	65	b	Dela.
Ruth	64	b	Pa.

<u>1850 Census</u>   Muskingum Co. Ohio   Perry Twp.

Hiram Virden	29	b	Ohio
Elizabeth	25	b	"
Ruth	5		"
Lewis	3		"
Marshall	2		"
Arthur	1		"
Lacy	8½		"

Note - Lacy was grandfather of Thomas Wilson (Virden) Breese, my husband. Hiram and Elizabeth were married 22 Feb 1844 in Muskingum Co. This is on record.

"1850 Census   Muskingum Co. Ohio   Perry Twp.

Delilah Virden	49	b	Pa.
Caroline	26		Ohio
Sarah	12		"

1860 Census   Muskingum Co. Ohio   Perry Twp.

Delilah Virden	59	b	Pa.
Caroline	39	b	Ohio
Sarah	23		"
Ruth	73		Pa.

1860 Census   Henry Co. Iowa   Mt. Pleasant Twp.

H.S. Virden	39	b	Ohio
Elizabeth	37		"
Ruth	14		"
Lewis	12		"
Robt	11		"
Arthur	10		"
Lacy	9		"
Jane	8		"
Isabelle	7		"
John	4		"
Benjamin	2		Missouri

Note - I have a land record for Hiram in Adair Co. Missouri for 1857. Apparently the family was in Iowa when the 1860 census was taken. The older Lewis must have died before 1860 in Missouri as there is a stone erected for him as the father of Hiram. This stone was placed by Benjamin Virden but no dates. Ruth, the wife of Lewis you will see is residing with Delilah.

1870 Census   Adair Co. Missouri   Nineveh Twp.

Hiram Virden	50	b	Ohio
Elizabeth	45		"
John	14		"
Benjamin	11		Mo
Margaret	9		"
Lacy Virden	19		Ohio
Louisa	18		Mo

Note - Lacy and Elvisa (Louisa, Wisey) Logston were married 29 Mar 1869 I have the marriage record.

"1880 Census   Adair County, Missouri   Nineveh Twp.

Lacy Virden	30	b	Ohio
Wisey	29		Mo
Laura	9		"
Milton	5		"
Harriett E.	1		"

Note - Tom's Father, William Thomas Virden was born 14 Feb 1886. I sent to the Census Bureau in Kansas for this information from the 1900 census as we were unable to find a birth record. William is the son of Lacy and Wisey.

William Thomas Virden, he was called Tom married Edna Cleo Evan daughter of Henry and Cornelia (Brunick) Evans 2 Apr 1913. My husband Thomas Wilson Virden also called Tom was born 7 July 1913. His parents were divorced and his mother remarried Albert Roy Breese. Tom grew up thinking Albert was his father and was given his name. Later because Tom needed proof of birth his mother and step-father signed an affidavit stating the real name was Virden. Tom and I were married 29 Jan 1935 in Chicago, Ill. We have two children Joan b 15 Sept 1935 & Thomas Jr. b 17 Sept 1937. Tom passed away 30 Aug 1974 here in Maryland. He was 61 years old.

Joan married James R. Bailey in 1954. Their children are:

Kurt Thomas Bailey	b 7 Apr 1955	b	Va.
Kim Elaine	17 Sept 1956		Ala.
Paula Jean	23 Aug 1958		Germany
Karl Frederick	26 Nov 1960		Germany

Father in Service

Thomas Jr. married Polly Ann Bevan 21 May 1960. Their children are:

Brandon Scott	b 15 Oct 1966	b	Ariz
Forrest Lee	5 May 1969		Calif.

"Shibley's Point Cemetery, Adair Co. Mo.

Virdens

Benjamin R.	b 20 Sept 1859	d	17 May 1912
Milton, son of L.B. and W.	18 Nov 1875		11 Aug 1897
Laura, dau. of L.B. and W.	7 July 1871		4 Sept 1890
John R.	30 Apr 1856		22 Mar 1899
Lewis, father of Hiram stone erected by Benj, R.			
Alice, dau. of H.S. & E.			15 Oct 1857
Florence, infant of H.S. & E.	1862		
Robert M.	1848		14 Sept 1867
Sarah	1865		1869"

Letter dated March 29, 1972, from Mrs. Minnie Surratt to James R. Virden

"Kind Sir:

My dad was Jim John Virden. Born, June 15, 1863. Died, Jan. 29, 1919, age 64. He was the only son. His father was killed in the Civil War. My dad was only 7 years old then. I don't know my grandfathers name. My mother was Julie Denson Virden. They were married July 30, 1877 in Georgia somewhere.

I am sorry I don't know more, but this is all I have a record of.

Your friend,

Minnie Surratt"

1820 Census of Delaware, New Castle County, Appoquinimink Hundred, shows

John Vardan, 1 male 0-10; 1 male 16-25; 1 male 45 up; one female 10-15; and one female 45 up.

* * *

1790 Census of Maryland shows

James Vardin, Worcester County, 2 males over 16; 1 male under 16; and 2 females.

John Vardin, Charles County, 2 males over 16; 3 males under 16; and 4 females.

William Verden, Caroline County, 1 male over 16; 1 male under 16; and 3 females.

* * *

1800 Census of Pasquotank County, North Carolina

Tully Vardin. 1 male 26-44. 1 female 26-44.

* * *

1800 Census of Edgecombe County, North Carolina

David Verden. 1 male 16-25. 1 female 16-25.

* * *

1810 Census of Jefferson County, Virginia

James Vardin. 1 male 45; 1 male 10-15; 3 males to 10; and 1 female 26-44; 2 females up to 10.

* * *

1850 Census of Christian County, Illinois shows

Isaac J. Verden, age 26, born in Ohio. Farmer.
Rachel Verden, age 26, born in Kentucky.

Ann E. Verden, age 2, born in Illinois.
Andrew Lockwood, age 39, born in Germany. Laborer.

* * *

William Verden, age 23, born in Illinois. Farmer.
Elisabeth J. Verden, age 21, born in Illinois.
James S. Verden, age 1, born in Illinois.

* * *

John Ishmael, age 30, born in Kentucky. Farmer.
Suka Ishmael, age 29, born in Illinois.
Nancy S.A. Ishmael, age 8, born in Illinois.
Julia Ishmael, age 6, born in Illinois.
Polly A. Ishmael, age 4, born in Illinois.
Amanda J. Ishmael, age 2, born in Illinois.
Patia M. Ishmael, age 6 months, born in Illinois.
James Verden, age 21, born in Illinois. Farmer.
Samuel Verden, age 19, born in Illinois. Farmer.
John Verden, age 13, born in Illinois. Farmer.

* * *

1850 Census of Sangamon County, Illinois, shows

Berryman Virden, age 24, born in Illinois. Plasterer.
Susan Virden, age 20, born in Illinois.
William H. Virden, age 2, born in Illinois.
George R. Virden, age 1 month, born in Illinois.
Sarah C. McKinney, age 9, born in Illinois.

* * *

Jacob Virden, age 48, born in Pennsylvania. Farmer.
Lydia Virden, age 55, born in New York.
Zoza Virden, age 13, born in Illinois.
Jacob Virden, age 11, born in Illinois.
Margaret Virden, age 8, born in Illinois.
Catharine Virden, age 4, born in Illinois.

* * *

Archibald Virden, age 27, born in Ohio. Farmer.
Henrietta Virden, age 23, born in Maryland.
Lamira Virden, age 3, born in Illinois.
Ann Virden, age 1, born in Illinois.
Wilson Virden, age 23, born in Ohio. Farmer.
Mary Virden, age 17, born in Ohio.
Lemuel Dixon, age 20, born in Ohio. Farmer.

1820 Census of Bond County, Illinois, shows

William Verden.
Levi Verden.

* * *

1830 Census of Bond County, Illinois, shows

William Verden.

    The 1939 records of Dane County, Illinois, show Samuel Verden, born in Ohio. He is shown on the 1850 Census of Grant County, Wisconsin. He was reportedly the son of Isaac Verden, and moved from Wisconsin to Missouri.

1840 Census of Christian County, Illinois, shows

Isaac Virden, 60-70 years of age; wife, 50-60 years; 2 sons, 20-30 years; 2 sons, 15-20 years; 1 son, 10-15 years; 1 son, 5-10 years; 1 daughter, 10-15 years.

William Virden, 40-50 years of age; wife, 30-40 years; 2 sons, 10-15 years; 2 sons, 5-10 years; 2 daughters, 15-20 years; 1 daughter, 5-10 years; 2 daughters, under 5 years.

    Note: This William Virden was probably the son of James and Sarah Virden.

William Virden, 30-40 years of age; wife, 20-30 years of age; 1 son, under 5 years; 1 daughter, under 5 years.

    Note: This William Virden was probably the son of Isaac Virden.

* * *

1840 Census of Fayette County, Illinois, shows

James Virden, pensioner, age 88 years; no wife; 1 male child, 10-15 years of age.

    Note: Age given is incorrect; Sarah Virden, his wife was not dead at this time; and the child living with him must have been a grandson.

R. Virden, 20-30 years of age; 1 female, 15-20 years; 3 males, under
    5 years; 2 males, 5-10 years.

    Note: This is probably Radford Virden, although the
    ages given for him and his wife are incorrect.
    But the ages for the children are correct. He
    was a son of James and Sarah Virden.

Elizabeth Ishmael, 40-50 years of age; 11 members in household.
    1 male, 10-15 years; 3 males, 15-20 years; 2 males,
    20-30 years; 1 female, under 5 years; 2 females, 10-15
    years; 1 female, 20-30 years.

    Note: This is probably the mother of the Ishmael
    family who married with the Virden family.

Levi Virden; 10 members in household, including 8 children; 1 male under
    5 years; 1 male, 5-10 years; 2 males, 15-20 years;
    Levi Virden, 40-50 years; 1 female under 5 years; 1
    female, 10-15 years; 1 female, 15-20 years; 1 female,
    20-30 years; 1 female, 30-40 years.

    Note: This is probably the son of James and Sarah Virden.

George Davis, age 60-70 years; wife, 50-60 years; 1 son, 15-20 years;
    1 daughter, 10-15 years.

    Note: This George Davis lived next to Levi Virden,
    above, and is the husband of Elizabeth (Virden)
    Davis, who was the daughter of James and Sarah
    Virden.

* * *

1850 Census of Christian County, Illinois, shows

James Card - age 26, born in Illinois. Laborer.
Minerva Card - age 24, born in Illinois.[1]
Sarah Card - age 3, born in Illinois.
America Card - age 1, born in Illinois.

[1] Minerva (Virden) Card, the daughter of William and Nancy Virden.

* * *

John Ishmael - age 30, born in Kentucky. Farmer.
Suka (Susan) Ishmael - age 30, born in Illinois.[1]
Nancy S.A. Ishmael - age 8, born in Illinois.

[1] Daughter of William and Nancy Virden.

Julia A. Ishmael - age 6, born in Illinois.
Polly A. Ishmael - age 4, born in Illinois.
Amanda J. Ishmael - age 2, born in Illinois.

Living in the same dwelling as property owners and farmers were these three sons of William and Nancy Virden:

James Verden - age 21, born in Illinois. 200 acres.
Samuel Verden - age 19, born in Illinois. 300 acres.
John Verden - age 13, born in Illinois. 250 acres.

* * *

William Verden - age 23, born in Illinois. Farmer.[1]
Elizabeth Verden - age 21, born in Illinois.
James S. Verden - age 1, born in Illinois.

[1] Probably son of William and Nancy Verden.

* * *

1850 Census of Sangamon County, Illinois, shows

William S. Verdin - age 39, born in Ohio. Tavernkeeper.[1]
Elizabeth Verdin - age 39, born in Ohio.
Amelia Verdin - age 13, born in Illinois.
Nelson Verdin - age 12, born in Illinois.
Francis Verdin (son) - age 9, born in Illinois.
William A. Verdin - age 6 months, born in Illinois.

[1] Probably son of Isaac Verdin.

* * *

Isaac Verden - age 26, born in Ohio. Farmer; property value, $900.00[1]
Rachel (Nester) Verden - age 26, born in Kentucky.
Anne Verden - age 2, born in Illinois.

[1] Probably the son of Isaac Verden.

* * *

1850 Census of Fayette County, Illinois, shows

James M. Ishmael - age 26, born in Illinois.
Margaret (Verden) Ishmael - age 20, born in Illinois.[1]
Catherine Ishmael - age 1, born in Illinois.
Elizabeth Ishmael - age 6 months, born in Illinois.

[1] Probably daughter of Levi Verden, who was son of James Verden.

Elizabeth Ishmael - age 60, born in Pennsylvania.
William Ishmael - age 34, born in Kentucky.
Nancy A. Ishmael - age 14, born in Illinois.
Lucy A.J. Ishmael - age 11, born in Illinois.
James G. Ishmael - age 8, born in Illinois.
Margaret Ishmael - age 3, born in Illinois.

* * *

Levi Verden - age 54, born in South Carolina.[1]
Catherine (Reese) Verden - age 38, born in South Carolina.
Mahala Verden - age 14, born in Illinois.
Levi Verden - age 11, born in Illinois.
Eli Verden - age 9, born in Illinois.

[1] Son of James and Sarah Verden.

* * *

1850 Census of Shelby County, Illinois, shows

James Verden - age 63, born in South Carolina. 720 acres.[1]
Elizabeth, "Nancy" Verden - age 60, born in South Carolina.
Ann Verden - age 35, born in Kentucky. 120 acres.
Norman Verden - age 30, born in Kentucky.
Luiza Verden - age 10, born in Illinois.
Elisha Verden (male) - age 8, born in Illinois.
James Verden - age 6, born in Illinois.
Jane Verden - age 2, born in Illinois.
Narcissa Verden - age 13, born in Illinois.
Jane Verden - age 15, born in Illinois.[2]

[1] Son of James and Sarah Verden.
[2] Daughter of William and Nancy Verden.

* * *

Levy Casey, Jr. - age 33, born in Illinois. 5,580 acres.
Sarah (Verden) Casey - age 29, born in Kentucky.[1]
Elizabeth Casey - age 8, born in Illinois.
Samuel Casey - age 6, born in Illinois.
Ann Casey - age 3, born in Illinois.
James Virden Casey - age 10 months, born in Illinois.

[1] Daughter of James and Nancy Verden.

* * *

William Virden - age 23, born in Illinois. 1,600 acres[1]
Sarah (Jacobs) Virden - age 26, born in Kentucky.
Lavina Virden - age 4, born in Illinois.
Margaret Virden - age 1, born in Illinois.

[1] Son of James and Nancy Virden.

* * *

Benjamin Gordon - age 30, born in Kentucky. 7,000 acres.
Elizabeth (Virden) Gordon - age 21, born in Illinois.[1]
Jacob Virden - age 25, born in Illinois.[2]

[1] Daughter of James and Nancy Virden.
[2] Son of James and Nancy Virden.

* * *

John McKinzie - age 50, born in Maryland.
Charity (Virden) McKinzie - age 27, born in Illinois.[1]
Matilda McKinzie - age 15, born in Illinois.
Aaron McKinzie - age 12, born in Missouri.
Samuel McKinzie - age 9, born in Illinois.
Lafiett McKinzie - age 5, born in Illinois.
Calhoun McKinzie - age 4, born in Illinois.
Lushid McKinzie (female) - age 1, born in Illinois.

[1] Daughter of William and Nancy Virden.

* * *

Isaac Verden - age 26, born in Illinois.[1]
Jane "Surelda" (Ishmael) Verden - age 24, probably born in Kentucky.
Samuel Verden - age 6, born in Illinois.
James Verden - age 4, born in Illinois.
Levy Verden - age 2, born in Illinois.
Martha Verden - age 1 month, born in Illinois.

[1] Son of Levy and Rachel Verden.

* * *

John Verden - age 28, born in Illinois.[1]
Elizabeth Verden - age 20, born in Illinois.
Melvina Verden - age 2, born in Illinois.
Levi Verden - age 6 months, born in Illinois.
Keziah - age 70, born in Indiana. (No last name; could be Elizabeth, a grandmother)

[1] Son of Levi and Rachel Verden.

* * *

Jackson Massey   -   born in Tennessee, and family.

* * *

John Massey   -   age 25, born in Illinois.
Catherine (Verden) Massey   -   age 25, born in Illinois.[1]

[1] Daughter of Levi and Rachel Verden.

* * *

Daniel Francisco   -   age 48, born in Alabama.
Charity Francisco   -   age 48, born in South Carolina.[1]
Jazah "Joseph" Francisco   -   age 21, born in Illinois.
Levi Francisco   -   age 18, born in Illinois.
Howard Francisco   -   age 15, born in Illinois.
John Francisco   -   age 12, born in Illinois.
James Francisco   -   age 11, born in Illinois.
Jacob Francisco   -   age 11, born in Illinois.
Peter Francisco   -   age 8, born in Illinois.

[1] Daughter of James and Sarah Verden.

* * *

John Verdon   -   age 35, born in Ohio.
Matey Verdon   -   age 31, born in Illinois.
Ann Verdon   -   age 17, born in Illinois.
Sheriah Verdon   -   age 7, born in Illinois.
Benjamin G. Verdon   -   age 6, born in Illinois.
Elela Verdon   -   age 2, born in Illinois.
William Verdon   -   age 2, born in Illinois.
Sarrah Gesphs   -   age 60, born in Kentucky.

* * *

1850 Census of Montgomery County, Illinois, shows

James Card   -   age 60, born in North Carolina.
Sarah Card   -   age 37, born in Kentucky.[1]
George Card   -   age 19, born in Illinois.
Joseph Card   -   age 17, born in Illinois.
John Card   -   age 13, born in Illinois.
Mary Card   -   age 12, born in Illinois.
Thomas Card   -   age 11, born in Illinois.
Ewing Card   -   age 9, born in Illinois.
Micajah Card   -   age 8, born in Illinois.
Margaret Card   -   age 5, born in Illinois.

[1] Daughter of Elizabeth Davis, granddaughter of James and Sarah Verden.

Henry Card   - age 3, born in Illinois.
Louisa Card   - age 1, born in Illinois.
Elizabeth Davis - age 16, born in Kentucky.

* * *

Benson Card   - age 37, born in Kentucky.
Nancy Card   - age 23, born in Kentucky.
Calvin Card   - age 9, born in Illinois.
Daniel Card   - age 7, born in Illinois.
James Card   - age 5, born in Illinois.
Synthia Card   - age 2, born in Illinois.
Levi Card   - age 1, born in Illinois.
William Card   - age 6 months, born in Illinois.

* * *

William Verden   - age 22, born in Illinois.[1]
Elizabeth Verden - age 21, born in Illinois.
Samuel Verden   - age 1, born in Illinois.

[1] Probably the son of William and Nancy Verden.

* * *

Benjamin Ishmael - age 23, born in Kentucky.
Sarah Ishmael   - age 21, born in Illinois.
James Ishmael   - age 2, born in Illinois.
Thomas Ishmael   - age 8 months, born in Illinois.
George Card   - age 18, born in Illinois.

* * *

Joseph Davis   - age 40, born in South Carolina.[1]
Mary Davis   - age 34, born in Kentucky.
George Davis   - age 10, born in Illinois.
Israel Davis   - age 8, born in Illinois.
Margaret Davis - age 8, born in Illinois.
Elizabeth Davis - age 67, born in South Carolina.[2]

[1] Son of George and Elizabeth Davis.
[2] Daughter of James and Sarah Verden.

* * *

Calvin Card   - age 39, born in Kentucky.
Nancy Card   - age 39, born in Kentucky.[1]
John Card   - age 17, born in Illinois.
Amaziah Card - age 13, born in Illinois.

[1] Daughter of Elizabeth Davis.

Henry Card - age 9, born in Illinois.
Silvester Card - age 7, born in Illinois.
Hamilton Card - age 5, born in Illinois.
Levi Card - age 3, born in Illinois.
Elizabeth Card - age 6 months, born in Illinois.
Jane Davis - age 14, born in Illinois.

* * *

Hugh Radford Verden - age 43, born in South Carolina.[1]
Margarett Verden - age 43, born in South Carolina.
James Verden - age 20, born in Illinois.
John Verden - age 17, born in Illinois.
Hiram Verden - age 14, born in Illinois.
Elisha Verden - age 13, born in Illinois.
Joseph Verden - age 11, born in Illinois.
Ruth Verden - age 9, born in Illinois.
Martha Verden - age 7, born in Illinois.
Bub Verden - age 9 months, born in Illinois.

[1] Son of James and Sarah Verden.

* * *

Wooten Harris - age 34, born in Tennessee.[1]
Anna Harris - age 27, born in Kentucky.
Elizabeth Harris - age 16.
William Harris - age 14.
Lucinda Harris - age 12.
Barsheba Harris - age 7.
Thomas Harris - age 5.
Sally Harris - age 3.
Isaac Harris - age 1.

* * *

William Ballard - age 52, born in Virginia.
Catherine Ballard - age 38, born in Kentucky.

Living with the Ballard family were:

Daniel Davis - age 28.
Benton Beck - age 30.
William Verden - age 19, born in Kentucky.
Marion Davis - age 22, born in Illinois.

* * *

1850 Census of Macoupin County, Illinois, shows

John W. Virden - age 38, born in Ohio. Farmer.[1]
Emily Virden - age 37, born in Ohio.
Eleanor Virden - age 12, born in Illinois.
Cornelia Virden - age 6, born in Illinois.
Harriet Virden - age 8, born in Illinois.
Emeline Virden - age 4, born in Illinois.

[1] Probably the son of Isaac Virden.

* * *

1850 Census of Wayne County, Illinois, shows

William Verden - age 65, born in Delaware.
Martha Verden - age 57, born in New Jersey.
Thomas Verden - age 19, born in Illinois.
Francis Marion Verden - age 14, born in Illinois.
Mary Verden - age 12, born in Illinois.

* * *

Osker Verden - age 30, born in Kentucky.[1]
Love Charity Verden - age 27, born in Massachusetts.
George Verden - age 4, born in Illinois.
Charles Verden - age 2, born in Illinois.

[1] Probably the son of William and Martha Verden.

* * *

1860 Census of Montgomery County, Illinois, shows

James Virden - age 30, born in Illinois. Farmer.[1]
Edy "Edith" Virden - age 22, born in Kentucky.
Hiram Virden - age 1, born in Illinois.

[1] Probably the son of Hugh Radford Virden.

* * *

Isaac Virden - age 38, born in Illinois. Farmer.[1]
Jane Virden - age 34, born in Kentucky.

[1] Probably son of Levi Virden.

Samuel Virden   - age 16, born in Illinois.
James Virden   - age 13, born in Illinois.
Levi Virden   - age 12, born in Illinois.
Martha Virden   - age 10, born in Illinois.
John Virden   - age 6, born in Illinois.
Bradford Virden - age 4, born in Illinois. (Could be "Radford")

* * *

1865 Census of Fayette County, Illinois, shows

Levi Verdin: 2 males, between 20-30; 1 male, between 60-70; 1 female, between 50-60.

   Note: Levi Verdin is probably the son of James and Sarah Verdin.

* * *

1850 Census of Shelby County, Illinois, shows

Levi Gordon   - age 31, born in Kentucky. (Son of Jane Gordon)
Mary Gordon   - age 30, born in Kentucky.
Nathaniel Gordon - age 5, born in Illinois.
Sariah Gordon   - age 3, born in Illinois.
Jane Gordon   - age 1, born in Illinois.
Jane Sern   - age 55, born in North Carolina.

* * *

Mary Gordon   - age 23, born in Illinois.[1]
Pheby Gordon   - age 22, born in Illinois.[1]
William Gordon - age 25, born in Illinois.[1]
Mary Gordon   - age 21, born in Illinois.
Melvina Gordon - age 2, born in Illinois.
Matilda Gordon - age 1, born in Illinois.

[1] Mary Gordon, Pheby Gordon, and William Gordon are children of Jane Gorden, a daughter of James and Sarah Verden.

* * *

William Smith   - age 30, born in Kentucky.
Lucinda (Virden) Smith - age 27, born in Illinois.[1]
Josephson Smith   - age 1, born in Illinois.

[1] Daughter of James and Nancy Virden.

1860 Census of Macoupin County, Illinois, shows

J.W. Virden   - age 32, born in Ohio. Plasterer. (Son of Isaac Virden)
Margarett Virden - age 31, born in Ohio.
Henery Virden   - age 11, born in Illinois.
Isaac Virden   - age 9, born in Illinois.
Fannie Virden   - age 4, born in Illinois.
Charles Virden   - age 1, born in Illinois.
Rebecca Cox   - age 25, born in Ohio.

* * *

1870 Census of Virden, Illinois, shows

Archibald Virden   - age 46, born in Ohio. Druggist.
Henrietta (Dyson) Virden - age 42, born in Maryland
Ann Virden   - age 21, born in Illinois.
William Virden   - age 18, born in Illinois.
Edgar Virden   - age 16, born in Illinois.

* * *

1880 Census of Virden, Illinois, shows

Henrietta Virden - age 52, born in Maryland
Ann M. Williams   - age 30. Boarder. Daughter.

* * *

Edward Virden - age 21, born in Illinois. (Son of Archibald Virden)
Jennie Piper - age 20, born in Illinois.

* * *

William Virden   - age 27, born in Illinois. (Son of Archibald Virden)
Sarah Virden   - age 26, born in Illinois.
Homer Virden   - age 4, born in Illinois.
Henrietta Virden - age 3, born in Illinois.

* * *

1880 Census of Audubon Township, Montgomery County, Illinois shows

John Virden — age 45, born in Illinois.
Ester Virden — age 35, born in Indiana.
M. Addie Virden — age 8, born in Indiana.
Mary Jane Virden — age 7, born in Indiana.
John R. Virden — age 4, born in Indiana.
Jacob C. Virden — age 56, born in Illinois.

* * *

1880 Census of Green County, Illinois, shows

Charles Virden — age 63, born in New York.
Freecy Virden — age 34, born in Illinois.
Charles Virden — age 11, born in Illinois.
Elisah Virden — age 9, born in Illinois.
Martha Virden — age 5, born in Illinois.

* * *

1880 Census of Hurricane Township, Fayette County, Illinois, shows

Levi Virden — age 38, born in Illinois.
Martha Virden — age 31, born in Illinois.
Emma Virden — age 5, born in Illinois.
William Edward Virden — age 3, born in Illinois.
Mary Virden — age 1, born in Illinois.
Catherine Virden — age 68, born in South Carolina. (Probably the wife of Lewis Virden)

* * *

Eli Virden — age 38, born in Illinois.
Susan Virden — age 40, born in Illinois.
William H. Virden — age 12, born in Illinois.
Joseph P. Virden — age 10, born in Illinois.
Mandy G. Virden — age 5, born in Illinois.
Melvina Virden — age 6 months, born in Illinois.
Celia Price — age 80, born in Illinois. (Probably mother-in-law)
Nancy Jane — age 19, born in Illinois. (Age may be wrong; may be a Price or a Virden)

* * *

1880 Census of Buckhart Township, Christian County, Illinois

Levi Virden - age 29, born in Illinois.
Francis N. Virden - age 28, born in Illinois.
William E. Virden - age 5, born in Illinois.
Amelda Virden - age 7, born in Illinois.
Fonarie B. Virden - age 3, born in Illinois.
Frederick H. Virden - age 1, born in Illinois.

    Note: This probably is Levi Virden, son of John Virden, grandson of James Virden, according to probate records.

* * *

1880 Census of Big Springs Township, Shelby County, Illinois

James Virden - age 30, born in Illinois.
Louisa Virden - age 25, born in Illinois.
William H. Virden - age 1, born in Illinois.

* * *

James F. Virden - age 34, born in Illinois.
Nancy P. Virden - age 25, born in Illinois.
Katie Virden - age 6, born in Illinois.
Orvie Virden - age 1, born in Illinois.

    Note: This James F. Virden is probably son of Isaac, grandson of Levi.

* * *

1880 Census of Oconee Township, Shelby County, Illinois

Samuel Virden - age 35, born in Illinois. (Son of Isaac Virden)
Sarah Virden - age 36, born in Illinois.
M.E. Virden (female) - age 5, born in Illinois.
William Virden - age 3, born in Illinois.
Surrelda Jane (Ishmael) Virden - age 54, born in Kentucky. (Isaac's wife)

* * *

1880 Census of Flat Branch Township, Shelby County, Illinois

George Virden - age 20, born in Illinois.
Mary J. Virden - age 19, born in Illinois.

Georgia Virden - age 4, born in Illinois.

> Note: "George Virden was enumerated with Hillary W. Snellgrove. According to Bible records this George Virden was the adopted son of Willis Virden, son of James Virden. The Virden descendants that gave me the Bible records could not make out all of the writing. But the Bible showed George A.D. Virden, born in 1867. He could have had two middle initials, A.D. Lucy Virden, age 4, was living with her grandmother, Elizabeth Housh, in Flat Branch Township, in 1880. Either many of the Virdens died off, or they moved further West. I didn't pick up the Virden spelling, but I did notice that there were some Virdenburg's listed."
>
> (From letter dated February 18, 1977, from James R. Virden, of Russia, Ohio.)

* * *

1880 Census of Shelby County, Illinois

John Virdon   - age 35, born in Connecticut. Collector
Mary Virdon   - age 31, born in Missouri.
Ann Virdon   - age 17, born in Illinois.
Sarah Virdon   - age 7, born in Illinois.
George Virdon - age 6, born in Illinois.
Eliza Virdon   - age 4, born in Illinois.
William Virdon - age 2, born in Illinois.
Sarah Gehspe   - age 60, born in Kentucky.

> Note: Sarah Gehspe is probably a mother-in-law.

* * *

1880 Census of Missouri shows

John Virden   - age 61, born in Kentucky.
Lizzie Virden - age 24, born in Kentucky.
Maggie Virden - age 19, born in Kentucky.
George Virden - age 14, born in Kentucky.
Mamia Virden   - age 12, born in Kentucky.
Mannie Virden - age 10, born in Kentucky.

* * *

Jacob Virden   - age 35, born in Illinois.
Alice Virden   - age 44, born in Missouri.
Anna L. Virden - age 4, born in Missouri.
Charlie Virden - age 2, born in Missouri.
Myrtle Virden   - age 2, born in Missouri.
Iva Virden   - age 2 months, born in Missouri.

> Note: Jacob Virden could be a son of John Virden, but John Virden would have to have gone to Illinois and then returned to Kentucky. John Virden is not found in the census records of Iowa with the other Virdens.

* * *

1850 Census of Wayne County, Illinois, shows

William Verden   - age 65, born in Delaware.
Martha Verden   - age 57, born in New Jersey.
Thomas Verden   - age 19, born in Illinois.
Francis M. Verden - age 14, born in Illinois.
Mary Verden   - age 12, born in Illinois.

> Note: There is a Benjamin Verden, age 24, born in 1826 in Illinois, listed on the 1850 Census of Illinois, who may also be a son. He is listed, also, on the 1880 Census of Iowa, together with Frank Verden.

* * *

Osker Verden   - age 30, born in Kentucky.
Love Charity Verden - age 37, born in Massachusetts. (Age should be 27)
George Verden   - age 4, born in Illinois.
Charles Verden   - age 2, born in Illinois.

* * *

1850 Census of Black Hawk County, Iowa, shows

Charles Mullin   - age 35, born in Pennsylvania.
America Mullin   - age 28, born in Kentucky.[1]
James Virden   - age 26, born in Kentucky.[1]
Daniel Virden   - age 25, born in Kentucky.[1]
Isaac Virden   - age 22, born in Illinois.[1]
Elizabeth Mullin - age 6, born in Illinois.
Charles Mullin   - age 4, born in Illinois.
William H. Mullin - age 2, born in Illinois.

Living in a separate dwelling from the above were:

William Virden - age 29, born in Kentucky.[1]
Rebecca Virden - age 26, born in Illinois.
Martha Virden - age 7, born in Illinois.
Louisa Virden - age 5, born in Iowa.

[1] The individuals thus marked were probably children of William Virden, born in Delaware.

* * *

1860 Census of Black Hawk County, Iowa, shows

James Virden - age 37, born in Kentucky.
Harriet (Rathbone?) Virden - age 27, born in New York
    (Probably his second wife)
George Virden - age 8, born in Iowa.
Willard Virden - age 6, born in Iowa.
Charlotte Rathbone - age 14, born in Indiana.

* * *

George Virden - age 10, born in Iowa. (He was living with another family than those listed in Black Hawk County.)

* * *

Oscar Virden - age 40, born in Kentucky.
Love Virden - age 27, born in Massachusetts. (Age should be 37)
George Virden - age 13, born in Illinois.
Charles Virden - age 11, born in Illinois.
Norman Virden - age 8, born in Iowa.
Elizabeth Virden - age 5, born in Iowa.
Emma Virden - age 3, born in Iowa.
William Virden - age 8 months, born in Iowa.

* * *

Eliza Virden - age 27, born in Indiana.
Estella Virden - age 2, born in Iowa.

    Note: Eliza Virden could be a widow of one of the Virden brothers.

* * *

Living with Charles and America Mullin in the 1860 Census was Martha Virden, age 68, born in New Jersey.

* * *

1880 Census of Iowa, Lucas County, White Breast Township, shows

Berryman Virden, born in Illinois.
Susan Virden   - age 48, born in Illinois. (Susan McKinney)
Lewis Virden   - age 20, born in Illinois.
Charles W. Virden - age 18, born in Illinois.
Ellen Phillips - age 31, born in Illinois. (Probably a niece)
George Virden   - age 2, born in Missouri.

        Note: Berryman Virden is shown as Benjamin Virden in the 1850 Census.

* * *

1880 Census of Iowa, Calhoun County, Butler Township, shows

Frank Virden   - age 44, born in Illinois.
Hattie Virden - age 24, born in Iowa.
Howard Virden - age 3, born in Iowa.
Martha Virden - age 87, born in New Jersey.

* * *

1880 Census of Iowa, Black Hawk County, Waterloo Township, shows

Charles Virden - age 31, born in Illinois.
Nelita Virden   - age 30, born in Illinois.
Bertrand Virden - age 3, born in Iowa.
Maud Virden   - age 10 months, born in Iowa.

* * *

1880 Census of Iowa, Henry County, Jackson Township, shows

Levi Virden   - age 41, born in Ohio.
Virginia Virden - age 30, born in Illinois. (Virginia Rowe)
Lewis Rowe Virden - age 8, born in Iowa.
Franklin Jerome Virden - age 5, born in Iowa.
William Elmer Virden - age 1, born in Iowa.

        Note: Levi Virden is the son of Jerome and Sarah (Flemming) Virden, a son of Lewis Virden of Delaware.

* * *

Records of Tolly Cemetery, Shelby County, Illinois

James F. Virden, son of _____ and M.J. Virden, died February 28, 1887, age 6 days.

J.T. Virden, died March 5, 1881, age 20 years, 3 days.

Elizabeth Virden, died October 2, 1881, age 63 years, 22 days.

Mary E. Virden, wife of Arne Virden, died January 6, 187_, age 19 years, 2 days.

Wilie Virden, son of A. and M.E. Virden, died October 6, 1878.

James Virden, died January 10, 1859, age 71 years, 6 months, 2 days.

Nancy Virden, wife of James Virden, died August 13, 1860, age 70 years.

Records of Linwood Cemetery, Christian County, Illinois (No Dates)

Elizabeth Virden
William J. Virden
Bertha Mae Verden
Catherine Virden
Mary Helen Virden
Lilly Ried Virden
Ivy Budds Virden

Records of Jacobs Cemetery, Christian County, Illinois

Nancy J. Virden, daughter of W. and S. Virden, died September 19, 1858.

Lovina Virden, daughter of W. and S. Virden, died September 6, 1867, age 18 years.

Willie Virden, born April 17, 1825, died September 18, 1901.

Tolly Cemetery, Flat Branch Township, Illinois, records

Levi Casey, born July 23, 1817, died March 6, 1893. Private in Illinois Mounted Militia, Military Volunteers, Black Hawk War.

Sarah (Virden) Casey, wife of Levi Casey, born January 13, 1831, died November 12, 1897.

Cynthia (Virden) South, wife of Andrew South, died April 9, 1855, age 45 years, 7 months, 18 days. (Note: Marriage index shows that she married Andrew Smith, so it is probably in error.)

James F. Virden, son of ___ and M.J. Virden, died March 6, 1881, age 16 days.

J.T. Virden, died March 5, 1881, age 20 years, 3 days.

Elizabeth Virden, died October 2, 1881, age 63 years, 22 days.

Mary E. Virden, wife of Arne Virden, died January 6, 187_, age 19 years, 2 days.

William Virden, son of A. and M.E. Virden, died October 6, 1878.

James Virden, died January 10, 1859, age 71 years, 6 months, 2 days.

Nancy Virden, wife of James Virden, died August 13, 1860, age 70 years.

Wright Cemetery, Moultrie County, Illinois, records

Daniel Francisco, died November 18, 1859, age 56 years, 6 months, 13 days.

Charity V. Francisco, wife of Daniel Francisco, died November 30, 1853, age 50 years, 6 months, 25 days.

Peter Francisco, died February 18, 1917, age 75 years, 6 months, 23 days.

Nancy E. Francisco, wife of Peter Francisco, died November 9, 1897, age 54 years, 7 months, 28 days.

C.A. Francisco, wife of P. Francisco, died October 23, 1865, age 22 years, 9 months, 4 days.

Elizabeth Francisco, daughter of P. and C.A. Francisco, died July 10, 1868, age 1 day.

Dennis Francisco, son of P. and C.A. Francisco, died August 6, 1861, age 7 days.

Mary A. Francisco, wife of A. Francisco, died August 1, 1851, age 29 years, 3 months, 20 days.

Lela M. Francisco, daughter of A. and D. Francisco, born October 16, 1893, died February 18, 1897.

Alfred Francisco, died May 12, 1864.

Susan J. Francisco, wife of Joseph Francisco, died October 11, 1886, age 54 years, 8 months, 26 days.

Jacob Francisco, Company K, 126th Illinois Infantry.

Jacob Francisco, son of J. and ___ Francisco, died June 13, 1864, age 2 years, 5 months.

Daniel Francisco, died August 22, 1879, age 24 years, 8 months, 4 days.

Mary Francisco, wife of Allen Francisco, died July 6, 1861, age 25 years, 8 months.

Charley Francisco, son of L. and M.J. Francisco, died April 16, 1864, age 2 years, 4 months, 28 days.

Martha A. Francisco, February 22, 1845 - October 8, 1927.

John Francisco, 1837 - 1916.

Mary J. Francisco, daughter of J. and M.A. Francisco, died January 7, 1897, age 3 years, 7 months, 22 days.

Mabel F. Francisco, 1894 - 1959.

Margaret I. Francisco, Mother, 1867 - 1948.

Peter L. Francisco, Father, 1862 - 1935.

Flossie Francisco, Daughter, 1904 - 1918.

Ramsey Cemetery, Fayette County, Illinois, Records

Bertha Virden, February 1, 1885 - October 26, 1916.

Freda Farber Virden, 1893 - 1953.

William Edward Virden, 1877 - 1964.

Eli M. Virden, July 19, 1900 - December 23, 1955.

Julia Elizabeth Virden, 1876 - 1958.

Marian A. Virden, 1919 - 1956.

Homer L. Virden, 1883 - 1947.

Martha Virden, his wife, 1888 - 1926.

Levi David Virden. His death certificate shows that he was born April 7, 1839, the son of Levi Virden who was born in Kentucky, and Catherine (Reese) Virden, who was born in North Carolina. He died February 5, 1917, age 77 years, 9 months.

William Edward Virden. His death certificate shows that he was born January 24, 1877, in Ramsey, Fayette County, Illinois, the son of Levi David Virden and Rachel (Thorpe) Virden. He died May 19, 1964. His wife was Hazel Virden.

Catherine Virden. She was born in 1830, and died September 22, 1855, in Fayette County, Illinois. She was the daughter of Levi D. Virden (who was born in 1796 in Kentucky) and Catherine (Reese) Virden, who was born in 1812 in North Carolina. Catherine Virden married John William Massey (born 1830, died September 22, 1855, in Fayette County, Illinois). John William and Catherine (Virden) Massey both died of cholera and are buried in a common grave. They left only one son, William Radford Massey.

Records of Bethel Baptist Cemetery, Buckhart Township, Sharpsburgh, Illinois

Alemeda Virden, 1873 - 1894.
Eugene Virden, 1875 - 1954.
Frances Sears Virden, 1852 - 1920.
Levi Virden, 1849 - 1941.
Melvina Virden Cearlock, wife of J.R. Cearlock, 1852 - 1888.

Greenwood Cemetery, Decatur, Macon County, Illinois, Records

Hiram P. Virden, 1859 - 1930
Emma J. Virden, his wife, 1863 - 1915.
Jesse P. Virden, 1888 - 1900.

Old Shedd Cemetery, Ramsey, Fayette County, Illinois, Records

Susan T. Virden, wife of E.T. Virden, April 20, 1839 - November 23, 1888.

Infant son of L.D. and M.A. Virden, died February 18, 1873, 1 month, 2 days.

Catherine Virden, daughter of J. and S.J. Virden, died September 30, 1854, 2 years.

Levi Virden, April 7, 1840 - February 5, 1917.

Martha Virden, his wife, May 13, 1844 - March 20, 1884.

A VIRDIN MARRIAGE CHRONOLOGY (DELAWARE)

These marriage records digested from the public files in the Hall of Records, Delaware Archives, Dover, Delaware, may be of assistance in tracing a particular line of ancestry.

1752 — John Virdin, Jr., married Sarah Barry. (Kent County, A-4, page 14)

1776 - 1781 — Elizabeth Virden, widow of Daniel Virdin, married Joseph Jackson. (Kent County, Chancery Case P-5)

June 1777 — Naomi Virdin, daughter of Daniel Virdin, married Enoch Jenkins. (Kent County, Chancery Case P-5)

1780 — Sarah Virden married William Gaskin. (Kent County, A-52, page 78)

Jan 25, 1781 — Levi Verdin married Shada Hall, daughter of Moses Hall. (Sussex County, Chancery Case W-40)

March 1781 — Sarah Virdin, daughter of Daniel Virdin, married John Jackson, son of Joseph Jackson. (Kent County, Chancery Case P-5)

1786 — Alice Virden married John Kilpatrick. (Kent County, A-52, page 88)

Jan 3, 1790 — Jemina Virden married Frederick Pratt. (Kent County, A-52, page 106)

Feb 8, 1790 — John Virden married Catherine Wright. (Kent County, Volume 2, page 7)

1790 — William Verden married Prudence Purdin. (Kent County, A-41, page 205)

1793 — Elizabeth Virden married Joseph Purdin. (Kent County, A-52, page 106)

1793 — Unity Virden married Thomas Lockwood. (Kent County, A-52, page 106)

1796 — Mary Virden married James Martin. (Sussex County, A-103, page 180)

Sept 25, 1797 — Polly Virden married Thomas Morris. (Sussex County, Vol. 87, page 237.7)

Oct 1, 1797 — Marnix Virden married Mary Fisher, widow of John Fisher. (Sussex County, Chancery Case F-4)

1798	- Elizabeth Virden married Samuel Coombe. (Kent County, A-2, page 108)
1800	- Sarah Virden married Thomas Green. (Kent County, A-52, page 94)
Jan 28, 1801	- Marrinix Virden married Frany Bostick. (Sussex County, Volume 87, page 237.18)
Nov 8, 1803	- Matthew L. Virden married Elizabeth Berry. (Kent County, Vol. 16, page 203)
1804	- Elizabeth Virden married Robert Young. (Kent County, Vol. A-52, page 101)
Jan 24, 1805	- Alice Virden married Josiah Martin. (Sussex County, Vol. 87, page 157)
1805	- Mitchell Virden married Neomi Bruice. (Sussex County, A-60, page 235)
Jan 5, 1806	- Mary Virden, widow of Marnix Virden, married Dennis Morris. (Sussex County, Chancery Case F-4)
1806	- Sophia Virden married Joseph Coulter. (Sussex County, A-103, page 173)
1807	- Daniel Virdin married Elizabeth Matthews. (Kent County, A-34, page 67)
Nov 23, 1815	- Elizabeth Virden married William Harrington. (Kent County, Vol. 20, page 259)
Dec 12, 1815	- Stratten Virden married Abigail Marec. (New Castle County Wills, Vol. 6, page 31)
Feb 12, 1818	- Samuel Virden married Anna McKimmey Smock. (Kent County, Vol. 87-A, page 203.10)
Jan 6, 1820	- Amoret Virden married Isaac Laws. (Sussex County, Vol. 41, page 199)
Sept 29, 1821	- Mary Virden married Phillip Barratt. (Kent County, Vol. 6, page 197)
Oct 21, 1821	- Thomas Virden married Ann Jane Robinett. (New Castle County, Vol. 36, page 59)
July 9, 1822	- Catharine Virden married Clement Morris. (Kent County, Vol. 21, page 66)
1826	- Allison Virden married Elizabeth Wilson, daughter of Piercy (Stockley) (Sussex County Chancery Case P-35)

1823 — Moses Virden married Matilda Prettyman. (Sussex County, Vol. A-94, page 75)

Mar 31, 1823 — Elizabeth Virden married Hugh Wilson. (Kent County, Vol. A-52, page 81)

Oct 8, 1829 — Eliza Virden married James F. Martin. (Sussex County, Vol. 56, page 41)

Feb 2, 1831 — Elizabeth Virden married William Baggo. (Kent County, Vol. 28, page 192)

Mar 1, 1834 — Susan Virden married William Skilenger. (Sussex County, Vol. 56, page 224)

Jan 18, 1835 — Susan Virden married Charles Holden. (Kent County, Vol. 14, page 246)

June 6, 1837 — William Virden married Mary Hargadine. (Kent County, Vol. 6, page 311)

1838 — Ann Virden, daughter of Mitchell M. Virden, married Ward S. Vandergrift. (Sussex County, Orphan's Court F-V-15)

1838 — Eliza Virden, daughter of Mitchell M. Virden, married James F. Martin. (Sussex County, Orphan's Court F-V-15)

1839 — Ann Virden married Ward Wainright. (Sussex County, A-103, page 183)

1841 — Nancy Virden married Peter Callaway. (Kent County, A-52, page 96)

Oct 11, 1842 — Samuel Virden married Eliza Ann Warren. (Kent County, Vol. A-53, page 148)

Jan 28, 1846 — Mary Jane Virden married William S. Wolfe. (Sussex County, Vol. 45, page 68)

Dec 27, 1848 — Lydia A. Virden married John Fisher. (Sussex County, Vol. 45, page 265)

Aug 28, 1849 — Alexander Virden married Ruthanna Virden. (Kent County, Vol. 90, page 8)

Mar 14, 1850 — Benjamin F. Virden married Sarah A. Marsh. (Sussex County, Vol. 74, page 54)

Dec 20, 1852 — Joseph B. Virden married Elizabeth F. Rust. (Sussex County, Vol. 89, page 31)

May 8, 1855 — Mary E. Virden married Beniah W. Truitt. (Sussex County, Vol. 36, page 59)

Jan 6, 1858 — Ellen Virden, daughter of Mitchell M. Virden, married Charles A. Rust. (Sussex County, Orphan's Court F-V-15)

Jan 5, 1858 — Ellen M. Virden married Charles H. Rust. (Sussex County, Vol. 47, page 267)

May 15, 1860 — William Virden married Caroline Polk. (Kent County, Vol. 90, page 45)

Jan 30, 1863 — Maggie C. Virden married Joseph B. Lyons. (Sussex County, Vol. 48, page 78)

1865 — Henry Virden married Lydia Hester Simpler, daughter of David Simpler. (Sussex County, Orphan's Court F-S-21)

Nov 8, 1865 — James Virdin married Mary Wallace. (Kent County, Vol. 31, page 261)

May 7, 1869 — Annie Virden married Benjamin F. Macintire. (Sussex County, Vol. 48, page 273)

Feb 21, 1871 — Harriet E. Virden married Nathaniel T. Veasey. (Sussex County, Vol. 49, page 76)

Sept 25, 1871 — Annie S. Virden married Horace E. Ashmead, Jr. (New Castle County, Vol. 82, page 269)

Dec 28, 1872 — James W. Virden married Sallie E. Lynch. (Kent County, Vol. 32, page 269)

1873 — Mary J. Virden, daughter of Mitchell M. Virden, married William S. Wolfe. (Sussex County, Orphan's Court, F-V-15)

1873 — Lydia A. Virden, daughter of Mitchell Virden, married John Fisher. (Sussex County, Orphan's Court F-V-15)

Feb 6, 1873 — William Virden, Jr., married Clementine Marvel. (Kent County, Vol. 32, page 275)

Apr 27, 1874 — John P. Virden married Louisa Maull. (Sussex County, Vol. 49, page 238)

Sept 15, 1875 — Mary Blanche Virden married Thomas A. Brown. (Kent County, Vol. 33, page 99)

Aug 14, 1877 — S.E. Virden (Lizzie M.) married John W. Hall, Jr. (New Castle County, Vol. 39, page 247)

Jan 19, 1877 — John W. Virdin married Sarah Williams. (Kent County, Vol. 33, page 204)

Apr 27, 1878 — William Virdin, Jr., married Emily Craig. (Kent County, Vol. 90, page 116)

Oct 10, 1878 — Laura E. Virden married William T. Holland. (Sussex County, Vol. 50, page 210)

June 1, 1880 — Peter R. Virden married Fannie E. Willey. (Sussex County, Vol. 37, page 247)

Oct 27, 1884 — Joseph E. Virden married Ella C. Lewis. (Sussex County, Vol. 51, page 191)

Jan 28, 1885 — Lizzie B. Virden married William H. Schafer. (Kent County, Vol. 35, page 66)

Sept 15, 1885 — Annie May Virden married Robert Scott at Philadelphia, Penna. (Kent County, Vol. 82, page 224)

Dec 3, 1885 — James Virden married Orra Hawkins. (Kent County, Vol. 82, page 228)

Dec 28, 1885 — Maggie C. Virden of Angola, Del. married William J. Wescott of Lewes, Del. at Camden, New Jersey. (Kent County, Vol. 82, page 229)

May 25, 1886 — Frank H. Virden married Mollie E. Dodd. (Sussex County, Vol. 57, page 102)

Oct 21, 1887 — John W. Virden married Annie Ford. (Kent County, Vol. 35, page 190)

Nov 13, 1888 — Clara H.F. Virden married William F. Marshall. (Sussex County, Vol. 57, page 279)

Feb 22, 1893 — Emma L. Virden married Walter R. Richardson (New Castle County, Vol. 84, page 3)

Dec 28, 1895 — Clarence Virden married Effie L. Davidson. (Sussex County, Vol. 89, page 92)

Dec 24, 1896 — Frank H. Virden married Sallie A. Black. (Sussex County, Vol. 77, page 66)

Jan 6, 1898 — Minnie Virdin married George W. Cook. (Kent County, Vol. 72, page 246)

Nov 16, 1898 — Charles A. Virden married Ruth E. Sharp. (Sussex County, Vol. 77, page 186)

Dec 28, 1898 - Lizzie Virdin married Charles A. Davidson. (Sussex County, Vol. 77, page 200)

July 19, 1899 - William E. Virden married Anna H. Reed. (New Castle County, Vol. 67, page 78)

Oct 25, 1899 - Walter T. Virden married Ara B. Hurdle. (Sussex County, Vol. 77, page 246)

Nov 15, 1899 - Hannah M. Virden married Arthur W. Marshall. (Sussex County, Vol. 36, page 89)

Dec 26, 1899 - Cora T. Virden married Harry C. Joseph. (Sussex County, Vol. 77, page 262)

Dec 26, 1900 - Harry Virden married Anna Belle Thompson. (Kent County, Vol. 90, page 204)

Oct 16, 1900 - Frank Virden married Margaret May Authors. (Kent County, Vital Statistics folder No. 3)

May 8, 1901 - Howard Virden married Ada E. Johnson. (Kent County, Vital Statistics folder No. 3)

Dec 18, 1901 - George W. Virden married Annie M. Hewitt. (New Castle County, Vol. 85, page 65)

June 10, 1902 - Thomas G. Virden married Elsie M. Start. (New Castle County, Vol. 80, page 171)

Dec 24, 1902 - Emma M. Virden married Marvil C. Davidson. (Sussex County, Vol. 78, page 141)

Nov 12, 1902 - Carrie Virdin married George Craig. (Kent County, Vital Statistics folder No. 1)

Apr 10, 1907 - Olen (Olin) Virdin married Nettie Bell Artis. (Kent County, Vital Statistics folder No. 2-F)

Apr 30, 1910 - Charles B. Virden married Lena M. Sllers. (New Castle County, Vol. 36, page 273)

Nov 30, 1910 - Brice Virden married Margaret E. Hobbs. (Kent County, Vital Statistics folder No. 3-E)

June 14, 1911 - Samuel A. Virden married Lela C. Ludwig. (Kent County, Vol. 36, page 284)

Feb 22, 1912 - Sarah Virden married Alva E. Hutchins. (Kent County, Vol. 36, page 295)

Marriage Licenses, 1821 - 1874, Fayette County, Illinois.
Records do not give any dates

Sally Verdin	- married James W. Gordon.
Margaret Verdin	- married Jonathan B. Howard.
Elizabeth Verdin	- married Wooten Harris.
Martha Ann Verden	- married William Henson.
Sarah Verdin	- married Thomas M. Ishmael.
Margaret Verdin	- married James M.C. Ishmael.
Catherine Verdin	- married John Massey.
Levi D. Virden	- married Mary T. Thorp.
Eli T. Verdin	- married Susan T. Price.
Isaac Verdin	- married Serilda Jane Ishmael.

Note: From letter dated January 6, 1977, to James R. Virden, from Mrs. Bruce Lloyd.

Some Marriages in White County, Indiana

Stratton Virden married Louisa Thompson, April 2, 1846.

Some Marriages in Fayette County, Illinois

Catherine Verdin married John Massey, April 28, 1845.
Elizabeth Verdin (his second wife) married Wooten Harris, November 22, 1854.
Isaac Verdin married Serilda Jane Ishmael, February 4, 1844.
Sarah Verdin married Thomas M. Ishmael, July 24, 1845.
Eli T. Verdin married Susan T. Price, February 10, 1867.
Margaret Verdin married James M.C. Price, July 1, 1847.

REVOLUTIONARY SOLDIERS FROM NATIONAL ARCHIVES

DAVID VARDEN — private, from North Carolina.

HUGH VARDIN — private, from Delaware. He enlisted January 20, 1776, in Col. John Haslet's Regiment. He was discharged at expiration of one year. He was on the muster roll in Lewes, Delaware.

JOHN VARDIN — was in the 3rd Artillery Regiment, Continental Troops.

JOHN VERDEN — was in Captain William Perry's Independent Company from Delaware.

LEVI VIRDEN — private, from Delaware. He enlisted January 20, 1776, in Col. John Haslet's Regiment. He was discharged at expiration of one year. He was on the muster roll in Lewes, Delaware.

LEVY VORDEN — Sergeant, from Delaware. He was in Captain Perry's Company, having enlisted April 24, 1777, at Lewes, Delaware.

MARNIX (MARNIT) VIRDEN — Corporal, enlisted January 16, 1776, for one year in Col. Haslet's Regiment.

SAMUEL VARDEN — private, was in the 2nd Massachusetts Regiment.

STEPHEN VARDEN — drummer, was in Willng's Regiment, Continental Troops. He was in the 3rd and 4th Virginia Regiments. He was also listed as Stephen Vardina, Corporal.

THOMAS VARDEN (VERDIN, VERDON) — private, was in the 1st Pennsylvania Regiment.

THOMAS VARDEN (VARDIN) — private, was in Gist's Regiment, Continental Troops.

THOMAS VARDIN — private, was in the 6th Pennsylvania Regiment.

A VIRDIN WILLS AND ADMINISTRATIONS CHRONOLOGY (Kent County)

March 27, 1769 — John Virden, Sr. (A-52, 90)
May 15, 1776 — Daniel Virden (A-52, 83)
Nov. 13, 1778 — Absalom Virdin (A-52, 76)
Jan. 20, 1785 — John Virden (Liber M, folio 39)
March 2, 1786 — Eleanor Virden (A-52, 88)

Feb. 27, 1787 — Eleanor Virdin (A-52, 89)
Feb. 27, 1787 — Alexander Virdin (A-52, 79)
Nov. 30, 1791 — William Virden (A-52, 105)
Sept. 30, 1793 — Peter Virden (A-52, 101)
Jan. 5, 1796 — John Virdin (A-52, 94)

Dec. 9, 1800 — Prudence Virden (A-52, 103)
March 24, 1804 — Daniel Virdin (A-52, 87)
Feb. 12, 1820 — William Virden (A-52, 109)
May 20, 1824 — Elizabeth Virden (Register of Wills, Book Q, page 29)
Aug. 31, 1831 — Andrew Virden (A-52, 80)

Dec. 5, 1831 — Matthew L. Virden (A-52, 99)
May 23, 1845 — John Virden (A-52, 96)

A VIRDIN WILLS AND ADMINISTRATIONS CHRONOLOGY (Sussex County)

Dec. 11, 1773	-	Huegh Virden (A-103, 175)
Apr. 15, 1796	-	Marnix Virden (A-103, 180)
Nov. 8, 1796	-	Levy Virdin (A-103, 176)
May 19, 1802	-	Manlove Virden (A-103, 179)
Feb. 11, 1803	-	Marrinix Virden (A-103, 181)
May 23, 1805	-	William Virden (A-103, 184)
Nov. 12, 1808	-	Elzey Virden (A-103, 173)
July 31, 1811	-	Amy Virden (A-103, 171)
Apr. 17, 1830	-	Lydia Virden (A-103, 177)
Feb. 20, 1840	-	Mitchell Virden (A-103, 182)

Some Virdins in State of Delaware Elective Offices

JAMES VIRDEN — was a member of the House of Representatives from Kent County, 1884. He was Recorder of Deeds for Kent County from 1891 to 1896.

SAMUEL VIRDEN — was a member of the House of Representatives from Kent County, 1840.

WILLIAM VIRDEN — was a member of the House of Representatives from Kent County, 1860.

WILLIAM VIRDIN — was Prothonotary for Kent County from 1899 to 1901. (History of State of Delaware, 1908, Conrad)

Some Shelby County, Illinois, Probate Records

ESTATE OF JAMES VIRDEN, Final Settlement, May 1861. Showed the following receipts and credits, each person or persons receiving $390.12, except as noted. Allen Snyder was administrator.

Beverly and Emiline Armstrong
Burrel Roberts (for J.B. and Margaret Howards' share)
William and Lucinda Smith
Levi and Sarah Casey
Willis Virden
John Virden
Francis and Polly Armstrong

Levi Casey Guard Receipt $234.07
John South 78.02
Henry and Nancy Hill 78.02

Note: See Probate Journal C, page 164, concerning above.

ESTATE OF NANCY VIRDEN, Further Settlement, October 1862. The following payments were made by Francis Armstrong, Administrator, each person or persons named receiving $8.33.

Jonathan and Margaret Howard
Cynthia South, deceased, children
Francis and Polly Armstrong
Levi and Sarah Casey
William and Lucy Smith
Willis Virden
John Virden
Beverly and Emaline Armstrong

    Note: See Probate Journal C, page 371, concerning above.
           Nancy Virden died intestate August 13, 1860.

MINOR HEIRS OF JOHN VERDIN, Guardianship, October 1853. Isaac V. Lee was named guardian for minor children, under the age of 14 years, of John Verdin. Children named were:

Melvina P. Verdin
Levi E. Verdin
Isaac H. Verdin

    Note: See Journal 4, page 332, concerning above.

GUARDIAN OF NANCY ANGELINE VIRDEN, May 1860. John Armstrong, Jr., was named guardian for her, minor child of William Virden, deceased, about 9 years of age.

    Note: See Guardians Record A. 1857 - 1869.

The History of Shelby and Moultrie Counties, Illinois, 1881,
  Contains Some References to the Virden Family

James Virden	- he settled on Section 33 in or about 1824, on the west side of the creek, now known as "Small Place." He later moved to Flat Branch Township where he died.
Willis Virden and John Virden	- two brothers. They were among the early settlers. Willis lived in Section 15. He was born in the South part of Shelby County in 1825. His father, James Virden, was one of the first settlers in that section of the county. He was a native of Georgia who moved to Flat Branch in 1842 and lived in Section 10. He died in 1859.
Levi Virden	- a brother of James Virden, was one of the early settlers of Ridge Township. He settled there in 1826.

Lucinda Virden — married William Smith March 2, 1843. She was born in Shoal Creek, April 17, 1823, the daughter of James and Nancy Virden. Her father was born in North Carolina and her mother in Alabama. William and Lucinda (Virden) Smith had five children: (1) Sarah Smith, the oldest, died at the age of three; (2) Josephus Smith, the oldest son, was a farmer in Tower Hill Township; (3) Nancy A. Smith married R.H. Bullington and lived in Rose Township; (4) Mary Smith died in February 1867 at the age of thirteen; and (5) Elizabeth Smith.

Charity Virden — married Allen Francisco and they had fourteen children. Charity Virden was born in Virginia but was living in Illinois at the time of her marriage. She died in 1854. Her husband, Allen Francisco was born May 30, 1825, in Robinson Creek, Shelby County, Illinois.

Daniel Francisco — the father of Allen Francisco, was a native of Alabama who went to Illinois in 1813, stopping at Greenville, at the Fort. He was a boy then, his father and mother were both dead. Some trouble had developed in the family as to the division of the property, which consisted of six dollars in money and a gun. As a result of the dispute Daniel Francisco picked up the gun, shouldered it, and walked out of the home, never hearing from any of his family afterward. He left the Fort at Greenville and went to Montgomery County in 1818, settling in Robinson Creek, afterwards part of Shelby County. He later moved to Todd's Point Township where he died in 1859.

Some Maryland Records

JOHN VARDIN of Charles County

November 31, 1761	- He gave a bill of sale involving chattles to Thomas Contee.
February 1, 1783	- James Vardin and Thomas Posey posted securities on the Estate of Elizabeth Simpson, of which Charles Simpson was administrator.
February 1783	- Letters of Administration were granted to James Vardin on the Estate of Elizabeth Montgomery.
August 1783	- John Vardin was made guardian of William Montgomery, an orphan about 10 years of age; John Montgomery, about eight years of age; and Mary Montgomery, about five years of age.
November 8, 1783	- John Vardin put up a guardian bond (in December Court) for Mary Montgomery, William Montgomery and John Montgomery.
October 1789	- An order was issued to show why there had been no final accounting on the estate of Elizabeth Montgomery. The final accounting was made December 14, 1789.
December 1787	- John Vardin was one of the securities on letters of administration granted on the estate of Henry Dixon.
1778 Census	- Port Tobacco, East Hundred, March Court Record, named John Varden.

RICHARD VARDIN of Charles County

June Court, 1786	- Richard Vardin purchased from the estate of William Maddox.
June 17, 1799	- Richard Varden was a witness to a sale of land from the estate of Joseph Clements.

JAMES VIRDIN of Worcester County

1762	- An addition to Salem was surveyed for German Gellitt. This survey was apparently of land belonging to John Virdin. (456 acres)
March 22, 1770	- Jerman Pillitt sold 89 acres of land to James Virdin.
1774	- James Verdin was listed in the Worcester County Debt Books concerning the Addition to Salem and Townsends Mistake (land which had been patented to John Payne in 1771)

June 15, 1793 — James Virden, of Salem, and others named agreed to boundaries on their two properties.

1783 — The tax assessment shows that James Virdin owned four separate parcels of land: Security, 33 acres; Townsends Mistake, 16 acres; Hog Quarter, 265 acres; and Salum 9 (?) acres. He also had 2 horses and 11 black cattle. His family had two white male inhabitants and 2 white female inhabitants.

JOSEPH VIRDON of Anne Arundel County

August Court, 1771 — Joseph Virdon was given an allowance of 100 pounds for his support until November.

Maryland Chancery Records

IGNATIUS VARDEN — 1796, was listed as a debtor (Book 35, page 203)

JOHN VARDEN — 1795 and 1796, was listed as a debtor (Book 31, page 303, and Book 35, page 203)

RICHARD VARDEN — 1796, was listed as a debtor (Book 35, page 203)

Note: Ignatius, John and Richard Varden were apparently related.

PHOENIX VARDEN — 1832, Queene Anne County, was listed in Book 145, page 209.

VERDEN AND CARROLL — 1791, were listed as debtor (Book 21, page 129)

VARDON, THEODORE AND CARROLL — 1794, were listed as debtor (Book 29, page 442)

Other Maryland Records

CAPTAIN W.W. VIRDIN — was the purchaser of Lot 211, Havre de Grace, Harford County, Maryland, in 1846.

WILLIAM V. VIRDIN et al — were listed on Maryland Rent Rolls.

1839 — Winters Island, Hartford County.
1846 — Virdin's Improvement.
1845 — Mariners Beacon, Cecil and Harford Counties.
1846 — Virdin's Enterprise, Cecil County.
1847 — Late Discovery.
1850 — Late Addition.

HENRIETTA VERDEN — was made reference to in some file in 1806.

Some Maryland Marriages (From Maryland Marriages, 1634-1777)

Ra'l Virgin	— married William Burges, October 30, 1750, in Talbot County.
Elizabeth Vernon	— married William Palmer, November 24, 1734, in Queen Anne Parish, Prince George's County.
Mary Virdian	— married Matthew Porter, January 8, 1752, in Coventry Parish, Somerset County.

MARY SIMPSON (VERDEN) of St. Mary's County

Ignatius Simpson married Elizabeth Mudd. His will was made August 9, 1767, and was probated February 4, 1768. Ignatius and Elizabeth Simpson had these children: (1) John Simpson; (2) William Simpson; (3) Ignatius Simpson; (4) Mary Simpson. She married ____ Verden; (5) Henrietta Simpson; (6) Monica Simpson; and (7) Elizabeth Simpson.

Apparently, Ignatius Simpson, who died in 1768, and whose will was probated in St. Mary's County, Maryland, was a descendant of Thomas and Elizabeth Simpson, of Warickshire, England, who came to Maryland in July 1649, and received a grant of some 450 acres of land in 1652, called "Simpson." (But the reference has been lost.)

Virden, New Mexico

The community of Virden, New Mexico, was founded originally in 1860, and was called San Antonio at that time. It is located along the Gila River valley. When the Mexican Revolution broke out in 1912 many people had to leave and they settled on a tract of land known as the Gila Ranch Property, which was owned by the Gila Ranch Company, of which Earnest W. Virden was the president and one of the owners. The land was sold to the new settlers for $50,000, $5,000 down and yearly payments of $5,000 at 7% interest. Earnest W. Virden was from Marshall County, Iowa, and died in Gillman, Iowa. According to a letter dated March 29, 1972, from the village clerk, Mr. Virden was so fair and considerate in his business dealings with the people there that the little community re-named the town "Virden" in his honor.

Virden, Manitoba, Canada

On September 1, 1882, a post office was established at Gopher Creek, one mile east of the present town of Virden. In 1883 a permanent townsite was established at the present location of Virden, and was called Manchester. But when application was made to the Postal Department for a post office, it was found that the name Manchester would cause duplication so the name Virden was submitted and on October 1, 1883 a post office was registered under that name. The Village of Virden was changed by Town Charter to be known as "The Town of Virden" on September 14, 1904. The town was originally named Manchester after the Seventh Duke of Manchester who was active in the land company in that area and helped select lands for the town. When the name Manchester proved unacceptable, the town was apparently named as a courtesy to his wife, Louise, daughter of a Count in Hanover, after the name of a beautiful cathedral in her homeland. (Letter dated February 22, 1972, from the Secretary-Treasurer of the Town of Virden; and The Virden Story, by Ida Clingan, Empire Publishing Company, Virden, Manitoba, Canada.)

Letter dated May 18th, 1866, on U.S. Steamship Burrville, At Sea, from Green Nickerson to Mr. Virdin, 606 Popular Street, Wilmington, Delaware

>U.S. Steamer Burrville At Sea
>May 18th, bound for St. Thomas

"Dear Friend:

At present I am enjoying very good health and am once more on the rolling deep bound for St. Thomas. This makes the third time we have visited this fine island. The second time we were there there were two U.S. Steamers. One had the Commodore on, which was the flagship of the Squadron. They went home, which broke up the West Indian Squadron and left us orders to cruise around among the principal islands and to return to this place (St. Thomas) and if there were no orders to the contrary to go to Aspinwall by the 10th of June.

So we go to St. Thomas to see if there is any orders and will get mail. We will lay at Aspinwall sixty days. There is a U.S. Ship there now; we will relieve her. I will finish my letter after getting to St. Thomas but it is very difficult to work while the ship is sailing around on the sea. We left St. Pine, Martinique, last night at 8 O'closk. It is a very busy place. The town is very antique looking, but the French are very kind and polite. Josephine, Napoleon's first wife, was here and lived there until twenty-three years old, and then went to France with Napoleon and was married. St. Croux is the first land that I ever seen, and very much like the French are kind and polite there. They are Danish and have very fine and clean soldiers. Every port we go in the Generals and officers visit the ship. On this island the people are very wealthy and own large plantations. Each one has a large windmill on it and they manufacture their own sugar, molassas, and rum, which is their principal production. Cultivation is carried on to a great extent. There the laboring men get fifteen cents a day and a peck of cornmeal which is intended for their families. Two classes: Very poor and very wealthy.

"It is tilled up the sides of the mountains, very near to the clouds which rest all over the top. Can see the green fields of corn and the large wings of the mills turning, and coconut trees which make it beautiful. Sugar is 4¢ and 5¢.

We then went to St. Bartholomews which is a Swedish island. This island is one solid mass of rock. The old Alabama and Florida used to lie here. They are very kind people, but rather dull and ignorant. Not a very productive place, but the finest pineapples that I have ever seen for a penny a piece. They grow very much like cabbage. Fishing is splendid. There are the largest sharks that I have ever seen. They treat us with great respect.

The next place to St. Kitts or St. Christopher, which is an English island. And of all the mean people I have seen them here. Called our ship a box. They'd say the Alabama was the ship....Then call us Yankee Son of Bitches! -all the names you could think of. I went ashore there to buy some things for the mess, potatoes, and went up and asked a fellow what was the price of the potatoes. They did not belong to him or to anyone else that I could find. Did not want to sell us anything. Went in the store to get some sugar and went up to the counter and the man turned on his heel and walked away. A big negro woman came in. He stepped up to her and waited on her. Did not know what she would say to him. Negros and all of us just alike; you could not say anything. If you did you would get a broken head. Natives were all along the street, half naked, with a cloth around their waist, would yell "There goes the damn Yankees."

I did not care to be affected with a broken head and held my peace. I was glad to leave there. Passed along the Islands near enough to see them all the way to Martinique. I will finish after getting in port, when we see where we are ordered.

                Green"

Letter from Mrs. Emily Virdin to Mr. David, written about 1875

"Mr. David:

I thought it would be my duty to write you a few lines as I would be very much granted to know why it is you have left Martha Thompson, as nice a young girl as she is and is well thought of by everybody in this neighborhood. To think that you have always been her only gentleman company she ever had. Why, she never went with any of the fellows around here. When we saw her in company she would be with you, and now to think you have treated her this way, it is certainly too bad. But we can't look on her for it at all; if she had been pushy or out of her place with others we might look on her, but she never was. She was always a quite modest and peaceable girl. I have known her ever since she was a child. I never saw any badness out of her in my life, nor none of that familiarity. The people all around here think it is awful mean in your acting as you are. They all saw you to camp and beach together and there were several compliments passed on. Both of you being so nice looking and so nice to each other, and the last I ever saw you together was out to the festival in the winter, and everybody in the Church admired you and Martha. I asked her if she was married and she said yes, and you would reside in Philadelphia. We all had a talk about her in the Church one Sunday, treating you so nice that night. Why they all said they never saw a married couple that acted so nice in their life before. I am sure I never did, and the other day I was out to Pearson's Corner and heard you had left her. And she showed me the last letter she ever had from you and cried over it.

Now, Mr. David, you had no cause to send her such a letter as that. There are people around here who knew Martha before she ever came down here. And if she had been around it would have been known on her. But she never was until you done it, and now it is known and her reputation can be proved by people around here.

Now, Mr. David, you come and take your wife with you, and take care of her as you should do.

"You will be more thought of if you do this.

From her friend,
        Emily Virdin

P.S. Why did you treat her this way? Can you tell, or are you ashamed of it?"

Letter dated January 26, 1880, to William Virdin, Jr., Hartly, Delaware, from Robert T. Ludwick, Philadelphia, Pennsylvania
___

"Cousin William:

I received your letter on the fifth. I was glad to hear from you. I was sorry to hear that your wife had the chills. I neglected answering your letter sooner, but I have been running around from one place to another until I forgot it. I am completely tired of the city. I don't believe I could live here anymore; it seems as if I can't be contented. I wish I was down with you again. Could you give me enough to earn my board if I was to come down, until you go to farming? I don't think I will go with Mr. Lyndale as I don't care about being so near Pierson's Corner. I will work for you for seven dollars a month and board, after farming commences.

I was up to the bazaar today and some very nice horses sold cheap. I don't know anything more except that you can't pick up the daily paper without your seeing a murder in it. There were two men hung the other day for killing their wives and there is another going to be hung next month.

I will now close by sending my best respects to you all. My mother and sister sends their love to you all.

        From your cousin,

        Robert T. Ludwick

        Rear 280 Catharine Street
        Philadelphia, Pennsylvania

P.S. Write soon. I will be glad to hear from you."

Chapter 3.   The Broadway Family

THE BROADWAY FAMILY

NICHOLAS BROADWAY is the first Broadway of record. He and his wife, Catherine, are referred to in the records of Talbot County, Maryland, on July 19, 1662. They had at least one son, Samuel Broadway, Sr., who died in 1699.

SAMUEL BROADWAY, SR., married Sarah Dudley. They bought from her father, Richard Dudley, on August 15, 1682, a tract of two hundred acres of land called "Dudley" located on the north side of the Choptank River and of the west side of Tuckahoe Creek. (Book 4, page 131, Talbot County Land Records) On November 10, 1692, Samuel Broadway bought from Vincent Lowe a tract of land for eight thousand pounds of tobacco. (Book 8, page 7, Talbot County Land Records) On July 31, 1699, the will of Samuel Broadway was probated in Talbot County, Maryland. (Book A1, 1501) The Broadways at one time owned most of the land located in Delaware on the road from the Maryland line to the farm of former Governor Robert J. Reynolds of Delaware. When Samuel Broadway died he left about six hundred acres of land. Samuel Broadway, Sr., and his wife Sarah (Dudley) Broadway had two children: (1) Sarah Broadway; and (2) Samuel Broadway, Jr., who married Sarah _____.

SAMUEL BROADWAY, JR., and his wife Sarah (____) Broadway, had eight children:

(1) James Broadway (he died in 1758) who married Julia Ann Campbell as his first wife in December 1737, and had four children: (1) Mary Broadway, born January 25, 1742, who married Thomas Hall of Queenstown, Maryland (he died in 1784); (2) James Broadway, born January 25, 1744; (3) Sarah Broadway, born February 14, 1745; and (4) Samuel Broadway. After his first wife, Julia, died, James Broadway married Mary _____ but there is no record of any children by this second marriage.

(2) Ambrose Broadway (he died in 1787) who married _____ Wilson and had Robert Broadway, a hatter, who married Ann Berry.

(3) Samuel Broadway (he died in 1764) who married Mary _____ (she died in 1773) and had three children: (1) Abner Wiles Broadway (he died in August 1777) who married Elizabeth _____ of Talbot County, Maryland; (2) Samuel Broadway who died young; and (3) Isaac Broadway who married Rebecca _____.

(4) William Broadway (he died in 1749) who married Mary _____ but had no children.

(5) Robert Broadway (he died in 1768) who married and had two children by his first wife, whose name is unknown: (1) Ambrose Broadway who died in 1789; and (2) Mary Broadway (March 4, 1762 - July 5, 1833) who married Edward Carter as her first husband and Joseph Dawson (1773 - 1824) as her second husband. As his second wife Robert Broadway married Sarah Russman and had four children: (1) Lydia Broadway who married Purnell Jump as her first husband, and Harrington Sylvester as her second husband; (2) Rachel Broadway who married Mark Hargadine as her first husband, and John Cohee as her second husband; (3) Elizabeth Broadway who married Benjamin Bradley; and (4) Catherine Broadway who married Elijah Dawson. The will of Robert Broadway was probated February 27, 1768; he left about four hundred acres of land.

(6) Sarah Broadway who married John Register on December 14, 1738, and had seven children: (1) Samuel Register, born June 7, 1739, who married Ann Wilson; (2) John Register, born September 23, 1743, who married Esther Wilson and had ten children; (3) Lydia Register, born May 10, 1746, who married Thomas Wilson; (4) Robert Register, born January 25, 1749, who married Ruth Stout on April 1, 1775; (5) Joshua Register, born October 11, 1850; (6) David Register, born January 17, 1752; and (7) Sarah Register, born January 27, 1754.

(7) Mary Broadway who married Giles Hicks in 1742.

(8) Ann Broadway (she died in 1798) who married Richard Cooper (he died in 1773) and had ten children: (1) John Cooper (1747 - September 6, 1749); (2) Mary Cooper, born July 6, 1750, who married Henry Ward, a Quaker, and had eight children; (3) Esther Cooper (1752 - 1752); (4) Ann Cooper, born in 1853, married John Hall as her first husband and had two children; as her second husband she married George Downs and had four children; (5) Richard Cooper who married as his first wife, Sarah Alford, and had two children; as his second wife he married Clarissa Taylor and had three sons; (6) James Cooper (1757 - 1767); (7) Nehemiah Cooper (1760 - 1789); (8) Ezekial Cooper (1763 - 1847) who became a Methodist Episcopal Preacher; (9) Thomas Cooper (1765 - 1806) who married Catherine Lowber (1765 - 1852); (10) Sarah Cooper (1767 - 1808) who married John Cooper, a cousin.

Samuel Broadway, Jr., left about seven hundred acres of land when he died in 1743. His will was probated March 18, 1743. His wife, Sarah, died in May 1744.

ROBERT BROADWAY (son of Ambrose Broadway) and Ann (Berry) Broadway had four children:

(1) Mary Broadway who married a cousin, Ezekial Cooper.
(2) Ambrose Broadway, a tanner, who married Ann Watson (she was born in 1851) of Philadelphia; he died in 1879.
(3) Sarah Ann Broadway (she died in 1861) who married Thomas J. Marvel (he died in 1895).
(4) Ruth Ann Broadway who married Nathan Marvel but had no children.

AMBROSE BROADWAY (son of Robert and Ann (Watson) Broadway) had eight children:

(1) Margaret Watson Broadway who married Isaac L. Cohee as her first husband and John W. Parvis as her second husband.

(2) William Broadway who married Susan Hall Sherwood and had six children.

(3) Emily Broadway who married Whiteley W. Meredith and had three children.

(4) Susannah Broadway who married Peter K. Meredith and had three children.

(5) Elizabeth Ann Broadway who married John Cooper Gooden and had eight children.

(6) Isabel Broadway who married Henry Moore Draper and had three children.

(7) Amanda Melvina Broadway who married Walter Booker but had no children.

(8) Watson Broadway who married Mary Clark but had no children.

Thomas J. and Sarah Ann (Broadway) Marvel had eight children: (1) Elizabeth Marvel who married Dr. Vincent Emerson; (2) Robert Berry Marvel, born in 1833, ran away at age 21 and nothing more is known about him; (3) William Berry Marvel who married Mary Powell in Missouri or Illinois; (4) Elphonsie Marvel (1838 - 1869) who died of "consumption"; (5) Ellen Marvel (1840 - 1859) who died of "consumption"; (6) Thomas Jefferson Marvel (1843 - 1853); (7) Sallie Ann Marvel (1845 - 1846); and (8) Philena Marvel who married Hezekial J. Baxter of Maryland.

Ezekial and Mary (Broadway) Cooper had eight children: (1) Thomas B. Cooper who married Emily Marvel and had sixteen children; (2) Robert B. Cooper who married Mary Hawkins; (3) Peter Stout Cooper who married Elizabeth Gooden and had six children; (4) Sarah Ann Cooper who married Alex Frasher; (5) Caroline Cooper who married John Sherwood; (6) Richard B. Cooper who married Mary F. Sherwood; (7) Catherine Lowber Cooper who married Tennessee Gooden and had six children; and (8) Ignatius Ezekial Cooper who married Margaret Pool and had "forty-two grandchildren."

ABNER WILES BROADWAY (son of Samuel and Mary (____) Broadway) and his wife Elizabeth (____) Broadway had three children: (1) Lydia Broadway; (2) Mary Broadway; and (3) Elizabeth Broadway.

ISAAC BROADWAY (son of Samuel and Mary (____) Broadway) and his wife Rebecca (____) Broadway had two children: (1) Ambrose Broadway; and (2) Samuel Broadway (February 11, 1765 - October 1, 1813) who married Mary Willoughby of Sandtown, Delaware. He was a Baptist preacher. They had eight children: (1) James Broadway; (2) Elizabeth Broadway; (3) Abner Broadway; (4) Rebecca Broadway; (5) Samuel B. Broadway; (6) Lurette Broadway; (7) Hester Broadway; and (8) Mary Skinner Broadway.

Mary Broadway (daughter of Robert Broadway) and her first husband, Edward Carter, had three children: (1) Nancy Carter, born July 28, 1787; (2) Rachel Carter, born November 22, 1788, who married as her first husband, John Carter, and as her second husband, James Frasher; and (3) Edward B. Carter who married Mary Register (1801 - 1836).

Rachel Carter and her first husband, John Carter, had two children: (1) George Carter who married Mary Ann Prettyman; and (2) Mary Broadway Carter who married as her first husband, John M. Killen, and as her second husband, James W. Jester.

Rachel Carter and her second husband, James Frasher, had four children: (1) Edward Frasher; (2) Debby Frasher who married Ezekial B. Clements; (3) Robert Frasher who married as his first wife, Catherine Jester, and as his second wife Roxanna Clough; and (4) William Frasher who married Ann Gooden.

Edward B. and Mary (Register) Carter had eight children: (1) Ann Carter; (2) Elizabeth Carter; (3) Edward Joseph Carter, who married Elizabeth Reynolds and had ten children; (4) Mary Ann Carter, who married Joseph O. McCalley and had ten children; (5) William Carter; (6) Thomas Carter; (7) Sarah Carter; and (8) Lydia Broadway Carter, who married William Vandyke of Odessa, Delaware, but had no children.

Mary Broadway (1762 - 1833) and her second husband, Joseph Dawson, had five children: (1) William Dawson, born May 15, 1791; (2) Sarah Dawson, born December 14, 1795; (3) Mary Dawson, born December 14, 1797; (4) Robert Dawson, born August 30, 1799, who married Miriam Cooper; and (5) Polly Dawson, born June 19, 1801, who married Isaac Gruwell (1792 - 1849).

Isaac and Polly (Dawson) Gruwell had six children: (1) Joseph Dawson Gruwell (March 9, 1828 - July 3, 1893) who married Caroline Lewis; (2) Eliza Ann Gruwell, born October 7, 1831, who married William Meredith but had no children; (3) John Gruwell, born August 8, 1833, who married Elizabeth Lewis; (4) Isaac Gruwell (May 8, 1836 - September 9, 1892) who married Mary Ann Bunt (1838 - 1887); (5) Elizabeth Gruwell who died single; and (6) William Gruwell who died single.

Purnell and Lydia (Broadway) Jump (he was her first husband) had five children: (1) Ann Jump who married John Killen and had six children; (2) Ambrose Jump who married in Springfield, Illinois; (3) John Jump who married Elizabeth Clements and had eight children; (4) Mary Jump who married Jonathan George, but had no children; and (5) Robert B. Jump who married as his first wife, Mary Barrett, and had eleven children; and who married, as his second wife, Elizabeth Draper, and had two children.

Mark and Rachel (Broadway) Hargadine (he was her first husband) had five children:

(1) Sarah Hargadine, born July 24, 1787, who married Will Chambers and went to Ohio.

(2) William Hargadine, born March 3, 1789.

(3) Samuel Hargadine (November 15, 1790 - July 6, 1832) who married Mary Lockwood on September 5, 1816.

(4) Robert Hargadine, born August 23, 1792, who married as his first wife, Mrs. Jarrell (who was a Miss Kenton) and had three children; (1) Henry Kenton Hargadine (1817 - 1890) who married Ruth Whitaker (1824 - 1893) and had eight children; (2) William Andrew Hargadine (1822 - 1892) who married Acrata McCrary and had five children; and (3) Julia Ann Hargadine who married Robert B. Wright and had nine children.

(5) John Hargadine, who married Sarah Cubbage.

John and Rachel (Broadway) (Hargadine) Cohee (he was her second husband) had two children: (1) Vincent Cohee, who married Miriam Cubbage; and (2) Rachel Cohee, who married James Raughley, of Duck Creek, and had nine children.

Benjamin and Elizabeth (Broadway) Bradley had seven children: (1) John Bradley who married in New York City; (2) Benjamin Bradley who married in New York City; (3) Margaret Bradley who married Thomas Cox of Lancaster, Pennsylvania; (4) Samuel Bradley who married Miss Stanbury of Baltimore, Maryland. He later became Mayor of Baltimore; (5) Philip Bradley who never married and died in North Carolina; (6) James Bradley who married in New York City; and (7) Mary Bradley who married Richard Cooper, a cousin.

Elijah and Catherine (Broadway) Dawson had a son, Greenberg Dawson, who married, but the name of his wife is unknown.

Thomas Cooper (1765 - 1806) (son of Richard and Ann (Broadway) Cooper) married Catherine Lowber (1765 - 1852). Thomas and Catherine (Lowber) Cooper had six children:

(1) Peter Lowber Cooper, born in 1790, who married Susannah Lowber, a second cousin, and had a daughter, Catherine Lowber Cooper, who married William Gooden.

(2) Mary Cooper, who married Samuel Cooper, a cousin, and had four sons and six daughters.

(3) Richard Cooper, who married Mary Bradley, a cousin, and had four sons and one daughter.

(4) Ezekial Cooper, who married Mary Broadway, a cousin.

(5) Sarah Cooper, who married Peter Meredith, and had seven sons and two daughters.

(6) Catherine Cooper, who married Alexander Frasher, a second cousin, and had eight sons and three daughters.

Richard and Mary (Bradley) Cooper (they were cousins) had four children:

(1) Benjamin Bradley Cooper, who married Hannah Sherwood and had two children: (1) Eugene Cooper who was killed in the Sioux Wars with General Custer; and (2) Dr. Thomas Cooper who died young.

(2) John Bradley Cooper, who married Mary Rash, and had two children: (1) Fletcher Ellsworth Cooper, who married Genevieve Gray and had ten children; and (2) Irving Cooper.

(3) Ezekial Vickers Cooper, who married and had two children: (1) Mary Cooper who married Josiah Evans but had no children; and (2) Ethel Cooper who married _____ Lloyd and had two children.

(4) Richard M. Cooper who married Miss Jefferson and had eight children.

Dr. Vincent and Elizabeth (Marvel) Emerson had three children: (1) Emma Marvel Emerson; (2) Gove Marvel Emerson; and (3) Ann Belle Marvel Emerson, who married James S. Dailey and had a son, J. Seward Dailey.

William Berry and Mary (Powell) Marvel had seven children:
(1) Ida Marvel; (2) Eva Marvel; (3) Mollie Marvel, who married and had three children; (4) Susan Marvel, who married and had one child; (5) Alice Marvel; (6) Philena Marvel, who married and had one child; and (7) Corliss Marvel.

Hezekial and Philena (Marvel) Baxter had five children:

(1) Herman Baxter, who married Ella Short and had three children: (1) Philena Baxter; (2) Elva Baxter; and (3) Thomas Rodney Baxter.

(2) Thomas G. Baxter, who married Emma Attix and had a daughter, Catherine S. Baxter.

(3) Alphonzo Baxter who married Sallie Artis and had two children: (1) William Marvel Baxter; and (2) Mildred F. Baxter.

(4) Ceasar Rodney Baxter who married Della Lowery and had a child, Myrtle Dove Baxter.

(5) Elphonsie Baxter.

Joseph Dawson and Caroline (Lewis) Gruwell had ten children: (1) Isaac Lewis Gruwell who married Margaret Castle; (2) Eliza Jane Gruwell who married George Cooper; (3) Melvina Gruwell who married Thomas Sipple; (4) Robert Broadway Gruwell; (5) Joseph Dawson Gruwell who married Sallie Bayles; (6) Herman Gruwell; (7) John M. Gruwell who married Adaline Needles; (8) Susan E. Gruwell who married Henry Vincent; (9) Ruth Ann Gruwell; and (10) Charles Gruwell.

John and Elizabeth (Lewis) Gruwell had seventeen children. John Gruwell was born June 8, 1833. (1) William W. Gruwell; (2) Joseph Edward Gruwell who married Mary S. Draper; (3) Mary Edward Gruwell who married Edward Dill; (4) Alda Gruwell; (5) Thomas Gruwell; (6) Luther Gruwell; (7) Peter Gruwell; (8) John Watson Gruwell; (9) L. Gruwell; (10) Henry Gruwell who married Martha Williams; (11) Jacob Gruwell; (12) Cooper Gruwell who married Eva Dill; (13) Jasper Gruwell; (14) Howard Gruwell; (15) Alice Gruwell; (16) and (17) names unknown.

Isaac and Mary Ann (Bunt) Gruwell had seven children: (1) Francis D. Gruwell; (2) William Bunt Gruwell who married Laura Lamb; (3) Frederic Gruwell; (4) Mary Gruwell who married Ezekial Moore; (5) Thomas Henry Gruwell; (6) Elizabeth Jane Gruwell; and (7) Susan Gruwell.

BROADWAY FAMILY NOTES

1. Nancy Broadway was mentioned as a daughter-in-law in the will of John Gray, probated June 23, 1783. (Kent County Wills, Book M, page 12)

2. Letters of administration were granted to Mary Broadway, on October 15, 1787, to administer the estate of Ambrose Broadway. Mary Broadway later married Israel Merrick.

3. The will of Ambrose Broadway, probated November 13, 1789, mentions his wife, Rebecca Broadway; an heir, Mary Broadway; a brother William Broadway; and the files indicate that Rebecca Broadway later married William Moore.

4. The will of William Broadway, farmer, of Caroline County, Maryland, was administered by Robert Broadway, November 25, 1790. Heirs mentioned were: Robert Broadway, Isaac Broadway, Elizabeth Broadway, Ambrose Broadway, Nancy Broadway, Abner Broadway, Sarah Broadway, and Samuel Broadway. (Kent County, Delaware, Archives, Vol. A5, page 246)

5. Sally Broadway was a witness to the will of John Gruwell, Sr., which was probated November 16, 1796. (Kent County Wills, Book N, page 156)

6. The will of Elizabeth Mors (Morris), probated December 14, 1796, shows as heirs: sons, Samuel Broadway, Abner Broadway, Robert Broadway; grandchildren, Ambrose Broadway and Samuel Broadway, children of Isaac Broadway, and Mary Broadway, daughter of Ambrose Broadway. (Kent County Wills, Book N, page 158)

7. Samuel Broadway was granted letters of administration for the estate of John Gray, Blacksmith, of Murderkill Hundred, on December 17, 1796. (Kent County Wills, Book N, page 158)

8. Letticia Broadway was named as a granddaughter in the will of William Morris, probated February 16, 1797. (Kent County Wills, Book N, page 167)

9. The files relating to the will of Rich Heald, probated February 22, 1797, show that his widow, Patients Heald, later married Robert Broadway. (Kent County Wills, Book N, page 168)

Chapter 4.   The Carter Family

THE CARTER FAMILY

The Carter family of Delaware is reportedly of English descent, although there is some indication that at least one family may have come from Ireland. For example, the will of Thomas Carter, probated November 10, 1796, in New Castle County, shows that he had two sons in Ireland. However, other evidence indicates that the Carters originally came from England to Virginia, after which part of the family moved to Maryland and Delaware.

On the assumption that the Carter family of Delaware was descended from the Carter family of Virginia, it may be of interest to include some early newspaper accounts of the family. A clipping from an unidentified newspaper dated July 20, 1908, states in part:

> "No man is better known traditionally and genealogically in the South than the celebrated 'King Carter of Virginia'. He was a prominent man in his day, and thousands of Virginians, as many others, are naturally proud of having his blood. He was Colonel Robert Carter of 'Carotoman', 1663-1732, a member and Speaker of the Virginia House of Burgesses; treasurer of the Virginia Colony, etc. From his great wealth and authority he came to be known as 'King Carter.' Of him, his family and his mansions, see Coat's Colonial Mansions. In recent years it has been claimed that he was a lineal descendent of the Plantagenet Kings of England. It is possible that he was, but...
>
> "In Pedigrees CCXX, fourth edition, and XLV, sixth edition of Browning's Americans of Royal Descent, Browning's Colonial Dames of Royal Descent, ..., in Keith's Ancestry of Benjamin Harrison, and Coat's Colonial Mansions, it may be seen that the descent from Kings of the Carter family of Virginia depends upon 'King Carter' being the son of Colonel John Carter by his wife Sarah Ludlow (who was the daughter of Gabriel Ludlow, 1587-1639, a lawyer, who was of a Wiltshire family of royal descent), and the only one of his four or five wives who was of royal descent.
>
> "Mr. Keith...places Colonel Robert Carter, or 'King Carter,' as the son of Colonel John Carter

"had no less than five wives, of whom the first four were buried near him in Christ Church, Lancaster County, Virginia, though others have allowed him only three.

"His first four wives are certainly named in the...epitaph.

"The aforesaid Colonel John Carter's parentage and the date and the place of his birth are unknown. He came to Virginia about 1643-1649. His will, dated January 3, 1669, was recorded at Lancaster Court House, Virginia, but not until January 9, 1722.

"From these statements, or the evidence, it may be presumed that 'King Carter' was the son of 'Sarah Ludlow,' and therefore a lineal descendant through her of kings of England and France."

Another unidentified newspaper clipping dated October 20, 1908, states in part:

"Colonel John Carter had five wives, his sons had several, but one of the wives of John, Jr., had no less than six husbands.

"Since the wealth of a man is figured as 'relative,' these Carters, father, Colonel John, and son, Colonel Robert, lived in a style in their day of which there is no counterpart in our day. Colonel John, the founder of the Virginia family, that is the 'King Carter,' Carter one, for there were others of this surname who removed, or were transported to the Old Dominion and founded Carter families, was a classical scholar and of refined manners and churchman and one who stood high in Government favor and filled without scandal throughout his active life many offices of trust in the Colony, and yet accumulated a remarkable fortune, whether by marriage or by thrift, it matters not. His son, who by his remarkable traits, immense possessions and almost amazingly innumerable official positions and authority, is still known as 'King' Carter, was a lad at his father's decease in 1669. In his will his father instructed that his executors should have him well educated...

> "For all the wonderful things we read of
> Colonel John Carter, the immigrant founder
> of this tribe in America, it is remarkable
> that neither he nor his contemporaries left
> a single hint as to whence he came and when
> came the first colonel of the Virginia Carters,
> nor do we know or have a suggestion who
> were the parents or the forbears, or even
> the father, of the founder of this noted
> family. Is it not remarkable that such a
> man with such sons and grandchildren did
> not leave a hint as to his antecedents and
> associates in the Old Country?...."

The preceeding discussion relating to the origin of the Carter family of Delaware, and the comments concerning the Carter family of Virginia, is not meant to imply that the two families are related, although it is possible that they are.

EDWARD CARTER (he died in November 1789) and his first wife, Ann Whitaker (daughter of Henry Whitaker whose will was probated September 25, 1794) had six children:

(1) John Whitaker Carter who married Sallie Wyatt as his first wife.
(2) Sarah Carter who married William Edmonson.
(3) Ruth Carter who married _____ Edmonson.
(4) William Carter.
(5) Edward Carter who married Rhoda Melvin.
(6) Mary Ann Carter who married William Case.

JOHN WHITAKER CARTER and his first wife, Sallie Wyatt, had two children: (1) Elizabeth Carter who married Noah Seward; and (2) Hannah Carter who married William Johnson as her first husband; Jeremiah Rusk as her second husband; and Benjamin Atwell as her third husband. She had no children by any of these marriages.

JOHN WHITAKER CARTER and his second wife, Miss _____ Clark, had one son, Noah Carter, an "old bachelor."

EDWARD CARTER and Rhoda (Melvin) Carter had six children:

(1) Henry Carter who went "West."
(2) Elizabeth Carter who married _____ Melvin.
(3) Mariah Carter who married William Jacobs, had a son, Isaac Jacobs, who married Sara E. Noble.
(4) Edward Carter who died of yellow fever.
(5) John Carter who died young.
(6) A child who died while a baby.

William and Mary Ann (Carter) Case had seven children:

(1) Louisa Case who died "an old maid."
(2) William Case who married Elizabeth Watson as his first wife and Elizabeth Simpson as his second wife.
(3) Edward Case.
(4) Rachel Case who married Stephen Catts and had a son, James E. Catts.
(5) John Case who married Sallie Credick.
(6) James Case.
(7) Mary Ann Case who married Caleb Clough and lived near Millington, Maryland, but had no children.

EDWARD CARTER and his second wife, Mary Broadway (March 4, 1762-July 5, 1828) had three children:

(1) Nancy Carter, born July 25, 1787, who died an infant.
(2) Edward Broadway Carter (July 29, 1790-September 6, 1849) who married Mary C. Register (July 9, 1801-August 23, 1836).
(3) Rachel Carter, born November 22, 1788, who married John Carter (not a relative) as her first husband.

EDWARD BROADWAY CARTER and his wife, Mary C. (Register) Carter, had eight children:

(1) Ann Carter, born June 28, 1822, at Slaughters, Delaware, who died while an infant.
(2) Elizabeth Carter, born March 27, 1823, at Slaughters, Delaware, who died an infant.
(3) Edward Joseph Carter, born November 3, 1824, who married Elizabeth Reynolds.
(4) Mary Ann Carter who married Joseph O. McColley.
(5) William Carter, born May 3, 1829, who died an infant.
(6) Thomas Carter, born August 4, 1830, died August 20, 1833.
(7) Sarah Carter.
(8) Lydia Broadway Carter, born February 26, 1833, who married William Vandyke of Odessa, Delaware.

Joseph and Mary (Broadway)(Carter) Dawson had five children. Mary Carter married Joseph Dawson as her second husband after the death of Edward Carter, her first husband. Joseph Dawson died in 1824 and Mary Dawson died in 1828. Their children were:

(1) William Dawson, born May 15, 1791.
(2) Sarah Dawson, born December 14, 1795.
(3) Mary Dawson, born December 14, 1797.

(4) Robert Dawson, born August 30, 1799, who married Miriam Cooper.

(5) Polly Dawson, born June 19, 1801, who married Isaac Gruwell (1792-1847) and had six children: (1) Joseph Dawson Gruwell (March 8, 1818-July 3, 1873); (2) John Gruwell, born August 8, 1833; (3) Elizabeth Ann Gruwell, born October 7, 1831; (4) Isaac Gruwell (May 8, 1836-July 9, 1872); (5) Elizabeth Gruwell and (6) William Gruwell both of whom died single.

Edward Joseph Carter was a farmer, fruit grower, and nurseryman living on more than one thousand acres of land in North Murderkill Hundred, Kent County. After attending the local schools he attended the Academy at New Castle, Delaware. On April 20, 1847, he married Elizabeth Reynolds.

EDWARD JOSEPH CARTER and his wife, Elizabeth Reynolds, had ten children:

(1) Mary Evelyn Carter, born May 18, 1848, who married Robert Whitaker Hargadine on October 30, 1872.

(2) Herman Carter, born October 2, 1849, who married Belle Cardiff.

(3) Sallie Gilder Reynolds Carter, born May 25, 1851, who married Dr. Edwin Buchanan on April 18, 1888.

(4) Robert W. Carter, born February 20, 1853, died June 10, 1853.

(5) Julia Carter, born August 9, 1854.

(6) Edward Broadway Carter, born October 12, 1856, who married Sarah May Scattergood.

(7) Luther Martin Reynolds Carter, born March 5, 1859, who married Mary Matilda Merrick (August 28, 1867-August 27, 1906).

(8) Frank Reynolds Carter who married Jeanie Thayre of East Hampton, Massachusetts.

(9) Lizzie Carter, born July 8, 1865, died July 30, 1866.

(10) Aimie Carter who married Charles O. Gregg, of Railey Park, Pennsylvania, on February 17, 1897.

Robert Whitaker and Mary Evelyn (Carter) Hargadine had seven children: (1) Edward Carter Hargadine, born November 12, 1873; (2) Mary Evelyn Hargadine, born September 12, 1875, who married George Heard; (3)

Elizabeth Reynolds Hargadine, born in 1877, died in 1881; (4) Robert Whitaker Hargadine, born October 4, 1879; (5) Julia Carter Hargadine, born August 17, 1883; (6) Annie Hargadine, born in February 1886; (7) Albert Henry Hargadine, born October 4, 1891.

HERMAN CARTER and his wife, Belle (Cardiff) Carter had four children: (1) Elizabeth Ann Carter, born May 31, 1886; (2) Mary Evelyn Carter, born September 30, 1888; (3) Edward Joseph Carter, born October 26, 1889; and (4) Reynolds Carter.

Joseph O. and Mary Ann (Carter) McColley had ten children:

(1) Truston P. McColley, born in 1844.

(2) Laura E. McColley, born in 1847, died January 25, 1908, who married Orlean DeWitt (he died in 1908) and had two children: (1) Lydia Carter DeWitt who married Dr. Frank Cripps; and (2) Anna Frasher DeWitt.

(3) Mary Carter McColley, born in 1848, who married Jacob Welden and had two children: (1) Mary Welden; and (2) Chatham Welden.

(4) Lydia Broadway Carter McColley, born in 1850, who married George Temple and had two children: (1) Clay Temple; and (2) Bessie Temple who married _____ Chapin and had two children, Dorothie Chapin and Bessie Temple Chapin.

(5) Edward Carter McColley, born in 1851, who married Elizabeth VanVorst and had one child, Sophia Carter McColley, who married _____ Harper.

(6) Josephine McColley.

(7) Lizzie Dutton McColley, born in 1858, who married Payne G. Green and had two children, Estel Green and Maybeth Green.

(8) Joseph McColley, born in 1860, who married Laura Long, and had a daughter, Elizabeth McColley.

(9) Hiram W. McColley, born in 1862.

(10) Nellie Register McColley, born in 1866, who married George Fetterolff and had three children, Agnes Fetterolff, J. Layton Register Fetterolff, and Estella Fetterolff.

LUTHER MARTIN REYNOLDS CARTER and his wife, Mary Matilda (Merrick) Carter, had eight children:

(1) Isabel Carter, born December 23, 1892.
(2) Luther Reynolds Carter, born March 24, 1894.
(3) Mary Merrick Carter, born April 27, 1896.
(4) Robert Shively Carter, born October 5, 1897.
(5) Mildred Carter, born May 3, 1900.
(6) Bernard Carter, born July 13, 1902.
(7) Dorothy Carter who died as an infant on January 20, 1903.
(8) James Merrick Carter, born January 9, 1905, died November 7, 1906.

John and Rachel (Carter) Carter (he died in 1813 and was her first husband) had two children:

(1) George Carter who married Mary Ann Prettyman and had seven children, none of whom married: (1) William Edward Carter; (2) Lydia Carter; (3) Sarah Emily Carter; (4) Francis Carter; (5) George H. Carter; (6) Albert Carter; and (7) George H. Carter (No. 2). The unmarried Carter girls lived in Camden, Delaware.

(2) Mary Broadway Carter who married John M. Killen as her first husband and had two children: (1) George M. Killen who married Rachel Case, a fourth cousin; and (2) William Edward Killen who married Sarah A. Needles.

James and Rachel (Carter) Frasher (he was her second husband) had four children:

(1) Edward Frasher.
(2) Debbie Frasher, born September 15, 1818, died December 4, 1843, who married Ezekial Clements on May 19, 1839.
(3) Robert Frasher, born January 20, 1821, died March 20, 1907, who married Catherine Jester as his first wife and Roxanna Clough as his second wife.
(4) William Frasher, born February 23, 1826, who married Ann Gooden.

Ezekial and Debbie (Frasher) Clements had three children: (1) James Thomas Clements, born January 19, 1840, who married Susan Jane Townsend; (2) Rachel Catherine Clements, born July 7, 1843, who married Henry C. Clark (February 17, 1837-August 24, 1884); and (3) Mary Ann Clements, born July 16, 1841, who died an infant.

Robert and Roxanna (Clough) Frasher had seven children:

(1) Mary Ellen Frasher, born June 12, 1850, who married Dr. John Marion Wilkinson.

(2) Emma Barzetta Frasher, born August 6, 1851, who married James Green (April 22, 1843- January 11, 1900).
(3) William Edward Frasher, born November 17, 1854, who married Emma J. Wright, and had a daughter, Louella Grace Frasher.
(4) Robert Emmet Frasher who married in California.
(5) James Augustus Frasher, born September 12, 1861, who married Hattie Smith.
(6) Harry O. Frasher, born May 31, 1865, who married Ann Huston.
(7) Calvin Rust Frasher, born February 24, 1858, died August 1907, who married Rachel Steel.

William and Ann (Gooden) Frasher had ten children. William was born February 23, 1826, and died July 13, 1882; Ann was born January 13, 1830, and died March 7, 1900. Their children were:

(1) John Raymond Frasher, born June 24, 1851, who married Mary E. Sargent, born January 28, 1860.
(2) Rachel Catherine Frasher, born May 27, 1853, who married David Heyd, born May 5, 1846.
(3) James Thomas Frasher, born February 17, 1855, who married Ida Maginnis.
(4) Isaac Gooden Frasher, born January 24, 1857, died in 1893.
(5) Ann Gooden Frasher, born March 21, 1859, who married Alexander Frasher Meredith.
(6) William Henry Frasher, born June 4, 1861, who married Ella Bayles.
(7) Wesley D. Frasher, born February 9, 1863.
(8) Benjamin Walter Frasher, born July 31, 1865, died December 24, 1867.
(9) Charles Oscar Frasher, born May 3, 1867, who married Goldie Reed, and had one child, Cecil Frasher, born July 23, 1896.
(10) Joseph Carrell Frasher, born February 26, 1870, who married Estella McMahon of Smithville, Indiana. She was born June 9, 1881.

James Thomas and Susan Jane (Townsend) Clements had two children: (1) Francis H. Clements, born December 2, 1874; and (2) Maggie J. Clements, born April 5, 1880, who married Lester L. Mills.

Henry C. and Rachel Catherine (Clements) Clark had two children: (1) Evelyn Clark, born April 9, 1872, who married Professor Griffith; and (2) John Dawson Clark, born November 12, 1873.

Dr. John Marion and Mary Ellen (Frasher) Wilkinson had two children: (1) Annie Lavenia Wilkinson; and (2) William Wilkinson.

James and Emma Barzetta (Frasher) Green had seven children: (1) Ethel Green; (2) Thomas Frasher Green; (3) James Olin Green; (4) Milton Green; (5) Robert Earl Green; (6) Eva Barzetta Green; and (7) Elizabeth Green.

James Augustus and Hattie (Smith) Frasher had three children: (1) Ida Smith Frasher; (2) Mary Ethel Frasher; and (3) Robert Lindale Frasher.

Harry O. and Ann (Huston) Frasher had two children: (1) Roxanna Huston Frasher; and (2) William Huston Clough Frasher.

Calvin Rust and Rachel (Steel) Frasher had one child, Edith Steel Frasher, born February 1, 1887, who married Lyle Tuckton.

John Raymond and Mary (Sargent) Frasher had five children: (1) Ina Etta Frasher, born in 1881; (2) Leaby Lewis Frasher, born in 1883; (3) William Frasher, born in 1886; (4) Thomas Everet Frasher, born in 1890; and (5) Matilda Ann Frasher, born in 1893.

David and Rachel Catherine (Frasher) Heyd had four children: (1) Alice Heyd, born in 1876; (2) Rose Heyd, born in 1878; (3) Bertha Heyd; and (4) Emma Heyd, born in 1882.

James Thomas and Ida (Maginnis) Frasher had five children: (1) Mable Frasher, born in 1886; (2) Rosell Frasher, born in 1890; (3) Lizzie Frasher, born in 1893; (4) Lillian Frasher, born in 1894; and (5) Susan Frasher, born in 1896.

Alexander Frasher and Ann Gooden (Frasher) Meredith had four children: (1) Ella Frasher Meredith, born in 1882; (2) Laura Ethel Meredith, born in 1883; (3) Amy Pauline Meredith, born in 1885; and (4) Lula Meredith.

William Henry and Ella (Bayless) Frasher had three children: (1) Edna Lobella Frasher, born in 1896; (2) Byron William Frasher, born in 1892; and (4) Virgil Raymond Frasher, born in 1893.

Joseph Carrell and Estella (McMahon) Frasher had four children: (1) Lester Marvel Frasher, born in 1897; (2) Jesse Marvel Frasher, born in 1899; (3) Ruby Ann Frasher, born in 1901; and (4) Victor Earl Frasher, born in 1903.

William and Elizabeth (Watson) Case, who was his first wife, had five children:

(1) Sarah Ann Case.
(2) Mary Elizabeth Case who married G.W. Anderson and had seven children: (1) Sarah E. Anderson; (2) Joseph W. Anderson; (3) Mary E. Anderson; (4) Sallie B. Anderson; (5) William Case Anderson; (6) Thomas Case Anderson; and (7) George E. Anderson.

(3) Rachel Case who married George W. Killen, a cousin, and had three children: (1) William Case Killen; (2) John Watson Killen; and (3) Thomas Edward Killen.
(4) Charles Case who married Emily Anderson.
(5) William Thomas Case who married Helena ____.

William and Elizabeth (Simpson) Case, who was his second wife, had three children: (1) Nora Case who married Thomas Bradley; (2) Louisa Case who married John Credick; and (3) Joseph Simpson Case, "an old bachelor."

John and Sallie (Credick) Case had nine children: (1) William James Case; (2) John Case; (3) Mary Ellen Case; (4) Emily Case; (5) Charles W. Case; (6) Rachel Case; (7) Sallie Case; (8) Samuel Case; and (9) Rosanna Case.

Willliam Edward and Sarah A. (Needles) Killen had four children: (1) Walter Killen who married Mary Danbery; (2) Elwood Killen who married Mary Wyatt; (3) Ann May Killen who married Willard Hickman, a merchant at Sandtown, Delaware; and (4) Estelle Varga Killen who married George P. Laister.

Isaac and Sarah E. (Noble) Jacobs had four children: (1) William Jacobs; (2) Truella Jacobs; (3) Lizzie Jacobs; and (4) Mollie Jacobs.

Noah and Elizabeth (Carter) Seward (she was the daughter of John Whitaker Carter and his first wife, Sallie Wyatt) had seven children: (1) Rebecca Ann Seward who married William A. Barwick; (2) William Seward; (3) John Seward who married Mrs. Mason; (4) Mary Ellen Seward who married John Golt but had no children; (5) Louisa Seward who married Mr. Sparks; (6) Joshua Seward who married and had children. His wife's name is unknown; and (7) Sarah Elizabeth Seward who married John Clough.

William A. and Rebecca Ann (Seward) Barwick had two children: (1) J. Frank Barwick, born October 17, 1847, who married Mary Ellen Reynolds, born February 23, 1849; and (2) Thomas Howard Barwick who married Alta Seward, and had two children, Henry Barwick and Rebecca Barwick.

J. Frank and Mary Ellen (Reynolds) Barwick had five children: (1) William Reynolds Barwick, born in 1872, died in 1874; (2) John Seward Barwick, born in 1874, who married Lola Elizabeth Bailey; (3) Margaret Rebecca Barwick, born in 1881, who married John Walter Paynter; (4) William Augustus Barwick, born in 1883; and (5) Wallace Clifton Barwick.

John and Sarah Elizabeth (Seward) Clough had six children: (1) Noah Herman Clouth; (2) John Clough who moved to Denver, Colorado; (3) Frank Clough; (4) Lizzie Clough; (5) Estella Clough; and (6) Josie Clough who moved to Denver, Colorado.

CARTER FAMILY NOTES

1. George Carter was a witness to the will of Martha Hill, of Calvert County, Maryland, March 2, 1676. (The Maryland Calendar of Wills, Vol. 1, page 190)

2. John Carter was a witness to the will of George Billingslay, of Upper Norfolk, Virginia, December 21, 1681. (The Maryland Calendar of Wills, Vol. 1, page 149)

3. Ann Carter was a witness to the will of John Cabley, made November 9, 1683. Not probated. (Kent County, Delaware, Wills, in Sylvania, Pennsylvania Historical Society Papers)

4. Valentine Carter was a witness to the will of Charles Stuart, of Kent Island, Maryland, signed August 26, 1688. (The Maryland Calendar of Wills, Vol. 2, page 31)

5. Philip Carter was a witness to the will of Michael Dusharoorn, of Somerset County, Maryland, October 23, 1690. (The Maryland Calendar of Wills, Vol. 2, page 124)

6. Valentine Carter was a witness to the will of Samuel Wheeler, Kent County, Maryland, May 15, 1693. (The Maryland Calendar of Wills, Vol. 2, page 90)

7. William Carter was a witness to the will of Joseph Fryt, of Calvert County, Maryland, January 26, 1694. (The Maryland Calendar of Wills, Vol. 2, page 77)

8. Joseph and Isaac Carter were witnesses to the will of Mauriss Baker, of Anne Arundel County, November 10, 1700. (The Maryland Calendar of Wills, Vol. 2, page 208)

9. A power of attorney was given to Valentine Carter of Kent Island by Thomas Whitup of Bristol, England, November 17, 1702. (Talbot County, Maryland Deeds, Book 9, page 133)

10. Richard Carter was a legatee in the will of John Burnam, of Talbot County, April 15, 1704. (The Maryland Calendar of Wills, Vol. 3, page 36)

CARTER FAMILY NOTES (cont.)

11. Sarah Carter was a witness to the will of John Smith, June 20, 1705. (The Maryland Calendar of Wills, Vol. 3, page 48)

12. The will of Richard Hutchins of Kent Island, probated June 18, 1706, named Henry Carter (son of Valentine Carter) and his wife, Mary, as legatees. (The Maryland Calendar of Wills, Vol. 3, page 75)

13. The will of Henry Carter of Talbot County names sons Valentine Carter, John Carter; and daughter, Elizabeth Ellicot, January 21, 1706/07. (The Maryland Calendar of Wills, Vol. 3, page 84)

14. Letters of administration were granted December 6, 1708, to Micaiah Perry, attorney for Elizabeth Carter, on estate of Richard Carter, late of Maryland in America. (From "Maryland Gleanings in England", Maryland Historical Magazine, Vol. II, page 377)

15. The will of Philip Carter of Stepency Parich, Somerset County, probated January 10, 1715/16, named: Wife, Mary; Sarah Acwith, Jr., and heirs: John Richards, Jr.; Tabitha Moore, Elizabeth and Philip Richards, and Sarah Acwith and her unborn child; John Richards, Sr. (The Maryland Calendar of Wills, Vol. 4, page 47)

16. Sarah Carter, a daughter, was a legatee in the will of John Burroughs, planter, of St. Marys County, March 13, 1715/16. (The Maryland Calendar of Wills, Vol. 4, page 170)

17. John Carter was a legatee in the will of Morris Morees of Somerset County, November 7, 1716. (The Calendar of Maryland Wills, Vol. 4, page 170)

18. The will of Robert Carter, yeoman, probated December 16, 1740, of Dover Hundred, Kenty County, Delaware, lists wife Jane Carter (who later married James Carbin), sons William Carter, Thomas Carter, and daughter Margaret Carter. (Kent County Wills, Book I, page 74)

19. Letters of administration were granted to Mary Carter, widow, for the estate of William Carter, Jr., on October 26, 1748. (Kent County Wills, Book I, page 241)

20. The will of Jacob Anderson, merchant, probated September 27, 1751, named as one of the executors of his estate in or near Maryland as Joseph Carter. (Kent County, Delaware, Wills, Book K, page 41)

CARTER FAMILY NOTES (cont.)

21. William Carter was a witness to the will of Abraham Mason, made May 1, 1754. (Kent County Wills, Book K, page 112)

22. The will of William Carter, probated, May 31, 1760, names heirs as: Elizabeth Carter; William Carter, Jr.; Jane Carter and Sarah Carter (daughters of William Carter); Mearrim Brown, Rachel Brown and Nyca Brown (daughters of Thomas Brown) and daughters Jane Brown, Comfort Powell, and Ann Donneho. (Kent County Archives, Vol. A8, page 44)

23. Letters of administration were granted to Jane Carbin, widow, and William Carter, for the estate of James Carbin, on August 13, 1760. (Kent County Wills, Book K, page 235)

24. The will of William Carter, probated April 5, 1765, names as heirs: James Carbine, brother; Jane, mother; sisters, Margret Carbine, Jane Carbine, Sarah Carbine, and Mary Carbine. (Kent County Wills, Book L, page 3)

25. Susanna Carter was named as an heir, a daughter, in the will of Peter Calloway, probated March 28, 1769. (Kent County Wills, Book L, page 80)

26. Edward Carter was a witness to the will of Samuel Mileham, probated May 29, 1772. (Kent County Wills, Book L, page 113)

27. Letters of administration were granted to Mary Carter, widow, for the estate of Edward Carter, November 26, 1789. Heirs mentioned are Ruth Carter, Mary Carter, William Carter, Edward Carter, Rachel Carter, John Whitacre Carter, Edward Broadway Carter, and Sarah Bailey. The widow, Mary Carter, later married Joseph Dawson. (Kent County Wills, Book M, page 210)

28. Mary Carter was named as one of the administrators of the estate of John Flynn, January 11, 1790. (Kent County Wills, Book M, page 217)

29. Henry Carter was a witness to the will of John Burton (Scully) Skulley, probated August 3, 1792. (Kent County Wills, Book N, page 24)

30. The will of Catherine Vanleuveneigh, spinster, probated October 22, 1792, mentioned the children of her sister, Elizabeth Carter, as Catherine Carter, Betsey Carter, Susanna Carter, and Hannah Carter. (New Castle County, Delaware, Wills, Book N, page 298)

CARTER FAMILY NOTES (cont.)

31. Henry Carter was a witness to the will of John Dill, farmer, probated April 17, 1793. (Kent County Wills, Book N, page 45)

32. Henry Carter was a witness to the will of John Longfellow, farmer, probated March 18, 1794. (Kent County Wills, Book N, page 81)

33. Letters of administration were granted for the estate of Daniel Carter on April 14, 1794. (Kent County Wills, Book N, page 84)

34. John Carter, William Carter, and Edward Carter, were named as heirs, and grandsons, in the will of Henry Whitaker, probated September 25, 1794. Sarah Carter, Ruth Carter, and Mary Carter were also listed as granddaughters. (Kent County Wills, Book N, page 112)

35. Letters of administration were granted to Mary Carter, for the estate of Samuel Carter, on April 7, 1796. (Kent County Wills, Book N, page 146)

36. The will of Thomas Carter, probated November 10, 1796, shows his wife as Elizabeth Carter, with a son, John Carter, and a daughter, Elizabeth McDonnal. His will also shows that he had two sons in Ireland, Alexander Carter and Thomas Carter. (New Castle County, Delaware, Wills, Book O, page 198)

37. Henry Carter was a witness to the will of John Greer, probated May 5, 1797. (Kent County Wills, Book N, page 161)

38. Letters of administration were granted to Nathan Scott, for the estate of Susannah Carter, on December 7, 1799. (Kent County Wills, Book N, page 248)

Chapter 5.   The Gilder Family

THE GILDER FAMILY

HENRY GILDER (who died in 1721) married Mary Clawson and they had at least one child, Reuben Gilder (who died in 1775).

REUBEN GILDER (son of Henry and Mary (Clawson) Gilder) bought from Caesar Rodney, Sheriff, on February 24, 1757, one hundred acres of land formerly belonging to Robert Caton, which was located about two miles west of Camden, Delaware, on the south side of the road to Willow Grove. Reuben Gilder's will was probated April 5, 1775. (Kent County Wills, Book L, page 168) The name of his wife is unknown, but he had five children:

(1) Henry Gilder (who died about 1784) married Tamar Dunning from Camden, Delaware, and had five children.
(2) John Gilder who married as his second wife, Unity (Lowber) Berry (1748-1825) and had four children.
(3) Dr. Reuben Gilder who fought a duel in February 1762 with a Mr. Barryford, a member of the South Carolina Assembly.
(4) Ann Gilder who married William Adkinson.
(5) Elizabeth Gilder.

HENRY GILDER and his wife, Tamar (Dunning) Gilder, had five children:

(1) John Gilder who died in 1799.
(2) Nancy Gilder who died in 1803.
(3) Elizabeth Gilder (1780-1875) who married David Marvel (1775-1866).
(4) Sarah Gilder who married Batchelder Chance.
(5) Reuben Gilder who married and had one son, William Hughes Gilder, who married Mary Howard of Baltimore.

JOHN GILDER and his wife, Unity (Lowber)(Berry) Gilder, had four children:

(1) Reuben Gilder who married Margret Wallace of Philadelphia.
(2) Henry Gilder who married Ann Murphy of Centerville, Maryland, and had one son, Clarence Philip Ludlow Murphy Gilder.
(3) John Gilder who married Magdaline Leonard.
(4) Unity Gilder (1781-1865) who married Daniel James Jackson (1782-1866)

Unity Lowber, whose second husband was John Gilder, married Joseph Berry as her first husband and they had two children: (1) Captain Peter Berry of Philadelphia who left no children; and (2) William Berry of Frederica, Delaware, a merchant, who married Mary Leach.

William and Mary (Leach) Berry had two daughters:

(1) Sarah Berry (1781-1831) who married Able Harris and had eight children.
(2) Ann Berry (1782-1864) who married Robert Broadway as her first husband, in 1803, and had one son and three daughters; who married a second time in 1814 and had one son and three daughters; and who married a third time to David Marvel, in 1826, and had one daughter, Emma Marvel (1827-1828).

REUBEN GILDER and his wife, Margret (Wallace) Gilder had nine children:

(1) John Gilder (1811-1844).
(2) Sarah Ann Gilder (1813-1857) who married John Stierley.
(3) Margret Jane Gilder (1815-1820).
(4) Unity Gilder (1818-1890) who married William Alford, Jr. (1813-1869).
(5) Ann Emaline Gilder (1818-1877) who married Caleb Scattergood on January 18, 1846.
(6) Margret Gilder (1822-1898) who married James Chambers (he died in 1884).
(7) Mary Amanda Pennell Gilder (1824-1850).
(8) Caroline Gilder (1826-1907) who married Christopher Jacoby.
(9) Reuben Gilder (1828-1832).

Daniel James and Unity (Gilder) Jackson had six children:

(1) Jane Berry Jackson, born in 1814, who married William Curtis Lowber.
(2) John Henry Jackson who married Mary Ellen Montague.
(3) Elizabeth Ann Jackson who married Elijah Morris.
(4) Henrietta Jackson who married Clement Novell as her first husband, and Jacob Graham as her second husband.
(5) Daniel James Jackson, born in 1824, who married Mary R. Firsthwait as his first wife, and Rachel Augur as his second wife, by whom he had a son, Frank Jackson.
(6) Unity Jackson who died at age 16.

David and Elizabeth (Gilder) Marvel had a daughter, Sarah Gilder Marvel (1812-1889) who married Robert W. Reynolds (1803-1863), and they had a daughter, Elizabeth Reynolds, who married Edward J. Carter.

JOHN GILDER and his wife, Magdaline (Leonard) Gilder, had six children:

(1) Rev. John Leonard Gilder who married Emma Holden.
(2) Rev. William K. Gilder who married but his wife's name is unknown.
(3) Ella Wright Gilder who married John Bottoroff and had a son, Gilder Bottoroff.
(4) Francis Ann Gilder.
(5) Unity Almire Gilder who married George Alfred West.
(6) Sarah Magdaline Gilder who married Captain Robert Little, but had no children.

William Curtis and Jane Berry (Jackson) Lowber had six children:

(1) Peter Edward Lowber who married and had six children.
(2) Elizabeth Ann Lowber who married and had three children.
(3) C. Henry Lowber who married Mary Louisa Carter and had three children.
(4) Daniel Whitely Lowber.
(5) John Gilder Lowber who married and had two children.
(6) Fannie Taylor Lowber who married and had one child.

John Henry and Mary Ellen (Montague) Jackson had five children: (1) Unity Jackson; (2) Charles Jackson; (3) John Henry Jackson; (4) Anna T. Jackson; and (5) Franklin Jackson.

Clement and Henrietta (Jackson) Novell had four children. (He was her first husband): (1) Alvina Novell; (2) Thomas Novell; (3) Emma Jane Novell; and (4) John S.W. Novell.

Henrietta (Jackson) Novell married Jacob Graham Lewis as her second husband, but there is no record of children.

Daniel James and Mary R. (Firsthwait) Jackson (his first wife) had seven children: (1) McElroy Jackson; (2) Gilda Davis Jackson; (3) Leonard Asbury Jackson; (4) Ernest Andrew Jackson; (5) Robert E. Jackson; (6) Annie E. Jackson; and (7) John Henry Frank Jackson.

John and Sarah Ann (Gilder) Stierley had four children: (1) William N. Stierley who had offices at 31 Broad Street, New York, in 1884; (2) Elmira Gilder Stierley who married Robert Lee but had no children; (3) Sarah Gilder Stierley who married Robert H. Taylor; and (4) Emma Lee Stierley who married Joseph Howard Klien.

William and Unity (Gilder) Alford, Jr., had seven children:

(1) George William Alford who married Emma Findlay.
(2) Augustus Alford who married Caroline Brooks but had no children.
(3) Henry Crawford Alford (1846-1855).
(4) Reuben Gilder Alford who married Ella Jane Brooke as his first wife and had two sons who died young; who married Mary Ellen duBree as his second wife and had a son, Newell Gilder Alford.

(5) Anna Margret Alford, born in 1851.
(6) Charles Morris Alford who married Caroline _____
    and had two sons and one daughter.
(7) Clara Virginia Alford who married E. Kunkle and
    had a daughter, Grace Alford Kunkle.

Caleb and Ann Emaline (Gilder) Scattergood had five children: (1) Joshua Scattergood, born in 1847; (2) Harry Scattergood, born in 1849; (3) Caleb Scattergood, born in 1860; (4) Sallie May Scattergood (May 21, 1871-1921) who married Edward B. Carter on February 21, 1898; and (5) Gilder Scattergood who died an infant.

James and Margret (Gilder) Chambers had two children: (1) James H. Chambers, born in 1858, who married Francis Rebecca Forman, but had no children; and (2) Errickson Chambers (1860-1890).

Christopher and Caroline (Gilder) Jacoby had four children: (1) Wallace Jacoby; (2) Mary Jacoby; (3) Margaret Jacoby; and (4) Linwood Jacoby.

REV. JOHN LEONARD GILDER and his wife, Emma (Holden) Gilder, had two children: (1) William Fiske Gilder who married and lived at 3632 Chesnut Street, Philadelphia; and (2) Henry Mulford Gilder who married Grace Bedwin.

REV. WILLIAM K. GILDER and his wife, whose name is unknown, had five children:

(1) John Francis Gilder, a musician.
(2) Major William Henry Gilder, a journalist, author,
    and arctic traveler.
(3) Richard Watson Gilder who married Helen duKey of
    New York and had five children: (1) Rodman Gilder;
    (2) Dorothy Gilder; (3) George Coleman Gilder; (4)
    Francesca Gilder; and (5) Rosamund Gilder.
(4) Jeanette Gilder, an author, critic, and journalist.
(5) Joseph Benson Gilder who married Gwendolen Jackson
    of Jamaica, New York.

George Alfred and Unity Almire (Gilder) West had four children: (1) Charles Henry West who had no children; (2) William E. West who had no children; (3) Henry West who had no children; and Ellen West who married Robert Webster Day, a greatgrandson of Noah Webster, and had three children: Madaline Day; (2) Emily Day; and (3) Rodney Day.

GILDER FAMILY NOTES

1. Henry Gilder emigrated to Barbados in 1635, at age 18, after which he came to the United States.

2. John Gilder died in Cecil County, Maryland, in 1698.

3. Ann Gilder is named as a daughter of Abraham Golden, Senior, in his will probated July 7, 1749. (New Castle County Wills, Gook G, page 320)

4. The will of Ann Gilder, St. Georges Hundred, New Castle County, probated July 4, 1761, names heirs: daughters, Mary Pierce, Ann Gilder, Elizabeth Gibbs, Sarah Gilder; son, Joseph Pierce.

5. The will of Ann James, New Castle Hundred, New Castle County, probated May 7, 1767, names as sons: Abraham Golden, and William Golden, the heirs of Ann Gilder.

6. The file relating to the will of Joseph Berry, blacksmith, of Murderkill Hundred, administered June 12, 1773, indicates that his widow, Unity Berry, later married John Gilder. (Kent County Wills, Book L, Page 137)

7. Letters of administration were granted Susanah Gilder, for the estate of Henry Gilder, June 16, 1789. The file shows that there was a daughter, Mary Gilder; and that the widow, Susanah Gilder, later married Alexander Hamilton. (Kent County Wills, Book M, page 195)

8. John Gilder was a witness to the will of Janet Mair, probated March 12, 1790. (Kent County Wills, Book M, page 228)

9. John Gilder was a witness to the will of William Virdin, probated November 30, 1791. (Kent County Wills, Book N, page 7)

10. John Gilder was named as a son-in-law in the will of Peter Lowber, Sr., as were Peter Berry and William Berry (sons of Eunity Gilder), probated December 4, 1794. (Kent County Wills, Book N, page 90)

11. Unity Gilder, wife of John Gilder, was mentioned as an heir in the estate of Peter Lowber, farmer, of Murderkill Hundred. (Kent County Wills, Book N, page 147)

12. The will of John Gilder, probated April 5, 1799, shows heirs: brother, Reuben Gilder; John Jenkins (son of Thomas Jenkins). It also should be noted that a John Gilder was listed as a witness to the will. (Kent County Wills, Book N, page 232)

Chapter 6.   The Lowber Family

THE LOWBER FAMILY

PETER LOWBER came to America from Amsterdam, Holland, and was a resident of New York City in 1677. He moved to Delaware in 1684 and purchased land near Dover. The first deed on record was September 15, 1684. He eventually owned much land in Kent County, Delaware. His will was probated May 2, 1698. Peter Lowber married Gertrude Nieuland and they had five children:

(1) Mary Lowber who married Robert Nicholls (he died in 1697), and had at least one child, William Nicholls, who inherited land from his grandfather in England. He sold his land in America and disappeared; he may have gone to England.

(2) Agnes Lowber who married John Smith June 15, 1693.

(3) Margaret Lowber who married Stephen Pardee November 4, 1697. She died in 1727; Stephen Pardee died in 1759. As his second wife Stephen Pardee married Lydia _____ and had three children: (1) Mary Pardee; (2) Stephen Pardee; and (3) Margaret Pardee. Both Mary and Stephen died young. Margaret Pardee married Daniel Lewis and had five children: (1) Daniel Lewis who died single; (2) Stephen Lewis who married four times and had many descendants; (3) Ruthannah Lewis who married Jonathan Pleasanton; (4) Hannah Lewis who married John Gooden; and (5) Mary Lewis who died single.

(4) Gertie Lowber who married William Thistlewood in 1732.

(5) Michael Lowber (1677-1746) who married Unity Pardee as his first wife.

MICHAEL LOWBER was born in 1677 and baptized in Old Dutch Church, New York, October 17, 1677. He went with his father to Delaware in 1684. Michael and Unity (Pardee) Lowber had ten children:

(1) Unity Lowber (1701-1773) who married John Emerson.
(2) Susannah Lowber (1702-1763) who married Benjamin Frisbie as her first husband, and Davis Lewis as her second husband.
(3) Michael Lowber (1705-1750).

(4) Grace Lowber, born in 1712, who was married three times.

(5) Peter Lowber (1708-1794) who married Catherine Caine.
(6) Matthew Lowber (1710-1772) who married Elizabeth Manlove as his first wife and Hannah Robinson as his second wife.
(7) Gertie (Gartry) Lowber who married Thomas Muncey (who died in 1802) and had five children.
(8) Agnes Lowber who married William Walker and had five children. Agnes died in 1782 and William died in 1769.
(9) Margaret Lowber who married Abram Manlove (who died in 1749) and had four children.
(10) Isaac Lowber who married Mary Bowers and had eleven children.

As his second wife Michael Lowber married Rachel Brooke and had one child, Isaac Lowber (1744-1802) who married and had children.

John and Unity (Lowber) Emerson had four children: (1) Gove Emerson who married, had children, but all had died by 1900; (2) Michael Emerson who married Sarah Crumpton but had no children; (3) Jonathan Emerson who married Ruth Bowers and had many descendants; and (4) Vincent Emerson who married Mary Russell and had many descendants.

PETER LOWBER (1708-1794) married Catherine Caine. Peter and Catherine (Caine) Lowber had these children:

(1) Michael Lowber (he died in 1788) who married and whose descendants lived in Philadelphia and New York.
(2) Matthew Lowber (he died in 1785) whose descendants included J. Frank Allee.
(3) Peter Lowber (he died in 1790) whose descendants included Coopers, Merediths, Fraziers and Goodens.
(4) Daniel Lowber (he died in 1795) whose descendants included Coopers, Merediths and Cohees.
(5) Unity Lowber (1748-1825) who married Joseph Berry as her first husband and John Gilder as her second husband.
(6) Agnes Lowber who married Judge Benjamin Caton and had four children who lived in Kentucky.

MATTHEW LOWBER (1710-1772) married Elizabeth Manlove as his first wife. Matthew and Elizabeth (Manlove) Lowber had five children:

(1) Unity Lowber (December 2, 1738-May 10, 1784) who married William Virdin and had thirteen children.
(2) Matthew Lowber (September 5, 1741-June 9, 1795) who married Elizabeth Walker, a cousin, and had six children.
(3) Peter Lowber (November 24, 1745-January 21, 1807) was married five times and left descendants including Youngs and Lowbers of Frederica; Loftons of Milford; and Dr. Lowber of Wilmington.

(4) Susannah Lowber, born in 1743, who married _____ Dunborough, and had one son.
(5) Elizabeth Lowber, born in 1748.

MATTHEW LOWBER (1710-1772) married Hannah Robinson as his second wife. Matthew and Hannah (Robinson) Lowber had two children: (1) Miriam Lowber who never married; and (2) Jonathan Lowber (1752-1804) who married Sarah Brown.

JONATHAN LOWBER and his wife Sarah (Brown) Lowber had four children: (1) Elizabeth Lowber who married Michael Hall; (2) Rachel Lowber who married Samuel Willoughby as her first husband and Philip M___ as her second husband; (3) Ruth Lowber who married Samuel Warren; and (4) Sally Ann Lowber who married James Ridgeway.

Thomas and Gertie (Gartry)(Lowber) Muncey had five children: (1) Ruth Muncey who married William Jackson and had eleven children; (2) Gartry Muncey who married Armwell Lockwood and had nine children; (3) Thomas Muncey who married Elizabeth Hyland; (4) Susannah Muncey who married Wheeler Meredith; and (5) Levi Muncey who married Margaret Patton and had eight children. They moved to West Virginia in 1798.

Grace Lowber married Daniel Reynolds as her first husband. Daniel and Grace (Lowber) Reynolds had three children: (1) John Reynolds (1732-1783) who married Elizabeth _____ but had no children; (2) Michael Reynolds (1735-1794) who married Mariana Blackshave (she died in 1798) and had seven children; and (3) Susannah Reynolds who married John Gooden.

As her second husband Grace (Lowber) Reynolds married Thomas Brown. Thomas and Grace (Lowber)(Reynolds) Brown had one son, Thomas Brown, who married Martha Carpenter.

As her third husband Grace (Lowber)(Reynolds)(Brown) married Anthony Pendegarst. There is no record of any children.

Michael and Mariana (Blackshave) Reynolds had seven children:

(1) Robert Reynolds (he died in 1798) who married Elizabeth Blackshave.
(2) Michael Reynolds (he died in 1811) who married Unity Pratt as his first wife and Mary Emerson as his second wife.
(3) Daniel Reynolds (he died in 1810) who married Susan Robinson.
(4) Thomas Reynolds who married Francis Smith and had two children: (1) John Reynolds who married Margaret Wallace; and (2) Robert W. Reynolds who married Sarah Gilder Marvel.
(5) John Reynolds who married Catherine Duhadaway.
(6) George Reynolds.
(7) Letitia Reynolds who married John Gruwell.

Robert W. and Sarah Gilder (Marvel) Reynolds had eight children:
(1) Luther Martin Reynolds; (2) Elizabeth Reynolds who married Edward J. Carter; (3) Ellen Reynolds; (4) Sarah Gilder Reynolds; (5) Fannie Smith Reynolds; (6) Thomas Gilder Reynolds; (7) Robert John Reynolds; and (8) David Marvel Reynolds.

Edward J. and Elizabeth (Reynolds) Carter had ten children:
(1) Mary Evelyn Carter; (2) Herman Carter; (3) Sallie Gilder Carter who married ____ Rodney; (4) Robert W. Carter; (5) Julia Carter; (6) Edward Broadway Carter; (7) Luther Martin Carter; (8) Frank Carter; (9) Lizzie Carter; and (10) Aimee Carter.

John and Susannah (Reynolds) Gooden had one child, Ruth Gooden, born in 1759, who married Moses (or Aaron) Gooden as her first husband and had two children: (1) William Gooden; and (2) John Gooden (1779-1867) who married Annie Price (1790-1875).

John and Annie (Price) Gooden had ten children:

(1) Daniel Gooden (1811-1852) who married Rebecca Longfellow and had eight children: (1) John Gooden; (2) Hince Gooden; (3) Ann Gooden; (4) Esther Gooden; (5) James Gooden; (6) Mary Gooden; (7) Edward Gooden; and (8) Daniel Gooden.

(2) Thomas Gooden (1813-1892) who married Ellen Marvel (a daughter of David Marvel) and had thirteen children.

(3) William Gooden (1815-1896) who married Catherine Lowber Cooper and had eleven children, including John C. Gooden who married E.A. Broadway.

(4) John Gooden (1807-1903) who married Lydia Gruwell as his first wife and had nine children; who married Susan Gruwell as his second wife and had four children; and who married Wilhelmina Harrington as his third wife.

(5) Benjamin Gooden (1819-1894) who married Sally Ann Marvel as his first wife and had seven children; and who married Martha Ford as his second wife and had seven children.

(6) George W. Gooden, born in 1821, who died as an infant.

(7) Sally Ann Gooden, born in 1823, who married Daniel Dunn.

(8) Elizabeth Gooden, born in 1827.

(9) Ann Gooden (1830-1900) who married William Frasher.

(10) Isaac Gooden (1832-1882) who married Margretta
Green and had four children.

As her second husband Ruth Gooden (born in 1759) married James Marker. James and Ruth (Gooden) Marker had four children: (1) James Marker who married four times; (2) Mary Marker who married Jesse Cullen; (3) Ann Marker who married Jacob Welsh; and (4) Charlotte Marker who married Isaac Marker.

As her third husband Ruth Gooden (born in 1759) married William Skinner. William and Ruth (Gooden) Skinner had four children: (1) Elizabeth Skinner who married Thomas P. Kemp and had two children; (2) Miriam Skinner who married Jacob B. Kemp and had fourteen children; (3) John Skinner who married Julia A. Hicks and had eight children; and (4) William Skinner who married Letitia Gruwell.

Thomas and Martha (Carpenter) Brown had a son, Thomas Brown, who married Rachel Hazard. Thomas and Rachel (Hazard) Brown had four children:

(1) William Brown who married Elizabeth Ridgeway as his first wife and had one child, Sarah Elizabeth Brown, who married John Satterfield of Dover. William Brown married Eliza Stayton as his second wife and they had four children: (1) William Brown; (2) James Brown; (3) Mary Brown; and (4) Maria C. Brown.

(2) Henry Brown who married Martha Walker and had three children: (1) James Brown; (2) William Brown; and (3) a daughter whose name is not known.

(3) James Brown who married and moved to California.

(4) Thomas Brown who died August 17, 1831.

Thomas and Martha (Carpenter) Brown had another son, William Brown, who married Sarah Reynolds. William and Sarah (Reynolds Brown had five children:

(1) Thomas Brown who married Mary Lockwood and had three children: (1) Joseph Brown; (2) Susan Ann Brown; (3) Thomas A. Brown who married Blance Virdin and had two children, Ethel P. Brown and Blanche Brown.

(2) Susan Ann Brown who married Samuel A. Shorts and had four children: (1) Sarah Shorts; (2) Samuel Shorts; (3) Susan Ann Shorts; and (4) Angaline Shorts.

(3) William C. Brown who married Julia A. Shorts and had three children: (1) Elizabeth Ann Brown; (2) Sarah C. Brown; and (3) Samuel Adams Brown.

(4) Emeline F. Brown who married Captain John Smithers and had three children: (1) Waitman Smithers; (2) Sally Ann Smithers; and (3) Emma B. Smithers.

(5) Sarah Brown who married Daniel Harrington and had four children: (1) Theodore Harrington; (2) Rosalee Harrington; (3) Jane Harrington; and (4) Susan Emma Harrington.

Thomas and Martha (Carpenter) Brown had a daughter, Sarah Brown, who married Samuel Harrington. Samuel and Sarah (Brown) Harrington had six children:

(1) Thomas Brown Harrington who married Agnes B. Moore and had three children: (1) James Henry Harrington; (2) Mary Elizabeth Harrington; and (3) Sarah Moore Harrington.

(2) William B. Harrington who married Elizabeth Luff Warren and had five children: (1) Warren Harrington; (2) Susannah Harrington; (3) Alex Lowber Harrington; (4) Anna Harrington; and (5) John Wesley Harrington.

(3) Henry Harrington who married Letitia Graham and had six children: (1) Isaac Harrington; (2) Samuel Harrington; (3) Thomas Harrington; (4) Martha Harrington; (5) Mary Elizabeth Harrington; and (6) Thomas Brown Harrington.

(4) Samuel Harrington who married Sally Ann Moore and had five children: (1) Sally Harrington; (2) Vincent Harrington; (3) Mary Catherine Harrington; (4) Samuel Harrington; and (5) Thomas Brown Harrington

(5) Peter Lowber Harrington who married Mary S. Moore and had three children: (1) Agnes Harrington; (2) Elizabeth Harrington; and (3) Mary Catherine Harrington.

(6) Mathilda Harrington who was born in 1804 and died in 1811.

Benjamin and Sally Ann (Marvel) Gooden (she was his first wife) had seven children: (1) Philip Gooden; (2) Elizabeth Ann Gooden; (3) Isaac Gooden; (4) David Marvel Gooden; (5) Sarah Catherine Gooden; (6) Charles Gooden; and (7) Thomas Gooden.

William and Catherine Lowber (Cooper) Gooden had eleven children: (1) John C. Gooden; (2) Peter L. Gooden; (3) Henry Gooden; (4) Susan Gooden; (5) Samuel Gooden; (6) Elvina Gooden; (7) Anna Gooden; (8) Susan Cooper Gooden; (9) William Cooper Gooden; (10) William Gilbert Gooden; and (11 Albert W. Gooden.

William and Agnes (Lowber) Walker had five children, one son, and four daughters whose names are unknown. The son, John Walker, married, moved to Maryland, and had five children: (1) John Walker; (2) Unity Walker who married _____ Vandever; (3) Elizabeth Walker who married Matthew Lowber, a cousin; (4) Alice Walker who married Caleb Sipple; and Susannah Walker who married Henry Harrington.

Abram and Margaret (Lowber) Manlove had four children, one daughter, and three sons. Only the name of one son, Mark Manlove, is known; he married Violet Cummins.

LOWBER FAMILY NOTES

1. Susanna Lowber was listed in the will of Catherine Miles, probated April 24, 1695. (New Castle County Wills, Book O, page 77)

2. Gartre Lober, the elder, and Margaret Lober, were witnesses to the will of William Nichols, probated March 6, 1697. (Kent County Wills, Book A, page 20)

3. Michael Lowber and Grace Lowber were witnesses to the will of Mary Lenton, probated March 28, 1727. (Kent County Wills, Book F, page 24)

4. Unity Lowber and Michall Lowber were witnesses to an affirmation concerning the will of James Brooks, probated June 26, 1727. (Kent County Wills, Book F, page 29)

5. Michael Lowber was a witness to the will of Nathaniel Lenton probated February 12, 1718. (Kent County Wills, Book D, page 6)

6. Michael Lowber was a witness to the will of Moses Whitaker, probated February 10, 1725. (Kent County Wills, Book F, page 1)

7. Peter Lowber was named as one of the administrators of the estate of William Thistlewood, May 10, 1733. (Kent County Wills, Book H, page 105)

8. Peter Lowber was a witness to the will of Owen Cain, probated December 9, 1741. (Kent County Wills, Book I, page 126)

9. Matthew Lowber was a witness to the will of William Trippet, probated November 26, 1744. (Kent County Wills, Book I, page 90)

10. Matthew Lowber was a witness to the will of David Lewis, probated January 12, 1744. (Kent County Wills, Book I, page 101)

11. The will of Michael Lowber, probated April 7, 1746, shows the following heirs: wife, Rachel Lowber; daughters, Unity Emerson, Gartry Muncy, Margarett Manlove, Agnes Walker, and Susannah Lewis; sons, Michael Lowber, Peter Lowber, Matthew Lowber, and Isaac Lowber; grandchildren of daughter Grace Brown; grandsons Michael Lowber (son of Peter Lowber), John Reynolds, Michael Reynolds, Michael Emerson (son of Unity and John Emerson); granddaughter Susannah Reynolds. (Kent County Wills, Book I, page 122)

LOWBER FAMILY NOTES (cont.)

    12. Peter Lowber was a witness to the will of Samuel Robinson, probated January 20, 1747. (Kent County Wills, Book I, page 177)

    13. Peter Lowber was executor of the estate of Daniel Cain, probated March 28, 1748. (Kent County Wills, Book I, page 192)

    14. Robert Lowber was a witness to the will of John Hawkins, probated November 23, 1748. (Kent County Wills, Book I, page 246)

    15. Matthew Lowber was a witness to the will of Thomas Dawson, probated January 12, 1754. (Kent County Wills, Book K, page 87)

    16. Elizabeth Clark, widow of John Clark, farmer, married Peter Lowber. (Kent County Wills, Book K, page 104) (Letters of Administration were granted to Elizabeth Clark January 25, 1755.)

    17. Mary Lowber was listed as a daughter in the will of John Bowers, probated June 25, 1766. (Kent County Wills, Book L, page 12)

    18. Michael Lowber was a witness to the will of Francis Cain, probated April 30, 1764. (Kent County Wills, Book K, page 340)

    19. The will of Matthew Lowber, Sr., probated July 29, 1772, named these heirs: wife, Hannah Lowber; sons, Matther Lowber, Jr., Peter Lowber, Jonathan Lowber; daughters, Susanna Lowber, Elizabeth Lowber, Meriam Lowber; son-in-law, William Virdin; granddaughter, Elizabeth Virdin, daughter of William Virdin; grandson, Hugh Durborrow. Related documents mention a daughter, Susanah Durbrow. (Kent County Wills, Book L, page 117)

    20. Letters of administration were granted to Mary Lober, widow of Peter Lober (Lowber) March 30, 1770. Related files show that Mary Lober later married Thomas Davis. (Kent County Wills, Book L, page 74)

    21. The will of William Brown, probated May 15, 1778, showed as an heir, a daughter, Sarah Lowber (wife of Jonathan Lowber). (Kent County Wills, Book L, page 200)

    22. Letters of administration were granted to Peter Lowber, Jr., for the estate of Mary Stuart, on March 9, 1782. (Kent County Wills, Book L, page 231)

LOWBER FAMILY NOTES (cont.)

23. Michael Lowber and Daniel Lowber were witnesses to the will of Martha Morris, made May 23, 1782. (Kent County Wills, Book L, page 263)

24. The file on the estate of Henry Harrington, probated February 4, 1784, showed that Agnes Harrington married Peter Lowber. (Kent County Wills, Book L, page 269)

25. Peter Lowber was an executor of the will of Alexander Huston, Murderkill Hundred, probated June 11, 1785; and Catherine Lowber was a witness to the will. (Kent County Wills, Book M, page 58)

26. Isaac Lowber was granted letters of administration on the estate of William Hefferman, August 12, 1785. (Kent County Wills, Book M, page 61)

27. Peter Lowber, Jr., was granted letters of administration on the estate of Caleb Sipple, January 4, 1788. (Kent County Wills, Book M, page 166)

28. Peter Lowber was granted letters of administration on the estate of Catherine Lowber, May 1, 1791. (Kent County Wills, Book M, page 274)

29. Isaac Lowber was a witness to the will of Winlock Hall, farmer, of Mispillion Hundred, probated April 4, 1791. (Kent County Wills, Book M, page 272)

30. The will of Peter Lowber, Sr., probated December 4, 1794, named heirs: son, Daniel Lowber; daughters, Catharine Duhadaway, Eunity Gilder; granddaughter, Catharine Cooper (daughter of Peter Lowber, deceased); grandsons, Benjamin Catron, Peter Catron, John Catron (sons of Benjamin Catron, deceased), Jacob Duhadaway (son of Catharine Duhadaway), Peter Lowber (son of Daniel Lowber), John Lowber (son of Mathew Lowber, deceased); daughter-in-law, Mary Lowber (wife of Daniel Lowber); son-in-law, John Gilder; John Hatfield and Sarah Hatfield (children of William Hatfield); William Berry and Peter Berry (sons of Eunity Gilder). (Kent County Wills, Book N, page 90)

31. Daniel Lowber was granted letters of administration on the estate of Peter Lowber, December 11, 1794. (Kent County Wills, Book N, page 95)

32. Peter Lowber was one of the administrators of the estate of John Gibb, January 27, 1790. (Kent County Wills, Book M, page 217)

LOWBER FAMILY NOTES (cont.)

33. Peter Lowber was granted letters of administration on the estate of Peter Virden, September 30, 1793. (Kent County Wills, Book N, page 55)

34. Peter Lowber was granted letters of administration of the estate of Mathew Lowber, July 30, 1795. Heirs mentioned were William Lowber, Peter Lowber, Agnes Jackson (wife of Jonathan Jackson), and Elizabeth Jackson (wife of _____ Jackson). (Kent County Wills, Book M, page 127)

35. The will of Daniel Lowber, probated February 18, 1796, named heirs: wife, Mary Lowber; sons, William Lowber, Peter Lowber. (Kent County Wills, Book N, page 142)

36. The estate of Peter Lowber, farmer, of Murderkill Hundred administered by Mary Lowber, May 9, 1796, mentioned heirs: Daniel Lowber, Peter Lowber, Catherine Duhadaway, Peter Caton, Benjamin Caton, John Caton, Sarah Vanburkeloe, and Unity Gilder (wife of John Gilder) (Kent County Wills, Book N, page 148)

37. Matthew Lowber was a witness to the will of Robert Clark, probated July 12, 1796. (Kent County Wills, Book N, page 149)

38. Peter Lowber was granted letters of administration on the estate of Nathaniel Summers, September 9, 1796. (Kent County Wills, Book N, page 153)

39. Letters of administration were issued to Letitia Lowber, widow, on the estate of William Lowber, October 31, 1796. Heirs mentioned were: Sarah Lowber, Susannah Lowber. The file shows that Letitia Lowber later married James Shaw. (Kent County Wills, Book N, page 154)

40. The will of William Morris, probated February 16, 1797, showed that one of the heirs was Mary Lowber, a widow. (Kent County Wills, Book N, page 167)

Lowber House;
Magnolia, Delaware

Chapter 7.   The Marvel Family

THE MARVEL FAMILY

ROBERT MARVEL appeared in Sussex County, Delaware, records in 1754, when he bought fifty acres of land. His will was probated July 25, 1755. The will of his wife, Rachel Marvel, was probated September 5, 1791. The Marvels came to Delaware from Worcester County, Maryland, and are believed to have been of Welch origin. Robert and Rachel Marvel had nine children: (1) Ann Marvel; (2) Thomas Marvel; (3) Robert Marvel; (4) Patience Marvel; (5) Philip Marvel who married Comfort Rodney; (6) Rachel Marvel; (7) Betsey Marvel; (8) Joseph Marvel; and (9) Chloeg Marvel.

PHILIP MARVEL (he died in 1795) and his wife, Comfort (Rodney) Marvel (1728-1802) had nine children:

(1) Thomas Marvel, born March 8, 1761.
(2) Rhoda Marvel, born February 18, 1763.
(3) William Marvel, born May 16, 1765, who married Sarah P____.
(4) Aaron Marvel, born December 12, 1767.
(5) Mary Marvel, born April 29, 1770.
(6) Alice Marvel, born May 17, 1772, who was married December 6, 1798.
(7) David Marvel, born January 18, 1775, who died September 13, 1866, and married Elizabeth Gilder (1780-1825).
(8) Philip Marvel, born February 9, 1779.
(9) Chloeg Marvel, born May 10, 1782.

WILLIAM MARVEL and his wife, Sarah (P____) Marvel had ten children, one of whom was Mary Marvel who married James Shiles (son of Eli and Rachel (Cardiff) Shiles). James and Mary (Marvel) Shiles had a son, John W. Shiles, who owned land in Broad Creek Hundred, Sussex County, which had been left to him by his grandfather, William Marvel.

THOMAS MARVEL (1761-1801), son of Philip and Comfort (Rodney) Marvel, married Mary ____ and had a son, Joseph Marvel, who married Mary ____. (Joseph Marvel died in 1817.)

JOSEPH MARVEL, son of Thomas and Mary Marvel, and his wife, Mary (____) Marvel, also had a son named Joseph Marvel, who married Sarah Ann ____. Joseph and Sarah Ann Marvel had a son, Joseph H. Marvel, who was elected Governor of Delaware in 1894, but died about three months after he was inaugurated. Governor Marvel had two sons, Joshua G. Marvel, and Joseph H. Marvel.

DAVID MARVEL and his first wife, Elizabeth (Gilder) Marvel, had fifteen children:

(1) Philip Marvel (December 9, 1799-May 28, 1885).
(2) Henry Marvel (January 20, 1801-March 13, 1801).
(3) John Gilder Marvel (1802-1847) who married Rachel Green.
(4) Sarah Gilder Marvel (June 5, 1803-May 4, 1874). who married Robert W. Reynolds.
(5) David Marvel, born October 8, 1804.
(6) Warner Marvel (April 15, 1806-June 13, 1818).
(7) Henry Gilder Marvel (November 16, 1807-December 14, 1891).
(8) Thomas Jenkins Marvel (May 15, 1809-February 22, 1895) who married Sally Ann Broadway.
(9) Elizabeth Ann Marvel (December 24, 1811-June 19, 1845).
(10) Susan Marvel, born June 15, 1813, who married Isaac Godwin.
(11) Ann Marvel (June 24, 1816-July 25, 1887) who married J. Williams.
(12) Ellen Marvel (June 24, 1816-October 15, 1880) who married Thomas Gooden (1813-1873).
(13) Rachel Marvel (July 25, 1818-August 4, 1818).
(14) Rembra G. Marvel (July 25, 1818-June 23, 1851) who married J.W. Dill and had two daughters.
(15) Harriet Marvel, born August 12, 1819, who married D.D. Dunn (a grandson of Governor Dondal of Pennsylvania) and had a daughter who married as her first husband John Carter.

As his second wife David Marvel married Mrs. Ann (Berry) Lockwood on January 19, 1826. They had a daughter, Emma Marvel, born July 4, 1827, who died in November 1828.

Mrs. Ann (Berry)(Lockwood) Marvel died in 1864. She was the daughter of William and Sarah (Leach) Berry. In 1803 she married Robert Broadway, who died in 1824. In 1816 she married Thomas Lockwood, who died in 1824. In 1826, as her third husband, she married David Marvel. Her father, William Berry, was the son of Joseph and Unity (Lowber) Berry.

Thomas and Ellen (Marvel) Gooden had thirteen children:

(1) George Henry Gooden (October 29, 1836-December 4, 1864) who married Mary Catherine Caulk and had three children: (1) Edgar Gooden; (2) George Gooden; and (3) Henry Gooden.

(2) Elizabeth Gooden, born April 9, 1838, who married Ezekiel L. Cooper.

(3) Caroline Cooper Gooden (July 30, 1840 - January 19, 1843).

(4) William Tennessee Gooden, born April 1, 1842, who married Catherine Lowber Cooper.

(5) Louise Gooden, born January 6, 1844, who married Charles T. Pepper.
(6) Robert Gooden (January 21, 1846-January 23, 1846).
(7) Sallie Gooden (December 27, 1846-April 18, 1865).
(8) Anna Gooden, born January 20, 1849.
(9) Ellen Gooden, born December 25, 1850, who married Henry Pratt.
(10) Thomas Marvel Gooden, born December 3, 1853, who married Annie R. Rust.
(11) Isaac Kline Gooden, born November 2, 1854, who married Lou Pepper.
(12) Clara Gooden (September 12, 1856-July 15, 1858).
(13) Fannie Reynolds Gooden, born July 18, 1858, who married Green Cooper.

Charles T. and Louise (Gooden) Pepper had eleven children: (1) Emile White Pepper; (2) Lola Pepper; (3) Byron Pepper; (4) Viola Pepper; (5) Thomas Gooden Pepper; (6) Lorenzo Pepper; (7) Norval Pepper; (8) Ellie Pepper; (9) Charles Pepper, who died young; (10) Zona Pepper; and (11) Lee Pepper.

Copy of undated newspaper clipping concerning Hon. David T. Marvel, Secretary of State

"Hon. David T. Marvel, Secretary of State, was born in Sussex County, Delaware, November 2, 1851. He is the son of ex-Sheriff Joshiah P. Marvel, who is now Prothonotary of Sussex County. Mr. Marvel was graduated at Princeton College in 1873. He registered as a law student under the direction of Hon. Thomas F. Bayard in the fall of 1873. During the school years of 1873 and 1874 he taught Higher Mathematics at Reynold's Academy, Wilmington. He then took a two year course at Harvard Law School and was for a time private Secretary for Mr. Bayard in Washington. He was afterwards admitted to the Bar in Sussex County, and has since practiced his profession in Georgetown. He was clerk of the House of Representatives of this State in 1881. He was Attorney for the Levy Court of Sussex County from 1883 until 1889. Governor Reynolds appointed Mr. Marvel, Secretary of State, January 20, 1891. The Legislature of 1891 directed him to codify the laws of the State, in which work he is now engaged. Mr. Marvel was married February 17, 1885, to Miss Mary R. Wootten, daughter of the late Attorney-General Wootten, and who was also a grand-daughter of the late Judge Wootten and ex-Governor Burton. Mr. Marvel has always been an active and influential Democrat."

Chapter 8.   The Register Family

THE REGISTER FAMILY

JEREMIAH REGISTER, of England, married Elizabeth Baron on July 23, 1743. He died in 1774. Jeremiah and Elizabeth (Baron) Register had eight children, as set forth in the will of Jeremiah Register, probated April 11, 1774. (Kent County Wills, Book L, page 152) (1) Rachel (Register) Crawford, wife of Oliver Crawford; (2) Leaer (Register) Cummins; (3) John Register; (4) Isaac Register; (5) Robert Register; (6) Jeremiah Register; (7) Francis Register; and (8) Elija Register.

ISAAC REGISTER (1765-1815) married Mary Ann Hatfield. Isaac and Mary Ann (Hatfield) Register had at least one child, Mary C. Register (1801-1836) who married Edward B. Carter (1790-1839).

Edward B. and Mary C. (Register) Carter had a son, Edward J. Carter, born in 1824, who married Elizabeth Reynolds daughter of Robert W. Reynolds and Sarah Gilder (Marvel) Reynolds.

REGISTER FAMILY NOTES

1. John Register was granted letters of administration on the estate of William Register, January 15, 1708. (Kent County Wills, Book B, page 70)

2. John Register was granted letters of administration on the estate of William Register March 5, 1719. (Kent County Wills, Book D, page 15)

3. John Register was a witness to the will of John Bell, probated December 17, 1729. (Kent County Wills, Book G, page 33)

4. The will of John Register, carpenter, probated May 20, 1734, shows heirs: wife, Sarah Register; son, John Register; daughter, Mary Clark; grandson, John Clark. (Kent County Wills, Book H, page 52)

5. Sarah Register was listed as an heir, and granddaughter, in the will of Joshua Clayton, probated January 26, 1761. (Kent County Wills, Book K, page 254)

6. Robert Regester was a witness to the will of Jonathan Ozbun, probated November 11, 1773. (Kent County Wills, Book L, page 143)

7. Robert Register was listed as executor in the will of William Porter, probated November 10, 1780. (Kent County Wills, Book L, page 219)

8. Ruth Register was granted letters of administration to the estate of Robert Register, April 19, 1784. (Kent County Wills, Book M, page 21)

9. John Register was one of the administrators of the estate of Samuel Long March 12, 1784. (Kent County Wills, Book M, page 20)

10. Thomas Corse was made administrator of the estate of Robert Register, November 9, 1790. (Kent County Wills, Book M, page 257)

11. Sophia Register, formerly Sophia Edmondson, was named as an heir in the will of Thomas Edmondson, administered October 17, 1796. (Kent County Wills, Book N, page 153)

REGISTER FAMILY NOTES (cont.)

12. Francis Register was granted letters of administration to the estate of Marian Fields on January 9, 1797. (Kent County Wills, Book N, page 161)

13. Francis Register was granted letters of administration on the estate of Maryann Mileham, May 12, 1798. (Kent County Archives, Vol. A35, page 55)

14. Francis Register was granted letters of administration on the estate of William Wyth, yeoman, of Murderkill Hundred, May 15, 1799. (Kent County Archives, Vol. A56, page 188)

Chapter 9.   The Reynolds Family

THE REYNOLDS FAMILY

JOHN REYNOLDS reportedly came from England to Delaware. On November 12, 1722, he purchased land in Kent County. When he died in 1729 he owned about four hundred acres of land. His will lists him as John Reynolds, Sr., a farmer. Some information indicates that he had two wives, with three children by the first wife, but this has not been verified. When his will was probated May 2, 1729, his wife was shown as Elizabeth Reynolds. His children were: (1) Daniel Reynolds; (2) George Reynolds; (3) Robert Reynolds; (4) John Reynolds; (5) Sara Reynolds; (6) Elizabeth Reynolds; and (7) Mary Reynolds.

DANIEL REYNOLDS (son of John Reynolds) married Grace Lowber. Daniel and Grace (Lowber) Reynolds had three children: He died in 1736; his will was probated June 14, 1736. Grace Lowber was born in 1712. Their children were:

(1) Susannah Reynolds who married John Gooden.
(2) John Reynolds who married Elizabeth _____ but had no children, and died in October 1773. His widow later married James White.
(3) Michael Reynolds who married Miriam Blackshave.

John and Susannah (Reynolds) Gooden had one child, Ruth Gooden, who married Moses (or Aaron) Gooden. Moses and Ruth (Gooden) Gooden had two children: (1) William Gooden; and (2) John Gooden (1779-1867) who married Anna Price (1790-1874) and had ten children.

MICHAEL REYNOLDS married Miriam Blackshave. He volunteered to serve in the French and Indian Wars on April 25, 1757. He was listed as No. 23 on the muster roll of Captain John Caton. Michael and Miriam (Blackshave) Reynolds had seven children:

(1) Robert Reynolds who married Elizabeth Blackshave.
(2) Michael Reynolds who married _____ Pratt as his first wife.
(3) Thomas Reynolds (1769-1816) who married Francis Smith.
(4) Daniel Reynolds who married Susan Robinson.
(5) John Reynolds who married Catherine Duhadaway and had two sons, Daniel Reynolds and John Reynolds. He died in February 1790.
(6) George Reynolds who married, settled on the Monongahalia River near Pittsburg, Pennsylvania and had three children.
(7) Letitia Reynolds who married John Gruwell.

MICHAEL REYNOLDS who married _____ Pratt had one child, Thomas Pratt Reynolds, who married Rebecca Maginnis as his first wife and Martha C. Willoughby as his second wife. Thomas Pratt and Martha G.

(Willoughby) Reynolds had two children: (1) Martha Willoughby Reynolds, born in 1851, who married John P. Emerson; and (2) Mary Elizabeth Reynolds, born in 1853, who married Paris M. Lenick.

MICHAEL REYNOLDS married as his second wife Mary Emerson. He died in 1811; she died in 1793. Michael and Mary (Emerson) Reynolds had four children: (1) George Reynolds who apparently never married; (2) Mary Elizabeth Reynolds who married Joseph Graham; (3) Miriam Reynolds who married Benjamin Graham as her first husband; and (4) Susan Ann Reynolds who married James G. Massey.

Joseph and Mary Elizabeth (Reynolds) Graham had six children. Joseph was born in 1803 and died in 1877; Mary was born in 1806 and died in 1857. Their children were:

(1) Michael Reynolds Graham who died in Arkansas in 1851, at age 21.
(2) Jonathan Graham who married Elizabeth Dailey of Cavsonville, Kentucky.
(3) Moses Graham who married Mary Dailey of Cavsonville, Kentucky. Moses Graham was born in 1840 and died in 1878.
(4) George R. Graham who married Mary L. Tinley. He was born in 1826 and died in 1889.
(5) Susan Graham who married Nathan Anthony.
(6) Mary Graham who married William A. Dill.

Benjamin and Miriam (Reynolds) Graham had one child, Thomas Reynolds Graham, who died young. As her second husband, Miriam (Reynolds) Graham married Thomas Sipple and had one child, John Reynolds Sipple, who lived near Felton, Delaware.

James G. and Susan Ann (Reynolds) Massey had three children. (Susan Ann (Reynolds) Massey was born in 1810 and died in 1895.) The names of their children are:

(1) Hannah Massey who is believed to have died young.
(2) Dr. James Thomas Massey who married Anna E. Massey but had no children.
(3) Rev. William A. Massey who married Mary Ann Coolbough, and had a son, William Everett Massey, who married and had two children, Sarah Massey and Jane Massey.

THOMAS REYNOLDS married Francis Smith (December 22, 1783-May 9, 1824) and they had two children:

(1) Robert Wright Reynolds (December 5, 1803-February 5, 1863) who married Sarah Gilder Marvel. He owned about fifteen hundred acres of land when he died.

(2) John Reynolds (August 22, 1809-January 7, 1874) who married Margaret Wallace (September 21, 1812-April 5, 1889).

ROBERT WRIGHT REYNOLDS and his wife Sarah Gilder (Marvel) Reynolds had eight children:

(1) Luther Martin Reynolds (1824-1890) who married Mary L. Willis.

(2) Elizabeth Reynolds (August 19, 1826-August 26, 1901) who married Edward J. Carter and had ten children: (1) Mary Evelyn Carter; (2) Herman Carter; (3) Sallie Carter; (4) Robert W. Carter; (5) Julia Carter; (6) Edward Broadway Carter; (7) Luther Carter; (8) Frank Reynolds Carter; (9) Lizzie Reynolds Carter; and (10) Simca Carter.

(3) Ellen Reynolds (1828-1846) who married William Thawley.

(4) Sarah Smith Reynolds (August 4, 1831-November 22, 1908) who married Robert D. Culbreth (1819-1908) and had a son, Dr. David Marvel Reynolds Culbreth, born December 4, 1855, who married Lizzie Gardner of Baltimore.

(5) Francis Smith Reynolds (August 26, 1833-February 10, 1906) who married William Clough (January 25, 1834-February 23, 1889).

(6) Thomas Gilder Reynolds (February 23, 1836-January 25, 1907) who married Julia Sutton as his first wife.

(7) Robert John Reynolds, born March 17, 1838, was Governor of Delaware. He married Lavenia L. Riggs (1840-1895) as his first wife.

(8) David Marvel Reynolds (January 30, 1846- July 3, 1851).

William and Francis Smith (Reynolds) Clough had one son, Reynolds Clough, born May 10, 1875, who married Annie Ethel Riggs on November 16, 1905, and had two children: (1) Frances Reynolds Clough, born August 5, 1906; and (2) David Culbreth Clough, born May 16, 1909.

THOMAS GILDER REYNOLDS and his first wife, Julia Sutton, had five children: (1) Lolo Reynolds who married Frank C. Mason of Easton, Maryland; (2) James N. Reynolds; (3) A. Edgerton Reynolds; (4) Fannie Reynolds; and (5) Julia Reynolds.

Thomas Gilder Reynolds as his second wife married Kate Geoghan.

ROBERT JOHN REYNOLDS and his first wife, Lavenia L. Riggs, had one son, Byron Reynolds (June 7, 1862-July 1898) who married Irene U. Williamson of Baltimore. As his second wife, Robert John Reynolds married Hester Thomas.

JOHN REYNOLDS and his wife, Margaret Wallace, had eight children:

(1) Margaret Jane Reynolds (1832-1902) who married O. Clifton (1827-1894).
(2) Robert Wallace Reynolds, born in 1834, who married A. Amerson, born in 1838.
(3) John Wallace Reynolds (1836-1892) who married S.G. Moore (1836-1894).
(4) Rebecca Burchell Reynolds, born in 1838, who married R.G. Dunn (1832-1893).
(5) Thomas Michael Reynolds.
(6) Francis Ann Reynolds, born in 1841, who married G.W. Graham.
(7) William Lewis Reynolds.
(8) Mary Ellen Reynolds, born February 23, 1849, who married Frank Barwick, born October 7, 1847.

DANIEL REYNOLDS and his wife, Susan Robinson, had five children. Daniel died in 1810. The names of their children were:

(1) Sarah Reynolds, born in 1788, who married William Brown and had six children.

(2) Letitia Reynolds who married Abner Wooters and had two children: (1) William Henry Wooters who died young, being killed in Arkansas; and (2) Elijah Wooters who married W.B. Dehorty.

(3) Barbara Reynolds (1803-1868) who married Thomas Tomlinson and had two children: (1) William Burton Tomlinson who married Lydia Burton; and (2) Daniel Reynolds Tomlinson, born in 1831, who married Ellen B. Kirk.

(4) Thomas Reynolds who married Emiline Foreman as his first wife; and who married Evetine Alliband as his second wife, by whom he had a son who was killed "by a cartwheel on the head."

(5) Daniel Reynolds (he died October 30, 1830) who married Sarah Tomlinson (she died in 1878) and they had a son, Thomas Reynolds, who married Sarah E. Salsbury.

William and Sarah (Reynolds) Brown had six children: (1) Thomas Brown (1812-1870) who married Mary Lockwood; (2) Susan Ann Brown (1814-1859) who married Samuel A. Short; (3) Martha Carpenter Brown who died young; (4) William C. Brown (1819-1896) who married Julia A.H. Short; (5) Emiline F. Brown who married Captain John Smithers; and (6) Sarah Brown who married David Harrington.

GEORGE REYNOLDS who settled on the Monongahalia River in Pennsylvania and his wife (whose name is unknown) had three children: (1) Robert Reynolds who married at Jefferson, Green County, Pennsylvania, and moved to Iowa had one son and three daughters; (2) Michael Reynolds who was living at Jefferson, Pennsylvania, in 1858; and (3) John Reynolds.

John and Letitia (Reynolds) Gruwell had four children:

(1) Daniel Gruwell who died single.

(2) Jacob Gruwell who died at Lafayette, Indiana.

(3) Jonathan Gruwell who married Kesiah Downham and had four children: (1) Letitia Gruwell who married Benjamin L. Reed; (2) Hannah Gruwell (1816-1881); (3) Isaac Gruwell who died young; and (4) Lydia Gruwell who married John Gooden and had nine children.

(4) Letitia Gruwell who married William Skinner and had three children: (1) Elizabeth Skinner who married Thomas B. Kemp; (2) Miriam Skinner who married Jacob B. Kemp; and (3) John Skinner who married Julia A. Kicks.

O. and Margaret Jane (Reynolds) Clifton had five children:

(1) John Clifton who married June E. Short and had two children, Florence Clifton and John Clifton, born in 1891.

(2) Dr. John W. Clifton, born in 1853, who married Emma Shaw Conner and had a son, Alfred Lee Clifton, born in 1881.

(3) Robert Clifton, born in 1855, who married Imogene Roe and had a son, Robert R. Clifton, born in 1898.

(4) Charles Curtin Clifton, born in 1857, who married Elizabeth Dehorty and had a son, Alfred Outen Clifton, born in 1887.

(5) Mary Clifton, born in 1864, who married Charles H. Burgess.

JOHN WALLACE REYNOLDS and his wife, S.G. Moore, had four children:

(1) Margaret Reynolds, born in 1858, who married Jacob Heyd and had a daughter, Susan George Heyd.
(2) John Wallace Reynolds, born in 1860, who married Mary Taylor.
(3) Annie Reynolds, born in 1869, who married William Credick, and had a son, Reynolds Credick, born in 1896.
(4) Clara Lacey Reynolds, born in 1871, who married Reynear Saulsbury.

R.G. and Rebecca Burchell (Reynolds) Dunn had four children:

(1) Laura Dunn, born in 1859, who died the same year.
(2) William Francis Dunn, born in 1860, who married Adalaid Hoffecker.
(3) Alfred Clifton Dunn, born in 1862, who married Margaret A. Grier and had three children: (1) Bertha R. Funn, born in 1887; (2) Robert George Dunn, born in 1889; and (3) Rebecca Dunn, born in 1892.
(4) George Heury Dunn, born in 1870, who died in 1889.

G.W. and Francis Ann (Reynolds) Graham had four children: (1) Thomas Reynolds Graham; (2) Catherine Clark Graham who married Francis A. Johns; (3) John Wallace Graham who married Sallie Hering; and (4) Margret R. Graham.

Frank and Mary Ellen (Reynolds) Barwick had five children: (1) William Reynolds Barwick, born in 1872, who died in 1874; (2) John Seward Barwick, born in 1874; (3) Margaret Rebecca Barwick, born in 1877; (4) William Augustus Barwick, born in 1883; and (5) Wallace C. Barwick, born in 1886, who died in 1887.

Thomas and Mary (Lockwood) Brown had seven children:

(1) Joseph Brown who married R.C. Clark and had two children, Elva Brown and Elizabeth Brown.
(2) Sarah E. Brown.
(3) Susan Ann Brown who married James Quillen and had three children: (1) Fannie Quillen; (2) Emma Quillen; and (3) Mary Quillen.
(4) Emelina F. Brown.
(5) Dr. Thomas Armwell Brown who married Blanche Virdin as his first wife and _____ Eckel as his second wife.
(6) Anthony W. Brown.
(7) Mary E. Brown.

Samuel A. and Susan Ann (Brown) Short had five children:

(1) Sarah Elizabeth Short who married William T. Sharp and had eight children: (1) Dr. James R. Sharp; (2) Ella P. Sharp; (3) Clara Sharp; (4) William W. Sharp; (5) H. Sharp; (6) Paddy F. Sharp; (7) Elijah Sharp; and (8) another whose name is unknown.

(2) Samuel A. Short who married a Miss Scott as his first and Miss Lofland as his second wife.

(3) Susan Ann Short who married Edmond Bailey and had four children: (1) Edmond E. Bailey; (2) Mary W. Bailey; (3) Edith Bailey; and (4) John Bailey.

(4) Angelina Short who married Alfred Harrington and had three children: (1) Susan Harrington; (2) Herman Harrington; and (3) Alfred Harrington.

(5) Jane H. Short who married John Clifton and had two children: (1) Florence Clifton; and (2) John Clifton.

William C. and Julia A.H. (Short) Brown had three children:

(1) Elizabeth Ann Brown who married Benjamin F. Burton and had four children: (1) Julia Burton; (2) Benjamin Burton; (3) William Burton; and (4) Mary Burton.

(2) Sarah Cathering Brown.

(3) Samuel Adams Brown, who married Anna Lord and had a son, William C. Brown, who died.

Captain John Smithers, of Chesapeake City, Maryland, and his wife Emiline F. (Brown) Smithers had four children:

(1) William Smithers, born in 1843, who married Minnie Smock.
(2) Sally Ann Smithers who married B. Harrington.
(3) Mary Smithers.
(4) Emma B. Smithers who married John M. Reed and had seven children: (1) Florence Reed; (2) Emma S. Reed; (4) Charles Reed; (5) Minnie Reed; (6) Lucy Reed; and (7) Emma Reed.

David and Sarah (Brown) Harrington had four children:

(1) Theodore Harrington who married Emeline Hughes and had four children.
(2) Sarah Rosalie Harrington who married Walter L. Jones and had four children.

(3) Ida Jane Harrington who married Albert Sapp and had five children.
(4) Susan Emma Harrington who married William Sapp Masten and had three children: (1) Virgia Masten; (2) James Masten; and (3) Pearl Bird Masten.

Elijah and W.B. (Dehorty) Wooters had two children: (1) Theodore J. Wooters; and (2) Lydia Wooters who married Eugene Long of Odessa, Delaware.

William Burton and Lydia (Burton) Tomlinson had two children: (1) William Tomlinson who became a New York lawyer; and (2) Virginia Tomlinson who married Charles E. Atkinson and had a child, Alena Atkinson.

Daniel Reynolds and Ellen B. (Kirk) Tomlinson had eleven children:

(1) Ella Tomlinson who married Ceasar B. Dennis and had five children.
(2) Elizabeth Kirk Tomlinson who married James H. Collins and had six children.
(3) Thomas Tomlinson who married Anna Wyatt.
(4) Albert Tomlinson.
(5) William Tomlinson who married Victoria Johnson and had two children.
(6) Josephine Tomlinson who married Ross M. Darrell and had two children.
(7) Gus Tomlinson.
(8) Albert Tomlinson.
(9) Minnie Tomlinson who married Jacob Darrell and had four children.
(10) Samuel Tomlinson who married Emma Morris of Dover, Delaware.
(11) Maud Tomlinson.

THOMAS REYNOLDS and his wife, Sarah E. (Salsbury) Reynolds had three children: (1) Anna T. Reynolds who married Livy Rogers and had two children; (2) John Salsbury Reynolds; and (3) James T. Reynolds who was killed in 1891.

Benjamin L. and Letitia (Gruwell) Reed had four children:

(1) Ezekiah G. Reed who married Anna Rebecca Newcomb and had four children: (1) John Reed; (2) Mary Emily Reed; (3) Gilbert J. Ree; and (4) another child whose name is unknown.

(2) John G. Reed who married Jane Morgan M____ and had two children: (1) Robert Rogers Reed; and (2) Mary Jane Reed.

(3) Lydia G. Reed who married John L. Boyd and had two children: (1) Robert S. Boyd; and (2) Ellen May Boyd.

(4) Letitia Reed who married George Johnson.

John and Lydia (Gruwell) Gooden had nine children:

(1) Ambrose Broadway Gooden who married Emma Clements and had ten children.
(2) Ellenor G. Gooden who married James E. Sapp and had eight children.
(3) Jonathan Gooden who married Carrie Johns and had two children.
(4) Lydia Ann Gooden.
(5) Hannah Felecia Gooden who married Francis M. Gooding and had seven children.
(6) Amanda Gooden.
(7) Thomas Walters Gooden who married Ann Cook and had two children.
(8) Lydia Gooden.
(9) Gove Gooden.

Thomas B. and Elizabeth (Skinner) Kemp had two children: (1) William Henry Kemp; and (2) Margaret Jane Kemp who married John Cook and had three children: (1) Emma Cook; (2) Mary Elizabeth Cook; and (3) William Cook.

Jacob B. and Mariam (Skinner) Kemp had thirteen children:

(1) Letitia Kemp who married John Fisher.
(2) Thomas J. Kemp who married Clarissa Wyatt.
(3) John Kemp who married Susan Killen.
(4) Matthew Kemp who married Elizabeth Minner.
(5) Jacob Kemp who married Mary A. Minner.
(6) Peter Kemp who married Sarah C. Stockley.
(7) Mary E. Kemp who married John Caball.
(8) William J. Kemp who married Louisa Smith.
(9) Deborah A. Kemp who married Charles Stubbs.
(10) Hannah Kemp who married Harrison Darting.
(11) Isaac Kemp who married Rachel Marker.
(12) Robert Kemp.
(13) Lydia Jane Kemp.

John and Julia A. (Hicks) Skinner moved to Grant County, Indiana, and had eight children: (1) Miriam Skinner; (2) Sarah E. Skinner; (3) Martha J. Skinner; (4) William T. Skinner; (5) Isaac Gruwell Skinner; (6) John A. Skinner; (7) Letitia A. Skinner; and (8) George W. Skinner.

Copy of undated newspaper clipping concerning Robert J. Reynolds, Governor of Delaware

"Robert John Reynolds, ...was born in the town of Smyrna, Kent County, Delaware, on the 17th day of March, A.D., 1838. His father, Robert W. Reynolds, was a man of considerable political prominence, and was first appointed by Governor Bennett, Sheriff of Kent County, in 1834, and was elected by the people to that same office in 1836. He was appointed Register of Wills for Kent County in 1853, and was beaten for the nomination for Governor by only four votes in the convention that nominated Samuel Jefferson of New Castle County in 1862. He died in 1863, leaving three sons and three daughters, Luther M. Reynolds, who is now a prominent lawyer in the city of Baltimore, Elizabeth, the wife of Edward J. Carter, of Kent County, Sarah G., the wife of Robert B. Culbreth, of Caroline County, Maryland, Frances R., the wife of the late William L. Clough, of Kent County, Thomas G., who is a successful farmer in Talbot County, Maryland, and Robert J., the subject of our sketch. Robert J. Reynolds was educated at Fairfield, in Herkimer County, New York. He began farming near Petersburg, in Kent County, Delaware, in 1861, and has continued in the business ever since. He has extensive peach orchards and is a successful farmer and fruit grower. He married Lavina L., the daughter of William E. Riggs, of New Castle County in 1861. They have but one child, Byron, who is practicing law in the city of Baltimore. Byron married Ulyssa I. Williamson, of Baltimore city. They have but one child, Herbert Byron Reynolds.

"Robert J. Reynolds was elected to the General Assembly in 1868, and was elected State Treasurer in 1879 and was re-elected to the same office in 1881. He has always taken an active part in politics and has frequently served as chairman of County and State Democratic committees. He was chairman of the Democratic State Central Committee when Richard Harrington was chairman of the Republican State Committee, and ran his campaign in a boat on wheels. He was also chairman of the State Committee in the campaign that elected Chas. C. Stockley, Governor, and Grover Cleveland, President. By reason of a split in the Democratic party in 1888, which sent Anthony Higgins, Republican, to the United States Senate to succeed Hon. Eli

"Saulsbury, Democrat, the party was in bad shape for the campaign of 1890, so much so, that a proper nominee for the office of Governor was a matter of serious consideration among party friends. The emergency of the times demanded a man who could harmonize the waring elements of his own party, and at the same time make inroads upon the opposition. The eyes of the public naturally turned upon a man of this kind, and when the primaries came and delegates elected for the approaching State Convention, it was found that a decided majority of those elected were favorable to the nomination of Robert J. Reynolds, of Kent County. Mr. Reynolds himself, however, not being fully persuaded in his own mind that he was the proper man to nominate, broke the established custom, and attended the convention in person, and while there did not hesitate to make his fears known to his party associates. In a speech before a caucus of delegates on that occasion Mr. Reynolds said:

> 'I feel that this nomination belongs to no man, nor to any particular section. It belongs to the whole Democratic party of Delaware and that while my friends have offered me as a probable candidate for the nomination, I say freely and I make no reservation, I am ready and willing at the proper moment to sacrifice my ambition upon the alter of my party. And in saying this, I further add, that I will support the choice of the convention and I only wish that those who are my opponents would say as much. If there is truth in a man's heart I assert I had rather be the man to unite the Democratic party and thereby send it to success and victory than to be Governor of the State.'

This action of the part of Mr. Reynolds intensified his friends and multiplied his admirers and when the convention met next day he received 150 votes on the first ballot out of a total of 180 delegates. The campaign that followed was a hard and bitter one, and contrary to the sanguine expectations of the Republicans and many Democrats besides, Mr. Reynolds came out of the fight with a majority of 543 votes in the State.

"Governor Reynolds was inaugurated January 20, 1891, for a term of four years. He never lost a political battle and has been in politics for thirty years."

REYNOLDS FAMILY NOTES

1. The will of Richard Reynolds, yeoman, probated May 19, 1708, named his wife, Ann Reynolds; and children, Mary Reynolds, John Reynolds, Sarah Reynolds, and Richard Reynolds. (New Castle County Wills, Book B, page 162)

2. The will of Col. John Frency, probated December 12, 1728, named John Reynolds as an heir. (New Castle County Wills, Misc. 1, page 352)

3. The will of John Reynolds, probated June 12, 1749, named his wife, Ann Reynolds; children, unnamed; and the three eldest children of his three brothers. William Reynolds, a brother, was one of the executors. (New Castle County Wills, Book G, page 316)

4. The will of George Houston, of Red Lion Hundred, probated February 19, 1761, named William Reynolds as one of the heirs. (New Castle County Wills, Misc. 1, page 213)

5. The will of William Reynolds, yeoman, of Mill Creek Hundred, probated August 7, 1777, named: daughter, Eleanor Ross, widow of John Ross; son, Thomas Reynolds; daughter, Ann Read, wife of William Read; daughter, Martha Carson, wife of Umphrey Carson; children of his daughter, Eleanor Ross, Thomas Ross, and Ann Ross. His son Alexander Reynolds was executor, though not named in the will. (New Castle County Wills, Misc., page 417)

6. The will of William Wilson, yeoman, of White Clay Creek Hundred, probated September 16, 1778, named a daughter, Mary Reynolds, wife of John Reynolds. (New Castle County Wills, Book L, page 71)

7. The will of Richard Reynolds, probated November 3, 1779, named his wife, Mary Reynolds; daughter, Bridget Reynolds; William Reynolds, Rebecca Reynolds, and Richard Reynolds, children of his brother Thomas Reynolds. (New Castle County Wills, Book L, page 154)

8. The will of John Cole, probated April 17, 1782, named a daughter, Mary Reynolds, and a grandson, John Reynolds. (New Castle County Wills, Misc., page 66)

9. The will of John Reynolds, farmer, probated June 1, 1784, named his wife, Mary Reynolds; children, George Reynolds, Benjamin Reynolds, Mary Reynolds, Margaret Reynolds, James Reynolds, and Temperance Reynolds. (New Castle County Wills, Book L, page 432)

REYNOLDS FAMILY NOTES (cont.)

    10. The will of Rachel Bird, Brandywine Hundred, probated June 2, 1789, named a daughter Rachel Reynolds. (New Castle County Wills, Book N, page 34)

    11. The will of Miss Mary Kneasborough, St. Georges Hundred, probated January 12, 1792, named cousins, Francis Reynolds, Thomas Reynolds and John Reynolds, sons of Francis Reynolds, deceased. (New Castle County Wills, Book N, page 237)

    12. The will of Henry Reynolds, probated July 30, 1792, named his wife, Mary Reynolds; sons, Joseph Reynolds, and Benjamin Reynolds; daughters, Sarah Reynolds, and Betty Reynolds; and Joseph Shallcross, Jacob Fussel, and Samuel Canby. (New Castle Wills, Book N, page 287)

    13. The will of Jane Reynolds, widow, of Brandywine Hundred, probated July 17, 1795, named: mother-in-law, Rachel Reynolds; sister-in-law, Sally Reynolds; father, Thomas Wilson; sons, William Reynolds and John Reynolds; brother-in-law, Jacob Reynolds; kinsman, Thomas Bird, son of John Bird. (New Castle County Wills, Book O, page 93)

    14. The will of John Reynolds, Fox Hall, probated December 8, 1691, named wife (Waddey Reynolds); sons, John Reynolds, Thomas Reynolds, William Reynolds, Joseph Reynolds; daughter, Waddey Reynolds. (Kent County Wills, Book A, page 7)

    15. Anna Reynolds, widow, was named administrator of the estate of Thomas Reynolds, March 9, 1697. (Kent County Wills, Book A, page 23)

    16. William Clark was named administrator of the estate of Francis Reynolds, January 13, 1700. (Kent County Wills, Book B, page 39)

    17. The will of John Reynalls, Sr. (Reynolds), farmer, probated May 2, 1729, named heirs: wife, Elizabeth Reynolds; sons, Daniel Reynolds, George Reynolds, Robert Reynolds, and John Reynolds; daughters, Sara Reynolds, Elizabeth Reynolds, and Mary Reynolds. (Kent County Wills, Book G, page 23, and Book H, page 61)

    18. The will of Elizabeth Reynolds (Renelds), probated March 17, 1732, named heirs: son, Robert Reynolds; two daughters, unnamed; cousin, Elizabeth Gordon. (Kent County Wills, Book H, page 56)

REYNOLDS FAMILY NOTES (cont.)

19. The will of Daniel Reynals (Reynolds), probated June 14, 1736, named heirs: sons, John Reynolds, Miyckel Reynolds; daughter, Susanah Reynolds; wife, Grace Reynolds. (Kent County Wills, Book H, page 147)

20. The will of John Reynalds (Reynolds), Duck Creek Hundred, probated August 18, 1742, named heirs: children, unnamed. (Kent County Wills, Book I, page 48)

21. Catherine Reynolds, widow, was made administrator of the estate of her husband, John Reynolds, December 17, 1745. (Kent County Wills, Book I, page 116)

22. John Reynolds (Reynalds) and Michael Reynolds, grandsons, were named heirs in the will of Michael Lowber, probated April 7, 1746. (Kent County Wills, Book I, page 122)

23. Rachael Reynolds, widow, was made administrator of the estate of her husband, Robert Reynolds, laborer, March 21, 1758. (Kent County Wills, Book K, page 179)

24. The will of Henry Reynalls (Reynolds), probated December 23, 1760, named heirs: wife, Sara Reynolds; sons, Ephriam Reynolds, Richard Reynolds; daughter, Elizabeth Williams, wife of Ezeliel Williams; daughter-in-law, Mary Reynolds, wife of son Ephriam; son-in-law, Ezekiel Williams; grandsons, John Reynolds (son of Ephriam and Mary); Thomas Williams (son of Ezekiel and Elizabeth). (Kent County Wills, Book K, page 249) Note: The files also show heirs, Rachel Turner, Milliset Bourke, and Lurania Darbe.

25. George Amos was named administrator of the estate of Catharine Reynolds, widow, December 13, 1763)

26. The will of Thomas Blackshear, probated March 12, 1768, named as heirs: daughters, Elizabeth Reynolds, Miriam Reynolds. (Kent County Wills, Book L, page 41)

27. The will of John Reynolds, farmer, probated October 7, 1773, named heirs: wife, Elizabeth Reynolds; John Reynolds, son of Michael Reynolds. File shows that widow, Elizabeth Reynolds, later married James White. (Kent County Wills, Book L, page 142)

REYNOLDS FAMILY NOTES (cont.)

28. Rachel Reynolds, widow, was named administrator of the estate of Samuel Reynolds, May 28, 1774. (Kent County Wills, Book L, page 154)

29. Henry Runnolds (Reynolds) was named as an heir, and grandson, in the will of John Brown, probated July 20, 1774. (Kent County Wills, Book L, page 155)

30. The will of Andrew Caldwell, probated April 8, 1775, named heirs: grandsons, Andrew Reynolds (son of daughter Ann Reynolds), William Reynolds, and granddaughter, Jean Reynolds. (Kent County Wills, Book L, page 162)

31. Ruth Reynolds, widow, was named administrator of the estate of Richard Reynolds, farmer, Mispillion Hundred, January 29, 1777. Heirs mentioned were Henry Reynolds and Elonor Reynolds. (Kent County Wills, Book L, page 186)

32. The will of Ruth Reynolds, probated January 11, 1785, named heirs: sons, William Reynolds, James Reynolds, John Christopher Reynolds; daughter, Elizabeth Cordray; son-in-law, Benjamin Dailey. (Kent County Wills, Book M, page 39)

33. William Brown was named administrator of the estate of Richard Reynolds, March 4, 1785. (Kent County Wills, Book M, page 49)

34. Sarah Reynolds was named administrator of the estate of William Reynalds (Reynolds), February 26, 1790. Heirs mentioned in file were: James Reynolds, William Reynolds, Eleanor Reynolds, Nancy Reynolds, Stephen Reynolds, Joanna Reynolds. (Kent County Wills, Book M, page 224)

35. The will of Thomas Blackshare, probated April 5, 1790, mentioned heirs: sister, Meriam Reynalds (wife of Michael Reynalds). (Kent County Wills, Book M, page 234)

36. Catherine Dyer, late Catherine Reynolds, widow of John Dyer, was named administrator of the estate of John Reynolds, March 31, 1791. (Kent County Archives, Vol. A43, page 108)

REYNOLDS FAMILY NOTES (cont.)

37. The will of Joseph Reynolds (Runnels) probated December 20, 1791, named heirs: Robert Reynolds; sister, Araminty Manning.

38. The will of Catharine Duhadway (of Somerset County, Maryland) probated January 17, 1797, named heirs: grandsons, Daniel Reynolds, John Reynolds (Rennolds). (Kent County Wills, Book N, page 165)

39. The will of Robert Reynolds, Murderkill Hundred, probated April 21, 1798, named heirs: mother, Miriam Reynolds; brothers, Thomas Reynolds, Daniel Reynolds, Michael Reynolds, George Reynolds; children of sister Leticia; children of John Reynolds. (Kent County Wills, Book O, page 215)

Chapter 10.   The Rodney Family

THE RODNEY FAMILY

The Rodneys of Delaware are believed to be descendants of William Rodney who emigrated from Bristol, England, to Lewes, Delaware. He was in the Lewes area from 1682 until 1690 with his father-in-law, Thomas Hollyman. William Rodney was born in 1652 and died in 1708.

WILLIAM RODNEY and his first wife, Mary Hollyman, were married January 28, 1688. They had two children: (1) William Rodney (1689-1732) who married Ruth Curtis, daughter of John Curtis; and (2) Thomas Rodney who died before he reached maturity.

William Rodney and his second wife, Sarah Jones, daughter of David Jones, were married February 20, 1693. William Rodney was in Kent County in 1692 since he received a grant of land there on August 15, 1692. William and Sarah (Jones Rodney had seven children:

(1) Thomas Rodney who died young.
(2) John Rodney who died in 1728, single.
(3) Anthony Rodney who died in 1720, single.
(4) George Rodney.
(5) Daniel Rodney who died in 1744.
(6) Caesar Rodney (October 12, 1706-May 3, 1745) who married Elizabeth Crawford on October 13, 1727. She died in October 1763.
(7) Sarah Rodney who died in 1709.

WILLIAM RODNEY and his wife, Ruth (Curtis) Rodney, had two children: (1) Comfort Rodney; and (2) John Rodney (1725-1792) who married Sarah Paynter as his first wife but had no children. As his second wife he married Ruth Hunn. She was the daughter of Caleb and Ruth Hunn. She died August 16, 1806.

JOHN RODNEY and his second wife, Ruth (Hunn) Rodney had twelve children:

(1) William Rodney.
(2) Mary Rodney, born in 1856, who married Isaac Turner.
(3) Penelope Rodney, born in 1758, who married W. Kollock.
(4) John Rodney, born in 1760.
(5) Hannah Rodney, born in 1762.
(6) Daniel Rodney, born in 1764, who married Sarah Fisher.
(7) Caleb Rodney, born in 1767, who married Elizabeth West.
(8) Ruth Rodney, born in 1770.
(9) John Rodney, born in 1771, who married Rebecca Shilds.
(10) William Rodney, born in 1773.

(11) Thomas Rodney, born in 1775, who married Sarah Burton.
(12) George Rodney, born in 1776.

CAESAR RODNEY and his wife, Elizabeth (Crawford) Rodney, had five children:

(1) Caesar Rodney (October 7, 1728-June 29, 1784) who signed the Declaration of Independence.
(2) Daniel Rodney who married Mimiam ____ and had a daughter, Sarah Rodney, who married John Ferguson and had four children: (1) Daniel Ferguson; (2) Henry Ferguson; (3) John Ferguson; and (4) James Ferguson. Daniel Rodney died in January 1764.
(3) William Rodney.
(4) Thomas Rodney who married Elizabeth Fisher.
(5) Mary Rodney who married Joshua Gooden.

THOMAS RODNEY and his wife, Elizabeth (Fisher) Rodney, had a son, Caesar Augustus Rodney, born January 4, 1772, in Dover, Delaware. He married Susan Hunn. Caesar Augustus Rodney was Attorney General of the United States; he commanded an artillery company in the War of 1812; he was the first Democratic Senator from Delaware; he died in South America June 10, 1824.

Joshua and Mary (Rodney) Gooden had three children:

(1) Elizabeth Gooden who married Dr. John Brinckle and had eight children.
(2) Sarah Gooden who married David Pleasanton and had a daughter, Mary Pleasanton, who married George Laws.
(3) Lavenid Gooden who married John Fisher, a lawyer, and had two sons.

NOTE: In the Virdin files from which this information came are to be found these comments:

"Mr. John C. Gooden says he fails to find Comfort Rodney with the Rodneys of Delaware. Mrs. W.K. Reynolds of Wilmington, Delaware, writes
'Judge Rodney says: We are not of the Rodneys of Delaware, but of William Rodney and Mary his wife, who had two daughters, Comfort and Hannah. Both married Marvels. William Rodney's will is at Snow Hill, Maryland, in which he mentions Comfort Marvel as the daughter of William Rodney, whose will was probated December 3, 1767. The Rev.

"'C.H.B. Turner, of Lewes, Sussex County, writes me the same.'

"According to Mr. John C. Gooden 'The Rodney family is very ancient. The earliest record is found in the Cathedral of Wills in which the name DeRodney occurs in the year 766.'"

RODNEY FAMILY NOTES

1. The will of Daniel Jones, probated March 21, 1694, named as an heir: William Rodney, son-in-law. (Kent County Wills, Book A, page 11)

2. William Rodney was a witness to the will of Daniel Brown (Browne), probated October 30, 1695. (Kent County Wills, Book A, page 16)

3. The will of John Betts, probated January 3, 1697, named William Rodeney, Jr., as an heir, and one of the executors. (Kent County Wills, Book A, page 22)

4. William Rodeney was one of the executors of the will of Maurice Smith, Sr., probated June 25, 1698. (Kent County Wills, Book B, page 30)

5. William Rodeney was one of the executors of the will of Richard Wilson, probated January 7, 1700. (Kent County Wills, Book B, page 38)

6. William Rodeney was granted letters of administration on the estate of Thomas Atthow, August 16, 1700. (Kent County Wills, Book B, page 37)

7. William Rodney was one of the executors of the will of George Hart, probated December 10, 1702. (Kent County Wills, Book B, page 45)

8. The will of John Richardson, Sr., of Little Creek, probated January 3, 1703, named as heirs: grandsons, Thomas Rodney, William Rodney. (Kent County Wills, Book B, page 50)

9. William Rodney was named executor of the will of Griffith Jones, Gentleman, probated May 24, 1703. (Kent County Wills, Book B, page 48)

10. The will of Simon Irons, Sr., probated December 16, 1706, named as an heir, Sarah Rodney, daughter of Captain William and Sarah Rodney. (Kent County Wills, Book B, page 56)

RODNEY FAMILY NOTES (cont.)

11. The will of William Rodeney, probated October 4, 1708, named as heirs: sons, William Rodeney, Thomas Rodoney, John Rodoney, Anthony Rodeney, George Rodeney, Caesar Rodeney; daughter, Sarah Rodeney; mother, Rachel Rodeney; sisters, Rachel Rodeney, Elizabeth Rodeney; wife, Sarah Rodeney; and orphans of Richard Willson. (Kent County Wills, Book B, page 63)

12. Sarah Rodeney, wife of William Rodeney, was named administrator of the estate of John Shepherd, October 4, 1709. (Kent County Wills, Book C, page 82)

13. William Rodeny was named as heir, and executor, in the will of David Smith, probated May 13, 1719. (Kent County Wills, Book D, page 9)

14. Daniel Rodeney was named administrator of the estate of Anthony Rodeney, May 7, 1720. (Kent County Wills, Book D, page 19)

15. William Rodeney and Ruth Rodeney, were witnesses to the will of William Coe, probated September 30, 1720. (Kent County Wills, Book D, page 24)

16. The will of Prissila Gilbert, widow, probated May 10, 1721, named Penelop Rodney, daughter of William and Ruth Rodney, as an heir. (Kent County Wills, Book D, page 44)

17. The will of William Cramer, probated December 13, 1726, showed William Rodney as an heir. (Kent County Wills, Book F, page 19)

18. The will of Elizabeth Morgan, probated April 19, 1727, named friend Daniel Rodney as an heir, and executor. (Kent County Wills, Book F, page 26)

19. Daniel Rodney was named as the son, and executor of the will of Sarah Nowell, wife of George Nowell, probated February 11, 1729. (Kent County Wills, Book H, page 2)

20. Ruth Rodeney was named administrator of the estate of William Rodeney, October 19, 1732. (Kent County Wills, Book H, page 32)

RODNEY FAMILY NOTES (cont.)

21. Ceasar Rodney was named administrator of the estate of Elizabeth Brinklee, May 31, 1733. (Kent County Wills, Book H, page 107)

22. Ceasar Rodney was named administrator of the estate of Thomas Cook, September 21, 1734. (Kent County Wills, Book H, page 81)

23. Elizabeth Rodeney, widow, was named administrator of the estate of Ceasar Rodeney, June 8, 1745. (Kent County Wills, Book I, page 111)

24. Margaret Rodeney was named administrator of the estate of Daniel Rodney, January 25, 1744. The file mentions John Bell, Jr., and his father's legacy. (Kent County Wills, Book I, page 96)

25. Elizabeth Rodeney was named administrator of the estate of Daniel Stevens, April 4, 1748. (Kent County Wills, Book I, page 200)

26. Elizabeth Rodeney, Jr., was named as an heir in the will of Jonathan Pleasanton, yeoman, of Dover Hundred, probated November 1, 1748. (Kent County Wills, Book I, page 236)

27. Meriam Rodney, widow, was named administrator of the estate of Daniel Rodney, January 18, 1764. (Kent County Wills, Book K, page 334)

28. William Rodney and Ledia Rodney were named administrators of the estate of John Edingfield, November 21, 1771. (Kent County Wills, Book L, page 103)

29. Thomas Rodney was named administrator of the estate of John Boyd, October 15, 1774. (Kent County Wills, Book L, page 157)

30. Margaret Rodney, widow, in her will, probated March 23, 1781, named Nathaniel Luff, grandson, as her heir. (Kent County Wills, Book L, page 226)

31. Ceasar Rodney (The Signer) (identified as the eldest son of Ceasar Rodney, deceased) in his will, probated August 14, 1784, named the following heirs: brothers, William Rodney, Thomas Rodney; half-sister, Sarah Wilson; half-brother, John Wilson; nephew, Caesar Augustus Rodney; nieces, Lavinia Rodney (daughter of brother Thomas Rodney), Letitia Rodney (daughter of brother William Rodney), Elizabeth Gordon (daughter of sister, Mary, deceased), Sarah Rodney (daughter of brother, Daniel Rodney), Caesar

RODNEY FAMILY NOTES (cont.)

Rodney Wilson (son of half-sister Sarah Wilson); children of sister Mary Gordon. (Kent County Wills, Book L, page 238)

32. William Rodney (son of Caesar Rodney) who was the youngest son of William Rodney, in his will, probated September 13, 1787, named as heirs: daughter, Letticia Rodney; niece, Elizabeth Wilson, daughter of sister, Sarah Wilson; granddaughter, Elizabeth Frazer; nephews, Caesar Rodney Wilson, Thomas Wilson, sons of sister Sarah Wilson; John Homestead; Sarah Edenfield. (Kent County Wills, Book M, page 155)

By Fields;
Ceasar Rodney's Birthplace

Bibliography

BIBLIOGRAPHY

Barnes, Robert. *Maryland Marriages 1634-1777*. Baltimore: Genealogical Publishing Co. Inc., 1976.

Beers, D.G. *Atlas of the State of Delaware*. Philadelphia: Pomeroy and Beers, 1868.

Conrad, Henry Clay. *History of the State of Delaware*. Wilmington: published by the author, 1908.

National Society of the Daughters of the American Revolution. *DAR Patriot Index*. Washington: National Society of the Daughters of the American Revolution, 1966.

Delaware Historical Society. Genealogical Surname File.

State of Delaware. Hall of Records. Rev. Joseph Brown Turner Genealogical Collection. Carter folder.

State of Delaware. Hall of Records. Marriage Records Files.

Delaware: A History of The First State. Volume III. New York: Lewis Historical Publishing Co., Inc., 1947.

Historical and Biographical Encyclopaedia of Delaware. Wilmington: Aldine Publishing and Engraving Co., 1882.

Colonial Dames of America. *A Calendar of Delaware Wills, New Castle County, 1682-1800*. New York: 1910. Reprinted by Genealogical Publishing Co., Baltimore, 1969.

deValinger, Leon, Jr. *Calendar of Kent County Delaware Probate Records 1680-1800*. Dover: Delaware Public Archives Commission, 1944.

Decatur Genealogical Society. *Fayette County, Illinois, Cemetery Inscriptions*. Decatur, Illinois: Decatur Genealogical Society.

Gannett, Henry. *The Origins of Certain Place Names in The United States*. Baltimore: Genealogical Publishing Co., Inc., 1977.

Hackett, J. Dominick, and Early, Charles Montague. *Passenger Lists From Ireland*. Baltimore: Genealogical Publishing Co., Inc., 1973.

Hancock, Harold B. *Liberty and Independence*. Wilmington: Delaware American Revolution Bicentennial Commission, 1976.

Kaminkow, Marion J., Editor. *Genealogies in the Library of Congress, A Bibliography*. Two Volumes. Baltimore: Magna Carta Book Co., 1972.

The Maryland and Delaware Genealogist, 1966-1976. St. Michaels, Maryland.

Decatur Genealogical Society. *Moultrie County, Illinois, Cemetery Inscriptions, Vol. II.* Decatur, Illinois: Decatur Genealogical Society.

Portrait and Biographical Record of Macoupin County, Illinois. Chicago: Biographical Publishing Company, 1891.

Illinois Genealogical Society. *Soldiers of the American Revolution Buried in Illinois.* Illinois Genealogical Society, 1976.

The History of Shelby and Moultrie Counties, Illinois. Philadelphia: Brink, McDonough and Co., 1881.

Sawin, Nancy C., and Carper, Janice M. *Delaware Sketch Book.* Hockessin, Delaware: The Holly Press, 1976.

Tepper, Michael. *Emigrants to Pennsylvania 1641-1819.* Baltimore; Genealogical Publishing Co., 1977.

Terrell, Dan. *Room For One More Sinner.* Rehoboth Beach, Delaware: The Duck Press, 1974.

Torrence, Clayton. *Virginia Wills and Administrations 1632-1800.* Baltimore: Genealogical Publishing Co., 1977.

Wheeler, Mrs. Eileen. *Moultrie County Heritage*, Vol. I, No. 2, February 1974. Moultrie County Historical and Genealogical Society.

Subject Index

SUBJECT INDEX

CEMETERY RECORDS

PAGE

Georgia

    Virden-Moore 6

Illinois

    Bethel Baptist 102
    Greenwood 102
    Jacobs 99
    Linwood 99
    Old Shedd 102
    Ramsey 101
    Tolly 99
    Wright 100

CENSUS RECORDS

Arkansas

    Pope County, 1850 56
                1860 57
                1870 56

Delaware

    New Castle County, 1820 80

Georgia

    Pike County, 1850 54
    Upson County, 1850 54

Illinois

    Bond County, 1820 82
              1830 82

    Christian County, 1840 82
                   1850 . . . . 80, 83
                   1880 94

    Fayette County, 1840 82
                 1850 84
                 1865 91
                 1880 93

SUBJECT INDEX (cont.)

    PAGE

Illinois cont.

    Greene County, 1880 93
    Macon County, 1870 . . . .
    Macoupin County, 1850 90
                  1860 92
    Montgomery County, 1850 87
                   1860 90
                   1880 93
    Sangamon County, 1850 . . . . 81, 84
    Shelby County, 1850 . . . . 85, 91
               1880 . . . . 94, 95
    Virden, Illinois, 1870 92
               1880 92
    Wayne County, 1850 . . . . 64, 90, 96

Iowa

    Blackhawk County, 1850 . . . . 62, 96
                1860 . . . . 63, 97
                1880 98
    Calhoun County, 1880 98
    Henry County, 1860 . . . . 62, 77
              1880 98
    Lucas County, 1880 98
    Soundex of Iowa, 1880 64

Maryland

    Worcester County, 1790 80

Missouri

    Adair County, 1870 77
             1880 . . . . 78, 95, 96
    Cape Girardeau, 1850 . . . . 54, 55

North Carolina

    Edgecombe County, 1800 80
    Pasquotauk County, 1800 80

Ohio

    Muskingum County, 1820 75
                1830 75
                1840 76
                1850 . . . . 60, 76
                1860 77
    Soundex of Ohio, 1880 67

SUBJECT INDEX (cont.)

PAGE

Virginia

Jefferson County, 1810 80

West Virginia

Soundex of West Virginia, 1880 65

DELAWARE RECORDS

A Marriage Chronology 103
Wills and Administrations, Kent County 111
Wills and Administrations, Sussex County 112

ILLUSTRATIONS

By-Fields: Caesar Rodney's Birthplace, Dover 194
The Lowber House, Magnolia 162

MARYLAND RECORDS 115

MARRIAGE RECORDS 103, 109

PENSION RECORDS 67

PHILADELPHIA RECORDS 46

PROBATE RECORDS 112, 113

REVOLUTIONARY WAR SOLDIERS 49, 67, 111

TOWNS

Virden, Manitoba, Canada 118
Virden, New Mexico, U.S.A. 118

SUBJECT INDEX (cont.)

                                                                                                       PAGE

OLD LETTERS

    1866, To Mr. Virdin from Green Nickerson 119
    1875, To Mr. David from Mrs. Emily Virdin 121
    1880, To Mr. William Virdin from Robert T. Ludwick . . . 122

Name Index

INDEX

- A -

ACETO

   Audrey, 18
   James, 18

ACWITH

   Sarah, 142

ADAMS

   Jerimiah, 6, 8
   Julia, 6, 8

ADKINSON

   Ann, 145
   William, 145

AGAZZI

   Jerry, 18
   Mary, 18

ALDRED

   Aaron, 5, 6

ALFORD

   Anna, 148
   Augustus, 147
   Caroline, 148
   Charles, 148
   Clara, 148
   George, 147
   Henry, 147
   Newell, 147
   Reuben, 147
   Sarah, 124
   William, 147

ALLEE

   J. Frank, 152

ALLIBAND

   Evetine, 174

AMOS

   George, 184

AMERSON

   A____, 174

ANDERSON

   Alice, 18
   Emily, 140
   George, 139
   G.W., 139
   Jacob, 142
   Joseph, 139
   Mary, 139
   Sallie, 139
   Sarah, 139
   Thomas, 139
   William, 139

ANGEL (ANGELL)

   Finn, 31
   Lulu, 31
   Winnifred, 32

ANTHONY

   Nathan, 172

ARMSTRONG

   Beverly, 15
   Emiline, 15

ATKINS

   Edna, 39

ATKINSON

    Alena, 178
    Charles, 178

ATTHOW

    Thomas, 190

ATTIX

    Emma, 129

ATWELL

    Benjamin, 133

ATWOOD

    Martha, 32

AUGUR

    Rachel, 146

AUTHORS

    Margaret, 40

- B -

BAILEY (BALEY)

    Edith, 177
    Edmond, 177
    Ethel, 40
    James, 78
    Joan, 78
    John, 177
    Karl, 78
    Kim, 78
    Kurt, 78
    Lola, 140
    Mary, 177
    Paula, 78
    Polly, 78
    Sarah, 143

BAKER

    Mauriss, 141

BALLARD

    William, 89

BARON

    Elizabeth, 167

BARRATT (BARRETT)

    Mary, 127

BARRYFORD

    Mr., 145

BARWICK

    Frank, 174
    Henry, 140
    J. Frank, 140
    John, 140, 176
    Margaret, 140, 176
    Mary, 174
    Rebecca, 140
    Thomas, 140
    Wallace, 140, 176
    William, 140, 176

BAYLES

    Ella, 138
    Sallie, 129

BAXTER

    Caesar, 129
    Catherine, 129
    Elphonsie, 129
    Elva, 129
    Herman, 129
    Hezekial, 125, 129
    Myrtle, 129
    Philena, 125, 129
    Thomas, 129

BEARD

    Samuel, 3

BEDWIN

    Grace, 148

BELL

   Edgar, 66
   John, 168, 192
   Susan, 66

BENNET

   Elizabeth, 40

BERRY

   Angelina, 18
   Ann, 123, 146
   Barbara, 17
   Catherine, 18
   Edward, 18
   Everett, 17
   Frederick, 17
   Gertrude, 18
   Helen, 18
   Jesse, 17
   Joseph, 145, 149
   Mary, 34
   Nonie, 17
   Patricia, 18
   Peter, 145, 149, 160
   Robert, 17
   Rose, 17
   Ruth, 18
   Sarah, 146
   Susan, 18
   Thomas, 17
   Unity, 145, 149, 152
   William, 145, 146, 149, 160, 164

BETTS

   John, 190

BEVERLY

   Sarah, 58

BEYNON

   Margaret, 31

BILLINGSLAY

   George, 141

BIRD

   John, 183
   Rachel, 183
   Thomas, 183

BLACKSHAVE (BLACKSHARE)

   Elizabeth, 153, 171
   Mariana, 153
   Miriam, 171
   Thomas, 184, 185

BLENDT

   Ruth, 40

BLY

   David, 30, 63
   Elizabeth, 30, 63

BODINE

   Bill, 20
   Mary, 20

BOGARD

   J.M., 66
   Mary, 66
   Thomas, 165

BOOKER

   Amanda, 125
   Walter, 125

BOURKE

   Millicent, 184

BOTTOROFF

   Gilder, 147
   John, 147

BOWERS

   John, 159
   Mary, 152
   Ruth, 152

BOYD

  Charles, 10
  Ellen, 179
  John, 179, 192
  Margaret, 67
  Robert, 179
  Virginia, 10

BRADLEY

  Benjamin, 124, 127
  Elizabeth, 124
  James, 127
  John, 127
  Mary, 127, 128
  Margaret, 127
  Philip, 127
  Samuel, 127
  Thomas, 140

BRADY

  Kathryn, 42

BREESE

  Albert, 75, 78
  Brandon, 78
  Edna, 78
  Forrest, 78
  Jean, 75, 78
  Polly, 78
  Thomas, 76, 78

BRINKLEE (BRINCKLE)

  Elizabeth, 188, 192
  John, 188

BROADWAY

  Abner, 123, 126, 130
  Amanda, 125
  Ambrose, 123, 124, 125, 126, 130
  Ann, 124, 125
  Catherine, 124
  E.A., 154
  Elizabeth, 123, 124, 126, 130
  Emily, 125
  Hester, 126
  Isaac, 123, 126, 130
  Isabel, 125

BROADWAY (cont.)

  James, 123, 126
  Lettecia, 130
  Lurette, 126
  Lydia, 124, 126
  Margaret, 125
  Mary, 31, 123, 124, 125, 126, 128, 130
  Nancy, 126, 130
  Nicholas, 123
  Patients, 130
  Rachel, 124
  Rebecca, 123, 126, 130
  Robert, 123, 124, 125, 146, 164
  Ruth, 125
  Sally, 130
  Samuel, 123, 126, 130
  Sarah, 123, 124, 125, 130, 164
  Susannah, 125
  Watson, 125
  William, 123, 125, 130

BROMLEY

  Howard, 34,
  Mary, 34

BROOKE

  Ella, 147
  Rachel, 152

BROOKS

  Caroline, 147
  James, 158

BROWN

  Anthony, 176
  Blanche, 155, 176
  Clifford, 32
  Daniel, 190
  Elizabeth, 156, 176, 177
  Elva, 176
  Emeline (Emiline), 156, 175, 176
  Ethel, 155
  Grace, 153, 158
  Henry, 155
  James, 155
  Jane, 143
  Jesse, 31, 32
  John, 185

BROWN (cont.)

   Joseph, 155, 176
   Lottie, 31
   Maria, 155
   Martha, 7, 175
   Mary, 155, 176
   Mearrim, 143
   Rachel, 143
   Richard, 7
   Rita, 32
   Samuel, 156, 177
   Sarah, 153, 155, 156, 175, 176, 177
   Susan, 155, 175
   Thomas, 153, 155, 156, 175, 176
   William, 155, 156, 159, 174, 175, 185
   Zilphey, 6, 8

BRUNICK

   Cornelia, 78

BRYCHEL

   Rita, 32

BUCHANAN

   Edwin, 135

BULLINGTON

   Nancy, 15
   R.H., 15

BUNT

   Mary, 127

BURGESS (BURGES)

   Charles, 175
   Ra'l (Rachel), 117
   William, 117

BURNAM

   John, 141

BURROUGHS

   John, 142

BURTON

   Benjamin, 177
   Julia, 177
   Lydia, 174
   Mary, 177
   William, 177

BUTLER

   Lucinda, 57

BYNUM

   Elizabeth, 58

- C -

CABALL

   John, 179

CABLEY

   John, 141

CAIN (CAINE)

   Catherine, 152
   Daniel, 159
   Francis, 159
   Owen, 158

CALDWELL

   Andrew, 185

CALLOWAY (CALLAWAY)

   Peter, 143

CAMPBELL

   Julia, 123
   Reuben, 57

CANBY

   Samuel, 183

CARBIN (CARBINE)

   James, 141, 143
   Jane, 141, 143
   Margaret, 143
   Mary, 143
   Sarah, 143

CARD

   America, 16
   Benson, 88
   Calvin, 88
   Elizabeth, 16
   Henry, 89
   Hester, 16
   James, 16, 83, 87
   Levi, 16
   Sarah, 16

CARDIFF

   Belle, 135
   Rachel, 163

CARNEY

   James, 59
   Willie, 59

CARPENTER

   Elizabeth, 47
   Martha, 153

CARSON

   Martha, 182
   Umphrey, 182

CARTER

   Aimee, 135
   Albert, 137
   Alexander, 144
   Ann (Annie), 126, 134, 141
   Bernard, 137
   Betsey, 143
   Catherine, 143

CARTER (cont.)

   Daniel, 144
   Dorothy, 137
   Edward, 124, 126, 133, 134, 135, 136
      143, 144, 148, 154, 167, 173
      180
   Elizabeth, 126, 133, 134, 136, 142
      143
   Francis, 137
   Frank, 135, 173
   George, 133, 143
   Henry, 133, 142, 144
   Herman, 1, 135, 173
   Isaac, 141
   Isabel, 137
   James, 137
   Jane, 142, 143
   John, 126, 131, 132, 133, 134, 141,
      142, 143, 144, 164
   Joseph, 141, 142
   Julia, 135, 173
   King, 131, 132
   Lizzie, 135, 173
   Luther, 135, 136, 137, 173
   Lydia, 126, 134, 137
   Margaret, 142
   Mariah, 133
   Mary, 124, 126, 133, 134, 135, 136,
      137, 142, 143, 144, 147, 173
   Mildred, 137
   Nancy, 126, 134
   Noah, 133
   Philip, 141, 142
   Rachel, 126, 134, 143, 173
   Reynolds, 136
   Ruth, 143, 144
   Richard, 141, 142
   Robert, 131, 132, 135, 137, 142
   Sallie, 135, 173
   Sarah, 126, 133, 134, 137, 142, 143,
      144
   Samuel, 144
   Simca, 173
   Susanna, 143, 144
   Thomas, 126, 131, 134, 142, 144
   Valentine, 141, 142
   William, 126, 133, 134, 137, 141, 142,
      143, 144

CASE

    Charles, 140
    Edward, 134
    Emily, 140
    James, 134
    John, 134, 140
    Joseph, 140
    Louisa, 134, 140
    Mary, 134, 139, 140
    Nora, 140
    Rachel, 134, 137, 140
    Rosanna, 140
    Sallie, 140
    Samuel, 140
    Sarah, 139
    William, 133, 134, 139, 140

CASEY

    Ann, 14
    Elizabeth, 14
    James, 14
    Levi, 14, 85
    Samuel, 14
    Sarah, 14

CASTLE

    Margaret, 129

CATER (CATEN)

    Sarah, 10

CATON (CATRON)

    Agnes, 152
    Benjamin, 152, 160, 161
    John, 161, 171
    Peter, 160, 161
    Robert, 145

CATTS

    James, 134
    Stephen, 134

CAULK

    Mary, 164

CHAMBERS

    Errickson, 148
    James, 146, 148
    Margaret, 146
    Will, 127

CHANCE

    Batchelder, 145
    Sarah, 145

CHAPIN

    Bessie, 136
    Dorothie, 136

CHENELLE

    Charles, 19
    Colin, 19
    David, 19
    Delsey, 19
    Francis, 19
    Gwenlyn, 19

CHERRY

    Dovie, 59
    Ernest, 59

CISCO

    Charity, 11

CLARK (CLARKE)

    Elizabeth, 159
    Evelyn, 138
    Henry, 137
    John, 138, 159, 168
    Mary, 168
    R.C., 176
    Robert, 161
    William, 183

CLAWSON

    Mary, 145

CLAYTON

    Joshua, 168

CLEMENTS

    Elizabeth, 127
    Emma, 179
    Ezekial, 126, 137
    Francis, 138
    James, 137, 138
    Maggie, 138
    Mary, 137
    Rachel, 137

CLIFTON

    Alfred, 175
    Charles, 175
    Florence, 175, 177
    John, 175, 177
    Margaret, 174
    Mary, 175
    O., 174
    Robert, 175

CLOUGH

    Caleb, 134
    David, 173
    Estella, 140
    Frances, 173
    Frank, 140
    John, 140
    Josie, 140
    Lizzie, 140
    Noah, 140
    Reynolds, 173
    Roxanna, 126, 137
    William, 173, 180

COFFMAN

    Delilah, 29, 75

COHEE

    Isaac, 125
    Margaret, 125
    John, 124
    Rachel, 124, 127
    Vincent, 127

COLE

    E.A., 33
    John, 182

COLLINS

    James, 178

CONNER

    Emma, 175

COOK

    Ann, 179
    Beatrice, 38
    Bessie, 38
    Elizabeth (Eliza), 38, 41
    Emma, 179
    George, 38, 41
    Herman, 41
    Jack, 43
    James, 38
    John, 179
    Mabel, 41
    Margaret
    Mary, 179
    Minnie, 38
    Thomas, 192
    Wallace, 41
    William, 179

COLLBOUGH

    Mary, 172

COONS

    Elizabeth, 63
    Emma, 30
    Jacob, 30, 63

COOPER

    Ann, 124
    Benjamin, 128
    Caroline, 126
    Catherine, 124, 126, 128, 154, 160
        164
    Clarissa, 124
    Elizabeth, 125

COOPER (cont.)

  Emily, 125
  Esther, 125
  Ethel, 128
  Eugene, 128
  Ezekial, 124, 125, 128, 164
  Fletcher, 128
  George, 129
  Green, 165
  Ignatius, 126
  Irving, 128
  James, 124
  John, 124, 128
  Mary, 124, 128
  Miriam, 126, 135
  Nehemiah, 124
  Peter, 125, 128
  Richard, 124, 125, 126, 127, 128
  Samuel, 128
  Sarah, 124, 125, 128
  Thomas, 124, 125, 128

CORDRAY

  Elizabeth, 185

CORIELL

  Leota, 32

CORLEY

  Elizabeth, 6, 7
  John, 7
  T.H., 1, 10

CORR

  Alice, 18
  Francis, 18

CORSE

  Thomas, 168

COVINGTON

  Leonard, 9
  Nettie, 9
  Queen Elizabeth, 9

COX

  Rebecca, 28
  Thomas, 127

CRAMER

  William, 191

CRAWFORD

  Elizabeth, 187
  Oliver, 167
  Rachel, 167

CREDICK

  John, 140
  Reynolds, 176
  Sallie, 134
  William, 176

CRIDER

  Gloria, 20, 25
  William, 20, 25

CRIPPS

  Frank, 136

CRUMP

  Charles, 43

CRUMPTON

  Sarah, 152

CUBBACE

  Miriam, 127
  Sarah, 127

CULBRETH

  David, 173
  Robert, 173, 180

CULLEN

  Jesse, 155

CUMMINS

   Leaer, 167
   Violet, 157

CURTIS

   John, 187
   Ruth, 187

CUSTER

   General, 128

- D -

DAILEY

   Ann, 128
   Benjamin, 185
   Elizabeth, 172
   J. Seward, 128
   James, 128
   Mary, 172

DANBERRY

   Mary, 140

DARNALL

   Annie, 29

DARBE

   Lurania, 184

DARRELL

   Jacob, 178
   Ross, 178

DARTING

   Harrison, 179

DAVIS

   Charity, 16
   Caniel, 89
   Elizabeth, 11

DAVIS (cont.)

   Emma, 23
   Franklin, 23, 32
   George, 11, 83
   John, 16
   Joseph, 88
   Mary, 159
   Thomas, 159

DAWSON

   Catherine, 124
   Elijah, 124, 128
   Greenburg, 128
   Joseph, 124, 126, 143
   Mary, 124, 126, 134
   Polly, 126, 135
   Robert, 126, 135
   Sarah, 126, 134
   Thomas, 159
   William, 126, 134

DAY

   Ellen, 148
   Emily, 148
   Madaline, 148
   Robert, 148
   Rodney, 148

DEHORTY

   Elizabeth, 175
   W.B., 174

DENNIS

   Caeser, 178

DENSEN

   Julia, 8

DEWEESE

   Betty, 18
   Effie, 18
   Eva, 18
   Marjorie, 18
   Ormand, 18
   Roy, 18

DeWITT

    Anna, 136
    Lydia, 136
    Orlean, 136

DILL

    Edward, 129
    Eva, 129
    J.W., 164
    John, 144
    Rembra, 164
    William, 172

DIXON

    Samuel, 28
    Lemuel, 81

DOILE

    Florence, 61

DONDAL

    Governor, 164

DONNEHO

    Ann, 143

DOWNHAM

    Kesiah, 175

DOWNS

    Ann, 124
    George, 24

DRAPER

    Elizabeth, 127
    Henry, 125
    Isabel, 125
    Mary, 129

duBREE

    Mary, 147

DUDLEY

    Richard, 123
    Sarah, 123

DUFF

    Hazel, 59
    Howard, 59

DUFFY

    James, 34

DUHADAWAY

    Catherine, 153, 160, 161, 171, 186
    Jacob, 160

DURBORROW (DUBROW)

    Hugh, 159
    Susannah, 159

duKEY

    Helen, 148

DUNBOROUGH

    Susannah, 153, 159

DUNNING

    Tamar, 145

DUNN

    Alfred, 176
    Bertha, 176
    D.D., 164
    Daniel, 154
    George, 176
    Harriet, 164
    Laura, 176
    R.C., 174
    Rebecca, 174, 176
    Robert, 176
    William, 176

DURBIN

  Gabe, 17
  Margaret, 17

DURR

  Charles, 20
  James, 20
  Mary, 20
  Mildred, 20
  Terry, 20

DUSHAROORN

  Michael, 141

DYER

  John, 185

DYSON

  Annie, 29
  Henrietta, 27, 28
  William, 28, 29

- E -

EDENFIELD

  John, 192
  Sarah, 193

EDMONDSON (EDMONSON)

  Ruth, 133
  Sarah, 133
  Sophia, 168
  Thomas, 168
  William, 133

ELDERDICE

  Augustus, 39
  Edna, 39
  Eunity (Unity), 35, 39
  Frances, 39
  James, 39
  John, 39
  Mabel, 39
  Robert, 39

ELLICOT

  Elizabeth, 142

ELLIOTT

  Eugenia, 8
  Pricilla (Priscilla), 6, 8
  Thomas, 6, 8

EMERSON

  Ann, 128
  Emma, 128
  Gove, 128, 152
  John, 151, 172
  Jonathan, 152
  Mary, 153, 172
  Michael, 152, 158
  Unity, 151, 158
  Vincent, 125, 128, 152

EVAN (EVANS)

  Cornelia, 78
  Edna, 75, 78
  Henry, 78
  Josiah, 128

- F -

FERGUSON

  Daniel, 188
  Henry, 188
  James, 188
  John, 188
  Sarah, 188

FETTEROFF

  Agnes, 136
  Estella, 136
  George, 136
  J. Layton, 136

FIELDS

  Marion, 168

FINDLAY

   Emma, 147

FIRSTHWART

   Mary, 146

FISHER

   Elizabeth, 188
   John, 179, 188
   Sarah, 187

FLEMING

   Sarah, 98

FLYNN

   John, 143

FOLSOM

   Nowassa, 58
   Woodrow, 58

FORD

   Martha, 154

FOREMAN

   Emiline, 174

FORMAN

   Francis, 148

FOSTER

   Micajah, 49
   Sally, 49

FRANCISCO

   Alfred, 23
   Allen, 24
   C.A., 24
   Charity, 11, 23, 24
   Daniel, 11, 23, 24, 87, 100, 114
   Dennis, 24

FRANCISCO (cont.)

   Elander, 23
   Eli, 24
   Elizabeth, 23, 24
   Ellen, 24
   Elsen, 23
   Howard, 24
   Izah (Izri), 24
   Jacob, 24, 101
   James, 24
   John, 24
   Levi, 24
   Mary, 23, 24
   Nancy, 24
   Peter, 24
   Rachel, 23
   Rosseline, 24
   Sarah, 23
   William, 24
   Zimeria, 23

FRASHER

   Alexander (Alex), 128
   Ann, 138
   Benjamin, 138
   Byron, 139
   Calvin, 138
   Cecil, 138
   Charles, 138
   Debby, 126, 137
   Edith, 139
   Edward, 137
   Emma, 138
   Harry, 138
   Ida, 139
   Ina, 139
   Isaac, 138
   James, 126, 137, 138, 139
   Jesse, 139
   John, 138, 139
   Joseph, 138, 139
   Leaby, 139
   Lester, 139
   Lillian, 139
   Lizzie, 139
   Louella, 138
   Mable, 139
   Mary, 137, 139
   Matilda, 139
   Rachel, 138

FRASHER (cont.)

   Robert, 126, 137, 138, 139
   Rosell, 139
   Roxanna, 139
   Ruby, 139
   Sarah, 126
   Susan, 139
   Thomas, 139
   Victor, 139
   Virgil, 139
   Wesley, 138
   William, 126, 137, 138, 139, 154

FRAZIER

   Elmer, 58
   Elizabeth, 193
   Lucinda, 58

FREENEY

   Alice, 39
   John, 39
   Laurence, 39
   Mabel, 39

FRENCY

   John, 182

FRISBEE

   Benjamin, 151
   Susannah, 151

FULLER

   Alice, 67

FUSSEL

   Jacob, 183

FRY

   Edna, 10

FRYT

   Joseph, 141

GAINOR

   Grace, 42
   Thomas, 42

GARCIA

   Christopher, 20
   John, 20
   Lori, 20
   Robert, 20
   Rochelle, 20
   Shelly, 20

GARDNER

   Lizzie, 173

GEOGHAN

   Kate, 174

GEORGE

   Jonathan, 127

GESPHS

   Sarrah, 95

GIBB (GIBBS)

   Elizabeth, 149
   John, 160

GILBERT

   Prissila, 191

GILDER

   Alford, 146
   Ann, 145, 146, 149
   Caroline, 146
   Clarence, 145
   Dorothy, 148
   Elizabeth, 145, 163
   Ella, 147
   Eunity (Unity), 145, 146, 147, 149, 160, 161
   Francesca, 148
   Francis, 147

GILDER (cont.)

  George, 148
  Henry, 145, 148, 149
  Jeanette, 148
  John, 145, 146, 147, 148, 150,
      152, 160, 161
  Joseph, 148
  Magdaline, 145
  Margaret, 146
  Mary, 145, 146, 149
  Nancy, 145
  Reuben, 145, 146, 150
  Richard, 148
  Rodman, 148
  Rosamund, 148
  Sarah, 145, 146, 147, 149
  Susannah, 149
  Tamar, 145
  William, 147, 148

GILES

  Mary, 10

GOLDEN

  Abraham, 149
  William, 149

GOLT

  John, 140

GOODEN

  Aaron, 154
  Albert, 157
  Amanda, 179
  Ambrose, 179
  Annie (Anna, Ann), 126, 137,
      154, 157, 165
  Benjamin, 154, 156
  Caroline, 164
  Charles, 156
  Clara, 165
  Daniel, 154
  David, 156
  Edgar, 164
  Edward, 154
  Elizabeth, 125, 154, 156, 164,
      188, 192

GOODEN (cont.)

  Ellen, 165
  Ellenor, 179
  Elvina, 157
  Esther, 154
  Fannie, 165
  George, 154, 164
  Gove, 179
  Hannah, 151, 179
  Henry, 157, 164
  Hince, 154
  Isaac, 155, 156, 164, 165
  James, 154
  John, 1, 125, 151, 153, 154,
      157, 171, 175, 179, 188, 189
  Jonathan, 179
  Joshua, 188
  Lavenid, 188
  Louise (Lou), 165
  Lydia, 179
  Mary, 154, 188
  Moses, 154, 171
  Peter, 157
  Philip, 156
  Robert, 165
  Ruth, 154, 155, 171
  Sallie, 165
  Sally, 154
  Samuel, 157
  Sarah, 156, 188
  Susan, 157
  Tennessee, 126
  Thomas, 154, 156, 164, 165, 179
  William, 128, 154, 157, 164, 171

GOODING

  Francis, 179

GORDON

  Benjamin, 15, 16, 86
  Elizabeth, 15, 16, 183
  Jane, 11, 15, 16
  John, 11, 15
  Levi, 16, 91
  Mary, 16, 91, 193
  Melissa, 16
  Melvina, 16
  Nathanial, 16
  Pheby, 16

GORDON (cont.)

  Sariah, 16
  Thomas, 16
  William, 16

GRAHAM

  Benjamin, 172
  Catherine, 176
  Francis, 174
  G.W., 174
  George, 172
  Jacob, 146
  John, 176
  Jonathan, 172
  Joseph, 172
  Letitia, 156
  Margret, 176
  Michael, 172
  Moses, 172
  Susan, 172
  Thomas, 172, 176

GRANT

  Paul, 59
  Willie, 59

GRAY

  Genevieve, 128
  Sally, 57

GREEN (GREENE)

  Amelia, 34
  Betty, 18
  Elizabeth, 139
  Estel, 136
  Ethel, 139
  Eva, 139
  James, 138, 139
  John, 130
  Kelly, 34
  Margretta, 155
  Maybeth, 136
  Milton, 139
  Oscar, 181
  Payne, 136
  Rachel, 139, 164
  Robert, 139
  Sarah, 34

GREEN (GREENE) (cont.)

  Thomas, 34, 139
  William, 34

GREER

  John, 144

GREGG

  Charles, 135

GRIER

  Margaret, 176

GRIFFITH

  Professor, 138

GRUWELL

  Alda, 129
  Alice, 129
  Charles, 129
  Cooper, 129
  Daniel, 175
  Eliza, 127, 129
  Elizabeth, 127, 129, 135
  Francis, 129
  Frederic, 129
  Hannah, 175
  Henry, 129
  Herman, 129
  Howard, 129
  Isaac, 126, 127, 129, 135, 175
  Jacob, 129, 175
  Jasper, 129
  John, 127, 129, 130, 135, 153,
      171, 175
  Jonathan, 175
  Joseph, 127, 129, 135
  L., 129
  Letitia, 155, 175
  Luther, 129
  Lydia, 154, 175
  Mary, 129
  Melvina, 129
  Peter, 129
  Robert, 129
  Ruth, 129
  Susan, 129, 154
  Thomas, 129
  William, 127, 129, 135

- H -

HALL

    Ann, 124
    Brig. Gen., 29
    Gertrude, 39
    Jackson, 9
    John, 124
    Mary, 123
    Michael, 153
    Thomas, 123
    Winlock, 160

HAMBLEN

    Bertha, 23

HAMILTON

    Alexander, 149
    John, 33
    Marial, 33
    Susannah, 149

HARGADINE

    Albert, 136
    Annie, 136
    Edward, 135
    Elizabeth, 136
    Henry, 127
    John, 127
    Julia, 127, 136
    Mark, 124
    Mary, 135
    Rachel, 124
    Robert, 127, 135, 136
    Samuel, 127
    Sarah, 127
    William, 127

HARMER

    Alfred, 45

HARPER

    Sophia, 136

HARRINGTON

    Agnes, 156, 160
    Alex, 156
    Alfred, 177
    Anna, 156
    B., 177
    Bertha, 33
    Daniel, 156
    David, 175, 177
    Elizabeth, 33, 156
    Henry, 156, 157, 160
    Herman, 177
    Ida, 178
    Isaac, 156
    James, 156
    Jane, 156
    John, 33, 156
    Lillie, 33
    Letitia, 156
    Martha, 156
    Mary, 156
    Mathilda, 156
    Peter, 156
    Rosalee, 156
    Sally, 156, 177
    Samuel, 33, 156
    Sarah, 156, 177
    Susan, 156, 177, 178
    Susannah, 156
    Theodore, 156, 177
    Thomas, 156
    Vincent, 156
    Warren, 156
    Wilhelmina, 154
    William, 33, 156

HARRIS

    Able, 146
    Wooten, 22, 89

HART

    George, 190

HATFIELD

    John, 160
    Sarah, 160
    William, 160

HAWKINS

  John, 159
  Irene, 39
  Mary, 125
  Orra, 39

HAYARD

  Rachel, 155

HEALD

  Patients, 130
  Rich, 130

HEARD

  George, 135

HEFFERMAN

  William, 160

HEFTY

  Ethel, 25
  Frances, 20, 25
  Otto, 25

HELLER

  Rebecca, 60

HENSON

  Ava, 9
  Ida, 9
  T. Cora, 10

HERRING

  Sallie, 176

HESS

  Henry, 45

HEYD

  Alice, 139
  Bertha, 139
  David, 138, 139

HEYD (cont.)

  Emma, 139
  Jacob, 176
  Rose, 139
  Susan, 176

HICKMAN

  Willard, 140

HICKS

  Giles, 124
  Julia, 155
  Mary, 124

HIGGINS

  Anthony, 180

HILLIS

  Louisa, 58
  Wiley, 58

HILL

  Dicey, 59
  Martha, 141

HINK

  Cordelia, 61
  Frank, 61

HINKLE

  Sydia, 15

HINSON

  Martha, 25
  William, 25

HOFFECKER

  Adalaid, 176
  Emma, 147

HOLLAND

  Ruth, 34

HOLLYMAN

    Mary, 187
    Thomas, 187

HOLMES

    James, 49

HOMESTEAD

    John, 193

HONIG

    Closetta, 61

HOOVER

    Lulu, 59

HORNE

    Gertrude, 18
    Harold, 18
    James, 18
    John, 18
    Sandra, 18
    Sharon, 18

HOUSTON

    George, 182

HOWARD

    Baltimore, 14
    De Kalb, 14
    Jonathan, 14
    Madison, 14
    Margaret, 14
    Mary, 145
    Nancy, 14
    Palashie, 14
    Rachel, 14
    Randolph, 14
    Thomas, 14

HUGHES

    Emeline, 177

HUNN

    Caleb, 187
    Ruth, 187
    Susan, 188

HUSTON

    Alexander, 160
    Ann, 138

HUTCHINS

    Richard, 142

HYLAND

    Elizabeth, 153

- I -

IRONS

    Simon, 190

ISHMAEL

    Amanda, 16
    Andrew, 21
    Benjamin, 21, 88
    Catherine, 22
    Elizabeth, 21, 22, 83, 85
    James, 22, 33, 84
    John, 16, 83
    Julia, 16, 81
    Margaret, 22
    Nancy, 16
    Nettie, 24, 32
    Patia, 16
    Polly, 16
    Rachel, 21
    Sarah, 21, 33
    Seraldi (Serilda, Surrelda), 22
    Susan (Suka), 16
    Thomas, 21, 33

- J -

JACKSON

  Agnes, 161
  Annie (Anna), 147
  Charles, 147
  Daniel, 145, 146, 147
  Elizabeth, 146, 161
  Ernest, 147
  Frank, 146
  Franklin, 147
  Gilda, 147
  Gwendolen, 148
  Henrietta, 146
  Jane, 146
  John, 146, 147
  Jonathan, 161
  Leonard, 147
  McElroy, 147
  Robert, 147
  Unity, 146, 147
  William, 153

JACOBS

  Isaac, 133
  Lizzie, 140
  Mollie, 140
  Sara, 15
  Truella, 140
  William, 133, 140

JACOBY

  Caroline, 146
  Christopher, 146, 148
  Linwood, 148
  Margaret, 148
  Mary, 148
  Wallace, 148

JAMES

  Ann, 149

JARRELL

  Mrs., 127

JEFFERSON

  Samuel, 180

JENKINS

  John, 150
  Pearl, 59
  Thomas, 150

JERRARD

  Matthew, 34
  Prudence, 34

JESTER

  Catherine, 126, 137
  James, 126

JOHNS

  Carrie, 179
  Francis, 176
  Thomas, 35, 38

JOHNSON

  George, 179
  Joseph, 66
  Martha, 66
  Victoria, 178
  William, 133

JONES

  Daniel, 190
  David, 187
  Fern, 58
  Flossie, 58
  Griffith, 190
  Sarah, 187
  Walter, 177

JUDD

  Mary, 61

JUMP

  Ambrose, 127
  Ann, 127
  John, 127
  Lydia, 124
  Mary, 127
  Purnell, 124
  Robert, 127

- K -

KATES

Bessie, 41
David, 41
John, 41
Joseph, 41
Sally, 41
Susanna, 41

KEEDER

Catherine, 65

KEESE

John, 9
Martha, 9

KEMP

Deborah, 179
Hannah, 179
Isaac, 179
Jacob, 155, 175, 179
John, 179
Letitia, 179
Lydia, 179
Margaret, 179
Mary, 179
Matthew, 179
Peter, 179
Robert, 179
Thomas, 155, 175, 179
William, 179

KENDALL

James, 29
Margaret, 27, 29

KENTON

Miss ___, 127

KERSHNER

Jesse, 31
Mildred, 32
Robert, 31

KICKS

Julia, 175

KILLEN

Ann, 140
Elwood, 140
Estelle, 140
George, 137, 140
John, 126, 127, 137, 140
Susan, 179
Thomas, 140
Walter, 140
William, 137

KING

Hattie, 59

KIRK

Ellen, 174

KLEIN

Emma, 147
Joseph, 147

KNEASBOROUGH

Mary, 183

KOLLOCK

Penelope, 187
W., 187

KREAGLE

Rose, 17

KUNKLE

E., 148
Grace, 148

- L -

LAISTER

Estelle, 140
George, 140

LAMB

Laura, 129

LANE

August, 40
Mary, 40
Penelope, 40
Phillip, 40

LAWS

George, 188
Mary, 188

LEACH

Mary, 145
Sarah, 164

LEE

Robert, 147

LENICK

Paris, 172

LENTON

Mary, 158
Nathaniel, 158

LENTZ

Mae, 59

LEONARD

Magdaline, 145

LEWIS

Caroline, 127
Daniel, 151
David, 158

LEWIS (cont.)

Elizabeth, 127
Hannah, 151
Jacob, 147
Margaret, 151
Mary, 151
Ruthannah, 151
Stephen, 151
Susannah, 158

LIDKE

Cynthia, 49
Maclyn, 49
Virginia, 48

LITTLE

Oniley, 15
Robert, 147
Sarah, 147

LITTS

Ellen, 32

LLOYD

Ethel, 128

LOCKWOOD

Andrew, 81
Ann, 164
Armwell, 153
Gartry
Mary, 127, 155, 175
Thomas, 164

LOFLAND

Catherine, 33
Miss, 177

LOGSTON

Elvisa, 77

LONG

Eugene, 178
Laura, 136
Samuel, 168

LONGFELLOW

    Rebecca, 154

LORD

    Anna, 177

LOWBER (LOBER)

    Agnes, 151, 152, 160
    C. Henry, 147
    Catherine, 124, 152, 160
    Daniel, 147, 152, 160, 161
    Dr., 152
    Elizabeth, 147, 152, 153, 159
    Fannie, 147
    Gartre (Gertie), 151, 152, 158
    Grace, 151, 153, 158, 171
    Hannah, 152, 159
    Isaac, 152, 158, 160
    Jane, 146
    John, 147, 160
    Jonathan, 153, 159
    Letitia, 161
    Margaret, 151, 152, 158
    Mary, 151, 152, 159, 160, 161
    Michael (Michall), 151, 152,
        158, 160, 184
    Miriam (Meriam), 153, 159
    Peter, 147, 149, 151, 152, 158,
        159, 160, 161
    Rachel, 152, 153, 158
    Robert, 159
    Ruth, 153
    Sally, 153
    Sarah, 153, 159, 161
    Susan (Susanna), 128, 151, 153,
        158, 161
    Unity, 145, 151, 152, 158
    William, 146, 161

LOWE

    Vincent, 123

LOWERY

    Della, 129

LUDLOW

    Sarah, 132

LUFF

    Elizabeth, 156
    Nathaniel, 192

- M -

MAIR

    Janet, 149

MAGINNIS

    Ida, 138
    Rebecca, 176

MAJOR

    Thomas, 2

MANLOVE

    Abram (Abraham), 152, 157
    Elizabeth, 152
    Margarett (Margaret), 152, 158
    Mark, 157
    Violet, 157

MANNING

    Araminty, 186

MARKER

    Ann, 155
    Charlotte, 155
    Isaac, 155
    James, 155
    Mary, 155
    Rachel, 179

MARQUES

    Virginia, 21

MARSHALL

    Arthur, 48

MARTIN

   Roy, 59
   Virginia, 59

MARVEL

   Aaron, 163
   Alice, 129, 163
   Ann, 163, 164
   Betsey, 163
   Chloeg, 163
   Comfort, 163, 188
   Corliss, 129
   David, 145, 146, 154, 163, 164
   Elizabeth, 125, 145, 163, 164
   Ellen, 125, 154
   Elphonsie, 125
   Emily, 125
   Emma, 146, 164
   Eva, 129
   Harriet, 164
   Henry, 164
   Hannah, 188
   Ida, 129
   John, 164
   Joseph, 163
   Joshua, 163
   Louisa, 40
   Mary, 125, 163
   Mollie, 129
   Patience, 163
   Philena, 125, 129
   Philip, 36, 163, 164
   Rachel, 163, 164
   Rembra, 164
   Rhoda, 163
   Robert, 125, 163
   Sally (Sallie), 125, 154
   Sarah, 125, 146, 153, 163, 164, 172
   Susan, 129, 164
   Thomas, 125, 163, 164
   Warner, 164
   William, 125, 163

MASON

   Abraham, 143
   Frank, 173
   Julia, 173

MASSEY

   Anna, 172
   Barbara, 24, 32
   Catherine, 22
   Elmer, 32
   George, 32
   Hannah, 172
   Jackson, 87
   James, 172
   Jane, 172
   John, 22, 87
   Sarah, 172
   Susan, 172
   William, 22, 24, 32, 172

MASTEN

   James, 178
   Pearl, 178
   Virga, 178
   William, 178

MATTHEWS

   Edward, 5, 6
   John, 9
   Nancy, 9

MEADS

   Patience, 17

MEIRE

   Ruth, 32

MELVIN

   Elizabeth, 133
   Rhoda, 133

MEREDITH

   Alexander, 138
   Amy, 139
   Ella, 139
   Emily, 125
   Laura, 139
   Lulu, 139
   Peter, 125, 128

MEREDITH (cont.)

    Susannah, 125
    Wheeler, 153
    Whitely, 125
    William, 127

MERRICK

    Israel, 130
    Mary, 130, 135

MERVIN

    Hassell, 62
    Lorena, 62

MILEHAM

    Maryann, 169
    Samuel, 143

MILES

    Catherine, 158

MILLER

    Beverly, 40
    Clyde, 40
    Donald, 40
    Helen, 40
    John, 40
    Patsy, 40
    Paula, 40
    Virginia, 40

MILLS

    Lester, 138

MINNER

    Elizabeth, 179
    Mary, 179

MITCHELL

    Lillie, 19

MONTAGUE

    Mary, 146

MOORE

    Ezekial, 129
    Rebecca, 130
    S.G., 174
    Sally, 156
    Tabitha, 142
    William, 130

MORGAN

    Elizabeth, 191
    Kate, 32

MOREES

    Morris, 142

MORRIS

    Elijah, 146
    Elizabeth, 130, 146
    Emma, 178
    Martha, 160
    William, 130, 161

MOUNTS

    Pamela, 20, 25

MULLIN (MULLEN)

    America, 63
    Charles, 63, 96
    Gertie (Gartry), 152, 153, 158
    Levi, 153
    Ruth, 153
    Susannah, 153
    Thomas, 152, 153

MURPHY

    Ann, 145

MYERS

    Eva, 18
    Harry, 18

- Mc -

McCALLEY (McCOLLEY)

  Edward, 136
  Elizabeth, 136
  Hiram, 136
  Joseph, 126, 134, 136
  Josephine, 136
  Laura, 136
  Lizzie, 136
  Lydia, 136
  Mary, 136
  Nellie, 136
  Sophia, 136
  Truston, 136

McCRARY

  Acrata, 127

McDANIEL

  Patience, 8

McKINZIE

  Charity, 16
  George, 17
  John, 16, 86
  Nancy, 17

McKINNEY

  Sarah, 81

McMAHON

  Estella, 138

McNEIL

  James, 34

- N -

NACALAZZI

  Angeline, 18

NEEDLES

  Adaline, 129
  Sarah, 137

NEIGHSWANDER

  Cora, 15

NESTER

  Rachel, 28

NEWCOMB

  Anna, 178

NICHOLS (NICHOLLS)

  Mary, 151
  Robert, 151
  William, 151, 158

NIEULAND

  Gertrude, 29, 151

NOBLE

  Sara, 133

NOVELL

  Alvina, 147
  Clement, 146, 147
  Emma, 147
  John, 147
  Thomas, 147

NOWELL

  George, 191
  Sarah, 191

- O -

OLLER

- Andrew, 17
- Marjorie, 18
- Patience, 17
- Paul, 18

OZBUM

- Jonathan, 168

- P -

PAINTER (PAYNTER)

- Christopher, 17
- John, 140
- Margaret, 17
- Mary, 17

PARADEE

- Lydia, 151
- Margaret, 151
- Mary, 151
- Stephen, 151

PARICH

- Stepency, 142

PARKER

- Benjamin, 9
- Edward, 9
- Ida, 9
- Mary, 9

PARVIS

- John, 125
- Margaret, 125

PATTON

- Margaret, 153

PAYNTER

- Sarah, 187

PELTIER

- Lucille, 20

PENDERGAST

- Anthony, 153
- Grace, 153

PEPPER

- Byron, 165
- Charles, 165
- Emile, 165
- Lee, 165
- Lola, 165
- Lou, 165
- Louise, 165
- Thomas, 165
- Viola, 165
- Zona, 165

PERRY

- Micaiah, 142

PHILLIPS

- Ellen, 65

PICO

- Pio, 21

PIERCE

- Joseph, 149
- Mary, 149

PIPER

- Jennie, 29, 92

PIRKLE

- Brian, 21
- Gerald, 21

PIRKLE (cont.)

  Joann, 21
  John, 21
  Kathleen, 21
  Robert, 21

PLATT

  Charlotte, 30

PLEASANTON

  David, 188
  Jonathan, 151, 192
  Mary, 188

POOL

  Margaret, 126

PORTER

  William, 168

POWELL

  Comfort, 143
  Love, 30
  Mary, 125

PRATT

  Ellen, 165
  Henry, 165
  Unity, 153

PRETTYMAN

  Mary, 126, 137

PRICE

  Annie (Anna), 154, 171
  Celia, 93
  Susan, 23

PULVER

  Zella, 19

- Q -

QUILLEN

  Emma, 176
  Fannie, 176
  James, 176
  Mary, 176

- R -

RATHBONE

  Harriet, 30, 31

RATHGEBER

  Dieter, 27
  Henrietta, 27
  Katheryn, 27

RAUGHLEY

  James, 127

REED (READ)

  Anna (Ann, Annie), 42, 182
  Benjamin, 175, 178
  Charles, 177
  Emma, 177
  Ezekiah, 178
  Florence, 177
  Gilbert, 178
  Goldie, 138
  Jane, 178
  John, 177, 178
  Letitia, 179
  Lucy, 177
  Lydia, 179
  Mary, 178
  Minnie, 177
  Robert, 178
  William, 182

REESE

  Catherine, 11, 22
  Reuben, 5, 6

REGISTER (REGESTER)

   Ann, 124
   David, 124
   Eliza, 167
   Elizabeth, 167
   Esther, 124
   Francis, 167, 169
   Isaac, 167
   Jeremiah, 167
   Joshua, 124
   John, 124, 167, 168
   Leaer, 167
   Lydia, 124
   Mary, 126, 134, 167
   Rachel, 167
   Robert, 124, 167, 168
   Ruth, 124, 168
   Samuel, 124
   Sarah, 124, 168
   Sophia, 168
   William, 168

REYNOLDS (RUNNOLDS, REYNALLS, RENELDS, REYNALS)

   A. Edgerton, 173
   Alexander, 182
   Andrew, 185
   Annie (Ann, Anna), 176, 178, 182, 183, 185
   Alexander, 182
   Barbara, 174
   Benjamin, 182, 183
   Betty, 183
   Bridget, 182
   Byron, 174, 180
   Catherine, 184, 185
   Clara, 176
   Daniel, 171, 174, 183, 184, 186
   David, 153, 154, 173
   Elizabeth, 126, 134, 146, 153, 154, 171, 173, 180, 184
   Ellen, 154, 173
   Elonor, 185
   Ephriam, 184
   Fannie, 154, 173
   Francis, 173, 174, 183
   George, 153, 171, 172, 175, 182, 183, 186
   Grace, 153, 171, 184
   Henry, 183, 184, 185

REYNOLDS etc. (cont.)

   Herbert, 180
   Hester, 174
   Irene, 174
   Jacob, 183
   James, 173, 178, 182, 185
   Jane, 183
   Jean, 185
   Joanna, 185
   John, 153, 158, 171, 173, 174, 175, 176, 178, 182, 183, 184, 185, 186
   Joseph, 183
   Julia, 173
   Kate, 174
   Lavenia, 173, 174
   Letitia, 153, 171, 174, 186
   Lolo, 173
   Luther, 154, 173, 180
   Margaret, 176, 182
   Martha, 172
   Mary, 140, 171, 172, 174, 182, 183
   Michael, 153, 158, 171, 175, 184, 185, 186
   Miriam (Meriam), 171, 172, 184, 185, 18
   Miyckel, 184
   Nancy, 185
   Rachel, 183, 184, 185
   Rebecca, 174, 182
   Richard, 182, 184, 185
   Robert, 123, 146, 153, 154, 164, 171, 172, 173, 174, 175, 180, 181, 184, 186
   Ruth, 185
   Sally (Sallie), 183
   Sara (Sarah), 154, 155, 171, 173, 174, 182, 183, 185
   Stephen, 185
   Susannah (Susan), 153, 158, 171, 184
   Thomas, 153, 154, 171, 173, 174, 178, 180, 183, 186
   Temperance, 182
   Waddey, 183
   William, 29, 174, 182, 183, 185

RHODES

   Allen, 20, 26
   Beverly, 20, 26

RICHARDS

    Elizabeth, 142
    John, 142
    Philip, 142

RICHARDSON

    John, 190

RIDGEWAY

    Elizabeth, 155
    James, 153
    Sally, 153

RIED

    Pearl, 61

RIGGS

    Annie, 173
    Lavina (Lavenia), 173, 174, 180
    William, 180

ROBINSON

    Hannah, 152, 153
    Samuel, 159
    Susan, 153, 171, 174

RODNEY (RODENEY, RODONEY)

    Anthony, 187, 191
    Caesar, 145, 187, 188, 191, 192, 193
    Caleb, 187
    Comfort, 163, 187, 188
    Daniel, 187, 188, 191, 192
    Elizabeth, 187, 188, 191, 192
    George, 187, 188, 191
    Hannah, 187, 188
    John, 187, 191
    Lavina, 192
    Ledia, 192
    Letitia (Letticia), 192, 193
    Margaret, 192
    Miriam (Meriam), 188, 192
    Penelope, 187, 191
    Rachel, 191
    Rebecca, 187
    Ruth, 187, 191

RODNEY etc. (cont.)

    Samuel, 185
    Sarah, 187, 188, 190, 191, 192
    Susan, 188
    Thomas, 187, 188, 190, 191, 192
    William, 187, 188, 190, 191, 192, 193

ROE

    Imogene, 175

ROGERS

    Livy, 178

ROSENGREN

    Maria, 48

ROSS

    Ann, 182
    Eleanor, 182
    John, 182
    Thomas, 182

ROWE

    John, 60
    Rebecca, 60
    Virginia, 60

RUSH

    Jeremiah, 133

RUSSELL

    Beatrice, 31, 152

RUSSMAN

    Sarah, 124

RUST

    Annie, 165

- S -

SACKETT

　Madeline, 39, 40

SADDLER

　Amelia, 26, 28

SALSBURY (SAULSBURY)

　Clara, 176
　Eli, 181
　Reynear, 176
　Sarah, 174

SAPP

　James, 179

SARGENT

　Mary, 138

SATTERFIELD

　John, 155

SCATTERGOOD

　Ann, 146
　Caleb, 146, 148
　Gilder, 148
　Harry, 148
　Joshua, 148
　Sallie, 148
　Sarah, 135

SCHAFER

　Lizzie, 35, 36
　William, 36

SCOUT

　Bessie, 40
　Jefferson, 40

SCOTT

　Dicey, 58
　Lucinda, 58
　Miss, 177
　Nathan, 144
　Wylie, 58

SCULLY

　John, 143

SEARS

　Frances, 22
　Louis, 49

SERAFINE

　Nora, 25

SERN

　Jane, 91

SEWARD

　Alta, 140
　John, 140
　Joshua, 140
　Louisa, 140
　Mary, 140
　Noah, 133
　Rebecca, 140
　Sarah, 140
　William, 140

SHALLCROSS

　Joseph, 183

SHANE

　Mary, 140

SHARP

　Clara, 177
　Elijah, 177
　Ella, 177

SHARP (cont.)

  H., 177
  James, 177
  Paddy, 177
  Sarah, 177
  William, 177

SHARTZER

  Gertrude, 32

SHAW

  James, 161
  Letitia, 161

SHEPHERD

  John, 191

SHELTON

  Dovie, 59
  Ode, 59

SHERWOOD

  Hannah, 128
  John, 126
  Mary, 126
  Susan, 125

SHIELDS

  Audrey, 18
  Oliver, 18
  Rebecca, 187
  Ruth, 18

SHILES

  Eli, 163
  James, 163
  Rachel, 163

SHORT (SHORTS)

  Angelina, 155, 177
  Barbara, 40
  Ella, 129
  Geraldine, 40
  Harry, 40
  Jane, 177

SHORT etc. (cont.)

  Julia, 156, 175
  June, 175
  Lucy, 40
  Samuel, 155, 175, 177
  Sarah, 155, 177
  Susan, 155, 177

SHOUP

  Cecil, 21, 25
  Edward, 21, 25
  Jeffrey, 21, 25
  Jennifer, 21, 25
  Kenneth, 21, 25
  Nora, 25
  Ruth, 21, 31, 69
  Thomas, 21, 25

SIMPSON

  Elizabeth, 117, 134
  Ignatius, 117
  Mary, 117
  Thomas, 117

SIPPLE

  Caleb, 157, 160
  Ellinor, 1, 3
  John, 172
  Mary, 34
  Ruth, 34
  Thomas, 34, 129, 172
  William, 34

SKINNER

  Elizabeth, 155, 175
  George, 179
  Isaac, 179
  John, 155, 175, 179
  Letitia, 179
  Martha, 179
  Miriam, 155, 175, 179
  Sarah, 179
  William, 155, 175, 179

SMITH

  Alfred, 45
  David, 191
  Elizabeth, 15

SMITH (cont.)

   Francis, 153, 171

   Hattie, 138
   John, 142, 151
   Josephson
   Josephus, 15
   Lucinda, 14
   Louisa, 179
   Mary, 15, 151
   Maurice, 190
   Nancy, 15
   Sarah, 14
   William, 14, 91

SMITHERS

   Emiline (Emeline), 156
   Emma, 156, 177
   John, 156, 175
   Mary, 177
   Sally, 156, 177
   Waitman, 156
   William, 177

SMOCK

   Minnie, 177

SMULLING

   Estelle, 42

SNELLGROVE

   Hillary, 95

SNOW

   Evlyn, 59
   Joseph, 59

SOUTH

   Andrew, 14
   Cynthia, 14, 100

SPARKS

   Mr., 140

STANSBURY

   Miss, 127

STAYTON

   Eliza, 155

STEEL

   Rachel, 138

STEINMAN

   Agnes, 31

STEPHENS (STEVENS)

   David, 192
   Maria (Monah), 8

STIERLEY

   Slmira, 147
   Emma, 147
   John, 146, 147
   Sarah, 146, 147
   William, 147

STOCKLEY

   Charles, 180
   Sarah, 179

STONE

   Ethel, 25

STOUT

   Ruth, 124

STUART

   Charles, 141
   Mary, 159
   Terry, 20

STUBBS

   Charles, 179

SUMMERS

   Nathaniel, 161

SURRATT

   Minnie, 8, 79

SUTTON

   Julia, 173

SWANN

   Martha, 7

SYLVESTER

   Harrington, 124
   Lydia, 124

- T -

TAYLOR

   Clarissa, 124
   Mary, 176
   Robert, 147

TEMPLE

   Bessie, 136
   Clay, 136
   George, 136

TEMPLETON

   Nancy, 14
   William, 14

TERRY

   Mary, 24

THAWLEY

   William, 173

THAYRE

   Jeanie, 135

THISTLEWOOD

   Gertie, 151
   William, 151, 158

THOESSEN

   Edythe, 1

THOMAS

   Hester, 174

THOMPSON

   Alice, 9
   Anne, 39
   Nancy, 61

THORPE (THORP)

   Ann, 32
   Cal, 32
   Martha, 23, 32

TINLEY

   Mary, 172

TOMLINSON

   Albert, 178
   Daniel, 174, 178
   Ella, 178
   Elizabeth, 178
   Gus, 178
   Josephine, 178
   Maud, 178
   Minnie, 178
   Samuel, 178
   Sarah, 174
   Thomas, 174, 178
   Virginia, 178
   William, 174, 178

TOWNSEND

   Susan, 137

TRIPPET

   William, 158

TRUDRUNY

    Charles, 32
    Richard, 32
    Winnifred, 32

TUCKTON

    Edith, 139
    Lyle, 139

TURNER

    Isaac, 187
    Rachel, 184
    Rev. C.H.B., 189

- U -

UPTON

    Emma, 59

- V -

VANBURKELOE

    Sarah, 16

VANDEVER

    Unity, 157

VANDYKE

    Lydia, 126
    William, 126, 134

VANLEUVENEIGH

    Catherine, 143

VAN VORST

    Elizabeth, 136

VINCENT

    Henry, 129

VIRDIN (VIRDEN, VERDEN, VARDIN, VERDUN, VERDAIN)

    Abner, 15
    Absolom, 65, 67
    Addie, 25
    Agnes, 31
    Ageniah, 3
    Alemeda, 22, 102
    Alexander, 7, 34, 35
    Alice, 9, 10, 17, 18, 31, 67
    Allen, 40
    Alfred, 42
    Amelia, 26, 71
    Amy, 11, 18
    Angela, 20
    Andrew, 33
    Annie, 14, 27, 28, 29, 39, 42, 47, 49,
    Archibald, 26, 27, 28, 72, 81, 92
    Archie, 27, 28, 29
    Artis, 48
    Ava, 9

    Barbara, 24
    Beatrice, 31
    Benjamin, 6, 7, 9, 53, 79
    Berryman, 65, 81, 98
    Bertha, 23, 101
    Bessie, 22, 38, 39
    Betty, 27
    Beverly, 20, 26
    Blanche, 155
    Bub, 25

    Calvin, 58
    Catherine, 11, 22, 102
    Charity, 11, 16, 23, 71, 114
    Charles, 15, 19, 28, 30, 64, 93, 98
    Charlotte, 30, 40
    Clifford, 42
    Clasetta, 61
    Christina (Christine), 20
    Christopher (Chris), 8, 15, 17, 18, 19,
    Cora, 15, 19, 61
    Cornelia, 27, 61
    Cynthia, 14

    Daniel, 46
    David, 66, 80
    Delilah, 29, 75, 77
    Dennis, 20
    Donald, 23
    Doris, 40
    Dovie, 59

VIRDIN etc. (cont.)

   E. Virgil, 61
   Earl, 28
   Edgar, 27, 29
   Edith, 32
   Edna, 10, 75
   Edward, 9, 10, 17, 66
   Effie, 17, 18
   Egenior, 3, 4, 5, 6, 51, 69
   Eleanor, 1
   Eli, 23, 33, 93
   Elisha, 14, 25
   Eliza, 6, 10, 30
   Elizabeth, 3, 6, 7, 15, 16, 21, 30, 33, 40, 47, 53, 57, 58, 63, 70, 159
   Ellen, 19, 21, 58
   Ellie, 32
   Ellinor, 27
   Elmina, 49
   Elvin, 59
   Elvisa, 77
   Emerson, 58
   Emiline, 15, 27
   Emily, 27, 35
   Emma, 8, 23, 30, 32, 63
   Ennis, 10
   Estella, 42
   Ester (Esther), 25
   Ethel, 40
   Eugene, 15
   Eva, 48
   Evlyn, 59

   Fannie, 8, 28, 61
   Felix, 58
   Fern, 48
   Flora, 6
   Flossie, 58, 61
   Fonaire, 22
   Frances, 25, 26, 40, 61
   Franklin (Frank), 38, 40, 41, 42, 46, 47, 61, 64, 98
   Frederick (Fred), 22, 28, 61

   George, 15, 30, 32, 42, 47, 94, 95
   Georgia, 10
   Gertrude, 32
   Glenn, 10, 62
   Gloria, 20, 25
   Grace, 39, 42
   Gwenlyn, 19

VIRDIN etc. (cont.)

   Hamilton, 65
   Harriet, 27, 28
   Harry, 38, 39
   Harold, 32
   Hazel, 23, 59
   Henderson, 57, 58
   Herbert, 61
   Henrietta, 27, 29, 92, 117
   Henry (Henery), 9, 28, 46, 47
   Hiram, 24, 25, 32, 71, 72, 75, 76, 77, 102
   Homer, 23, 27, 29, 32
   Howard, 39
   Hugh, 3, 11, 14, 24, 52, 57, 58, 71, 72, 89

   Ignatius, 116
   Ira, 22
   Irene, 39
   Isaac, 11, 22, 26, 28, 30, 33, 46, 47, 70, 71, 72, 80, 82, 86, 90
   Iva (Ida), 15

   J.W., 26, 28, 72, 92
   Jacob, 15, 81, 96
   James, 1, 4, 7, 11, 14, 17, 19, 20, 22, 24, 30, 34, 38, 39, 40, 41, 46, 52, 53, 57, 58, 59, 69, 70, 79, 80, 82, 85, 90, 94, 97, 113, 115, 116
   Jane, 4, 11, 14, 17, 70
   Jason, 6
   Jeanne, 20
   Jeffery (Jeffry), 20, 25
   Jennifer (Jennefer, Jennie), 8, 20, 25, 27, 29
   Jerome, 61, 72, 76
   Jessie, 31
   Joann, 19, 21
   John (Johnnie), 1, 4, 7, 8, 17, 18, 19, 20, 21, 22, 25, 26, 27, 33, 35, 42, 44, 45, 46, 49, 53, 58, 61, 64, 67, 72, 80, 87, 90, 93, 93, 113
   Josiah, 64
   Joseph, 10, 19, 20, 23, 25, 116
   Judith, 20, 25
   Julia, 6, 7, 8, 25, 53
   Julius, 9

VIRDIN etc. (cont.)

  Kate (Katie), 22, 33
  Kathryn, 42
  Kenneth, 40

  Lacy, 29, 60, 75, 78
  Laura, 7, 27
  Lavina, 15
  Lewis, 61, 75, 76
  Levi, 11, 21, 22, 23, 32, 33, 60, 61, 65, 71, 83, 85, 91, 93, 94, 98, 113
  Lidonia, 61
  Lodina, 61
  Lorena, 61
  Lottie, 31
  Louisa, 40, 58, 59
  Love, 30
  Lucinda, 14, 58, 114
  Lucy, 39, 40
  Luiza, 14
  Lulu, 23, 31, 32, 59
  Luther, 23

  Madeline, 39, 40
  Mahala, 22, 33
  Mandy, 23
  Margaret, 11, 14, 15, 22, 24, 27, 28, 29, 30, 31, 33, 40, 47, 58, 67, 71
  Maria, 8, 48
  Marilyn, 20, 26
  Marjorie, 40
  Marion, 39
  Marilla, 66
  Martin, 22, 66
  Martha, 6, 7, 8, 9, 10, 23, 25, 53, 63, 66
  Mary, 6, 7, 8, 9, 10, 11, 15, 17, 18, 23, 25, 28, 31, 33, 34, 39, 40, 42, 47, 52, 58, 61, 71
  Matthew (Mattew), 20
  May, 28
  Melvina, 21, 23
  Michael, 20
  Mildred, 19, 20
  Minnie, 38
  Mina, 23
  Minerva, 16
  Milton, 8
  Molly, 28

VIRDIN etc. (cont.)

  Monah, 8
  Moses, 49

  Nancy, 7, 8, 11, 14, 15, 17, 61, 113
  Narcissa, 14
  Nellie, 10, 24, 28
  Nelson, 26
  Noel, 20
  Nolan, 58
  Nonie, 17
  Nora, 10
  Norman, 14, 30
  Nowassa, 58

  Onee, 32
  Orra, 27, 39
  Orville, 22
  Oscar (Osker), 8, 30, 63, 64, 90, 96, 9

  Pamela, 20
  Patience, 8, 17
  Paul, 42, 48
  Pearl, 59, 61
  Peter, 47, 161
  Phoenix, 116
  Pricilla, 6, 7, 8, 53
  Prudence, 34

  Queen Elizabeth, 9

  Rachel (R'al), 11, 21, 28, 117
  Radford, 11, 22, 71, 83
  Ralph, 31, 32, 38, 40
  Ray, 31, 40
  Richard, 46, 49, 115
  Rita, 10
  Robert, 10, 39, 40, 66
  Rochelle, 20
  Ronald, 40
  Roscoe, 32
  Roxanne (Roxane), 21
  Russell, 48
  Ruth (Rutha), 1, 19, 21, 25, 75
  Ryan, 10

  Sally, 49
  Samira, 27
  Samuel, 1, 7, 17, 22, 26, 27, 29, 30, 52, 91, 94
  Sarah, 7, 14, 16, 21, 22, 27, 29, 33, 41, 46, 53, 58, 59

VIRDIN etc. (cont.)

  Serilda (Surrelda), 22
  Stella, 28, 42
  Steven, 49
  Susan, 16, 23, 48, 66, 102
  Sydia, 15

  Theodore, 33
  Thomas (Tommy), 6, 7, 8, 10, 46, 47, 48, 53, 57, 58, 59, 65, 66, 75
  Thornton, 66
  Tully, 80

  Unity, 39

  Victoria, 42
  Virginia, 10, 21, 39, 48, 58, 60
  Vivian, 40

  Walter, 47
  Willard, 30, 31, 32
  William (Willie), 4, 6, 7, 8, 10, 11, 15, 16, 22, 26, 27, 28, 29, 30, 32, 33, 34, 35, 39, 40, 41, 42, 46, 47, 48, 49, 52, 53, 58, 59, 61, 63, 64, 70, 72, 75, 78, 81, 82, 84, 86, 88, 90, 92, 96, 97, 102, 115, 116, 149, 152, 159
  Willis, 15
  Wilson, 26, 28, 72

  Zella, 19
  Zilphey (Zilphia), 6

- W -

WADE

  Asa, 58
  Mary, 58

WALKER

  Agnes, 152, 158
  Alice, 157
  Elizabeth, 152, 157

WALKER (cont.)

  John, 157
  Martha, 155
  Susannah, 157
  William, 152, 157
  Unity, 157

WALLACE

  Ellen, 34, 41
  Evelyn, 41
  Florence, 41
  Hannah, 41
  Henry, 41
  Herman, 41
  Margaret (Margret), 145, 153, 173, 174
  Mary, 38, 41, 173
  Nellie, 41
  Samuel, 34, 41

WALLER

  Ellen, 24

WARD

  Henry, 124
  Mary, 124

WARREN

  Ruth, 153
  Samuel, 153
  Willie, 66

WATKINS

  James, 59
  Willie, 59

WATSON

  Arthur, 58, 59
  Arvie, 59
  Benjamin, 59
  Decatur, 59
  Dicey, 59
  Elizabeth, 134
  Emma, 59
  Hattie, 59
  James, 59

WATSON (cont.)

    Louisa, 59
    Mae, 59
    Oliver, 59
    Sarah, 58, 59
    Thomas, 59
    Wiley, 59
    William, 59

WEATHERBY

    Septimus, 6

WEBBER

    Clifford, 59
    Evlyn, 59

WEBSTER

    Noah, 148

WEIDMAN

    Fannie, 61

WELDEN

    Chatham, 136
    Mary, 136

WELLS

    Cora, 19
    John, 19
    Lillie, 19
    Marilla, 66

WELSH

    Jacob, 155

WEST

    Charles, 148
    Elizabeth, 187
    Ellen, 148
    George, 147, 148
    Harrison, 30
    Hannah, 30
    Henry, 148
    William, 148

WHEELER

    Samuel, 141

WHITAKER

    Ann, 133
    Henry, 133, 144
    Moses, 158
    Ruth, 127

WHITE

    Agnes, 31
    Elizabeth, 3, 171, 184
    James, 171, 184
    Philip, 31

WHITUP

    Sarah, 27, 29

WILDER

    Joseph, 136

WILGUS

    Stella, 42

WILKINSON

    Annie, 138
    John, 137, 138
    William, 137, 138

WILLIAMS

    Anna (Ann), 27, 29, 92, 164
    Archie, 29
    Elizabeth, 184
    Ezekiel, 184
    J., 164
    Lamira, 29
    Martha, 129
    Muriel, 29
    Otho, 27, 29
    Thomas, 184

WILLIAMSON

    Irene, 179
    Margret, 58

WILLIAMSON (cont.)

  Martha, 34, 66
  Ulysses, 180

WILLOUGHBY

  Martha, 171
  Mary, 126
  Rachel, 153
  Samuel, 153

WILSON (WILLSON)

  Ann, 124
  Caesar, 193
  Elizabeth, 193
  Esther, 124
  John, 192
  Margaret (Margarett), 11, 24, 71
  Richard, 190, 191
  Sarah, 192, 193
  Thomas, 124, 183, 193
  William, 182

WOOD

  David, 7
  Laura, 7

WOODALL

  Mary, 7

WOOTEN

  Attorney General, 165
  Judge, 165
  Mary, 165

WOOTERS

  Abner, 174
  Elijah, 174, 178
  Lydia, 178
  Theodore, 178
  William, 174

WRIGHT

  Helen, 39
  David, 39

WRIGHT (cont.)

  Emma, 138
  John, 3
  Robert, 127

WYATT

  Anna, 178
  Clarissa, 179
  Mary, 140
  Sallie, 133

WYTH

  William, 168

- Y -

YOUNG

  Daniel, 3

YOUNGBLOOD

  Willie, 7

Other Heritage Books by Donald O. Virdin:
Civil War Correspondence of Judge Thomas Goldsborough Odell
Colonial Delaware Wills and Estates to 1800: An Index
Delaware Bible Records, Volume 2
Delaware Bible Records, Volume 3
Major General Alfred Thomas Archimedes Torbert: Delaware's Most Famous Civil War Hero
Maryland and Delaware Genealogies and Family Histories
Pennsylvania Genealogies and Family Histories: A Bibliography of Books about Pennsylvania Families
Some Pioneer Delaware Families
The Virdins of Delaware and Related Families
Virginia Genealogies and Family Histories: A Bibliography of Books about Virginia Families

With Lu Verne V. Hall:
Delaware Bible Records, Volume 5
New England Family Histories and Genealogies: Miscellaneous New England States
New England Family Histories and Genealogies: States of Maine and Rhode Island
New England Family Histories and Genealogies: States of New Hampshire and Vermont
New England Family Histories: State of Connecticut
Texas Family Histories and Genealogies

With Donald M. Hehir:
CD: Delaware Bible Records, Volumes 1-4

www.ingramcontent.com/pod-product-compliance
Lightning Source LLC
Chambersburg PA
CBHW081151290426
44108CB00018B/2514